THE DEVELOPMENT OF INTERNATIONAL INSURANCE

FINANCIAL HISTORY

Series Editor: Robert E. Wright

Forthcoming Titles

THE DEVELOPMENT OF INTERNATIONAL INSURANCE

EDITED BY
Robin Pearson

Routledge
Taylor & Francis Group
LONDON AND NEW YORK

First published 2010 by Pickering & Chatto (Publishers) Limited

Published 2016 by Routledge
2 Park Square, Milton Park, Abingdon, Oxfordshire OX14 4RN
711 Third Avenue, New York, NY 10017, USA

First issued in paperback 2015

Routledge is an imprint of the Taylor & Francis Group, an informa business

© Taylor & Francis 2010
© Robin Pearson 2010

BRITISH LIBRARY CATALOGUING IN PUBLICATION DATA

The development of international insurance. – (Financial history)
1. Insurance – History. 2. Financial institutions, International – History.
I. Series II. Pearson, Robin, 1955–
368'.009-dc22

ISBN-13: 978-1-138-66138-7 (pbk)
ISBN-13: 978-1-8489-3075-9 (hbk)
Typeset by Pickering & Chatto (Publishers) Limited

CONTENTS

PREFACE

This book contains a selection of essays that derive from papers presented at the session 'Insurance in History', held at the XVth World Economic History Congress in Utrecht in 2009, and at a related pre-conference meeting held in Zurich. The theme of both meetings was deliberately left general with the object of casting the net as widely as possible. One aim of the organizers was to find out what historical research on the insurance industry was currently being carried out around the world and who was involved. The call for papers produced a result that surprised even the optimists among us. Altogether 18 papers from 22 authors were presented at the Utrecht and Zurich meetings. The authors came from Italy, Spain, Switzerland, the Netherlands, Sweden, France, Germany, the USA, Argentina, Chile, Brazil, Japan, Australia and South Africa. There were further offers of papers from researchers in the USA, Canada, Japan, France, the UK, Singapore, Hungary, Morocco and Nigeria that could not be included in either meeting or that were withdrawn, often for funding reasons. One outcome was that the existing pockets of insurance historians, hitherto working in a fairly small and specialized field of business and financial history, were now connected to a truly global network of researchers.

This is the latest stage in a process that has been gathering pace over several years. It began in 1995 with a conference in Kyoto, organized by Takau Yoneyama, where Japanese scholars were brought together with a small number of historians from the UK – David Jenkins, Peter Mathias, Robin Pearson, Clive Trebilcock and Oliver Westall – to discuss aspects of insurance history in both countries. In 1998 a more broad group met in a session at the World Economic History Congress in Madrid, from which several publications resulted (see *Risques* 31 (July–September 1997); and C. E. Núñez (ed.), *Insurance in Industrial Societies: Economic Roles, Agents and Markets from Eighteenth Century to Today* (Seville: University of Seville, 1998)). In the same year Peter Borscheid established a regular workshop on insurance history under the auspices of the German Society for Business History. In 2005 there was a session on insurance in Spain held at the conference of the Spanish Economic History Conference in Santiago de Compostela, organized by Jerònia Pons Pons and María Ángeles

Pons Brías, from which a collection of essays has recently been published (*Investigaciones Históricas sobre el Seguro Español* (Madrid: Fundación Mapfre, 2010)). Since then there have been conference sessions and dedicated workshops on insurance history held in Madrid, Melbourne, Hanover and Zurich, in addition to the meetings last year. Scholars have been very fortunate in that much of the recent impetus has come from industry sources, notably the corporate history project of Mapfre, authored by Leonard Caruana, José Luis Garcia-Ruiz and Gabriel Tortella (*De Mutua a Multinacional: Mapfre 1933–2008* (Madrid: Mapfre, 2009)), and the large ongoing project at the Swiss Re, led with great energy and skill by Rudolf Frei and Niels-Viggo Haueter. Several of the authors in the present volume are also involved in the Swiss Re corporate history, and we owe a debt of gratitude to Rudolf and Niels for their outstanding support, particularly in hosting our pre-conference meeting at the Swiss Re Centre for Global Dialogue in Rüschlikon.

As editor of this volume, I would also like to thank my colleagues Leonardo Caruana and Robert Wright for co-organizing the meetings in Utrecht and Zurich. Leonardo had the original idea for an international session on insurance history at the WEHC, and Bob kindly suggested that we publish this volume in the Financial History series that he edits for Pickering & Chatto. I would also like to thank Daire Carr of Pickering & Chatto for being such an efficient and supportive commissioning editor and for holding me to deadlines. Finally, I must also thank the contributors to this volume. They turned their chapters around to tight deadlines and answered all the queries set for them, despite various language barriers. This was all the more remarkable for the fact that at least two of them have had to cope with new arrivals to their families while revising their chapters. The future of insurance history, as well as the babies, would appear to be in safe hands.

Robin Pearson
Hull, April 2010

LIST OF FIGURES AND TABLES

LIST OF CONTRIBUTORS

Liselotte Eriksson is a PhD student at the University of Umeå, Sweden. Her research focuses on the development of life insurance in Sweden from the mid-nineteenth to the mid-twentieth century. Her main interests are the cultural and social implications of life insurance. Her most resent research focuses on women as life insurance policyholders and the marketing strategies of life insurance companies. Her article 'Life Insurance and Income Growth: The Case of Sweden 1830–1950' is forthcoming in the *Scandinavian Economic History Review*.

Adrian Jitschin, MA, studied and graduated at Philipps-University Marburg, Germany. He has been working in a research project on the internationalization of insurance. Since 2007 he has worked at the Department of Economic History, Philipps-University, where his job involves giving lectures and writing articles. His research interests cover the development of international trade, insurance history and history of the family. He is currently preparing his PhD thesis on life insurance in India.

Martin Lengwiler is Professor of Modern History at the University of Basle, Switzerland. He has published on the history of the welfare state, with a specific interest in the relation between public and private actors. His habilitation thesis on the history of accident insurance in Switzerland has been published as *Risiko-politik im Sozialstaat: Die schweizerische Unfallversicherung 1870–1970* (2006). His recent work is reflected in his essay 'Competing Appeals: The Rise of Mixed Welfare Economies in Europe, 1850–1945', in G. Clark (ed.), *The Appeal of Insurance* (2010). He currently works on the history of international networks of insurance experts.

Manuel Llorca-Jaña is a lecturer in Latin American history at Birkbeck College, University of London. He recently finished a PhD in International Economic History at Leicester University, supervised by Professor Philip L. Cottrell, on Britain's textile exports to Chile and Argentina during the 1810s–50s. He published his masters dissertation, 'Knowing the Shape of Demand: Britain's Exports of Ponchos to the Southern Cone, c. 1810s–70s', as an article in *Business History*,

51 (2009). He is also a contributor to the *Oxford Dictionary of National Biography*. He is currently adapting his PhD thesis to be published as a monograph.

Robin Pearson is Professor of Economic History at the University of Hull, UK. He has published widely on various aspects of British and international economic and business history, with a particular focus on insurance. His first book, *Insuring the Industrial Revolution: Fire Insurance and the British Economy, 1700–1850*, won the 2004 Wadsworth Prize for Business History. He has recently finished a book, *Shareholder Democracies? Corporate Governance in Britain and Ireland before 1850*, co-authored with Mark Freeman (University of Glasgow) and James Taylor (Lancaster University), forthcoming with University of Chicago Press. He is currently working on a project entitled *Insuring America: Multinational Insurance Companies in the United States, 1850–1920*.

Jerònia Pons Pons is senior lecturer in economic history at the University of Seville (Spain). Her research focuses on the economic history of insurance in Spain. She is author of *Companyies i mercat assegurador a Mallorca, 1650–1715* (1996), *El sector seguros en Baleares* (1998), and has edited with M. Angeles Pons a collection of essays, *Investigaciones Históricas sobre el Seguro español* (2009). Her work on insurance history has also been published in *Internationalisation and Globalisation of the Insurance Industry in the Nineteenth and Twentieth Centuries* (2007), edited by P. Borscheid and R. Pearson, and in *The Appeal of Insurance*, edited by Geoffrey Clark et al. (2010, forthcoming). Currently she is working on *Spanish Insurance History* sponsored by the Fundación Mapfre.

Christofer Stadlin is a historian and archivist working in the Corporate Archives of Zurich Financial Services. He holds a masters degree from the University of Zürich in history, philosophy and informatics. Since working in an insurance archive he has commenced research on business and insurance history. On various occasions he has presented the results of this research to scientific conferences. He is currently working on a doctoral thesis on the history of actuarial techniques and actuarial science in non-life insurance.

Grietjie Verhoef is Professor in Economic and Accounting History in the Department of Accountancy, University of Johannesburg, South Africa. Her research specialization lies in the economic, business and accounting history of South Africa. She has completed research projects on the development of Afrikaner business in South Africa, and is currently engaged in research on the insurance industry in that country, with a case study of SANLAM. She is also conducting research on the professionalization of the accounting profession in South Africa. She has published 47 articles in peer-reviewed journals and contributed chapters to seven books.

Welf Werner is Professor of International Economics at Jacobs University, Germany. He works in the fields of international trade, international trade policy and economic history. He has published widely on international trade in services, trade policy on financial services and the development of international insurance markets. In recent years he has advised the Federal Ministry of Economics and Labour in Berlin and the Ministry of Industry and Trade in Amman, Jordan, on the GATS negotiations at the World Trade Organization. Before joining Jacobs University in 2004 he worked at the Freie Universität Berlin, the School of Advanced International Studies, Johns Hopkins University and, as a John F. Kennedy Memorial Fellow, at Harvard University.

Takau Yoneyama is Professor of Risk Management and Insurance at Hitotsubashi University, Tokyo. He has published widely on various approaches to risk management and insurance. He compiled the eight-volume edition of the *History of Insurance* (2000) together with David Jenkins (University of York). Recently he has been involved in the revision of insurance contract law in Japan as a non-juridical member of the Legislative Council of the Justice Ministry. He is a co-editor, together with Professor Tomonobu Yamashita of Tokyo University, of *A Commentary on the Insurance Act of Japan*. He is a member of the executive committee of Asia-Pacific Risk and Insurance Association as well as the organizer of an international project on corporate forms in insurance, supported by the Dai-ichi Life.

INTRODUCTION: TOWARDS AN INTERNATIONAL HISTORY OF INSURANCE

Robin Pearson

Preamble: Culture, Trust and Risk

Unlike commodity trades, where the object of exchange is visible and tangible, insurance is a business based entirely on trust and expectation. Money is handed over in return for a promise to pay back a larger sum in the future, contingent upon the occurrence of an uncertain event, or in one unique case – death – contingent upon a certain event occurring at an uncertain point in time. In the case of whole-term life assurance, for example, the insured by definition will not be around to ensure that his or her claim is paid. Trust in the individual or institution selling the insurance product therefore has to run deep. The purchaser has to have confidence that the product is fairly priced – a much more complicated problem than the pricing of most commodities – and that the insurer will remain solvent over the duration of the policy.[1] The seller has to have confidence that the risk taken is an insurable one and that the moral hazard embodied by the policyholder is at an acceptable level. Why, therefore, should such a business ever take place beyond the boundaries of local communities or outside close-knit groups characterized by high levels of transparency and reputational knowledge? How and why did this trust-based invisible product become traded over long distances and across political, ethnic, religious and cultural borders, and, since the early nineteenth century, in such vast quantities?

The short answer is the need to spread risk. But risk can be diffused in many ways, not all of which involve 'modern' forms of social security and insurance. For centuries poor communities in the Philippines have reduced the risks and limited the effects of typhoons and flooding through mutual assistance associations and forms of cooperation denoted by the Tagalog word *turnahan* – literally 'doing a turn'.[2] Mutual aid includes cooperative irrigation and rotating credit societies. Less formal reciprocity includes collective actions (known as *bayanihan*) such as helping with the rebuilding of houses after typhoons, moving houses onto higher ground before storms, and dam building to protect barrios from floods. Long-run data for the twentieth century suggests a close correlation between the *per caput* density of mutual aid associations and those regions with historically the highest frequency of disasters, so that the latter seems to have been the primary determinant of the former.

This example suggests that different political and cultural environments can shape attitudes to risk and levels of trust.[3] With the exception of a few pioneering works on life insurance,[4] historians have not really begun to explore how consumers and suppliers of insurance in the past have factored in world views and cultural bias when buying or selling cover against different types of risk. The relative balance of influence between cultural perceptions of hazards and scientific knowledge of hazards is likely to have changed considerably over time in different societies, according to a wide variety of external factors such as education, standards of living, lifestyle, economic structures and political institutions. Cultural theorists have begun to examine the ways in which popular perceptions of risk are culturally determined and impact upon power relations in a society, but little of this has found its way into insurance history.[5] There is no space here to discuss cultural theory at any length, but its principal message warns us against assuming the inevitable triumph of scientific risk assessment with the global diffusion of Western forms of insurance. It also suggests there may be a strong path-dependent effect determining how national markets develop and respond to the arrival of suppliers of insurance from other nations and other cultures. The great variety of such markets and the institutional vehicles through which different forms of insurance have been delivered is highlighted in the survey below.

The Rise of National Markets

Marine and Inland Transport Insurance

The protection of goods and people in transit provided an early motive for various types of mutual association offering non-actuarial forms of insurance. From the middle ages there were, for instance, mutual societies of shipowners in Chinese ports and armed escort services for trade caravans passing along bandit-infested roads between Chinese provinces.[6] Similarly, merchants in the Habsburg territories paid fees for the military protection of trade convoys travelling along designated routes, the so-called *Geleitregal*, formalized by the imperial law of Henry VII in 1231.[7]

The insurance of ships and their cargoes, however, was the earliest form of premium insurance and, from the outset, the most international. Ocean shipping usually passed between borders and operated under internationally accepted legal codes. Nevertheless, one can still speak of national markets in so far as recognized centres of marine insurance emerged in different states, and were subjected to taxation by their respective rulers. Such centres were first strung out along the northern Mediterranean, Italian and Adriatic coasts. By the 1600s there were also specialist communities of insurance brokers in London, Antwerp, Amsterdam, Bruges and Hamburg. In London some 150 private marine underwriters were joined in 1720 by two new chartered monopoly companies, the Royal Exchange Assurance and the London Assurance, but these failed to displace the underwriters operating out of Edward Lloyd's coffee house. By this date the London market had extended to include the slave trade and so-called 'cross risks', that is ships or cargoes travelling between two or more foreign destinations outside the United Kingdom.

While private underwriters and brokers continued to operate in many ports, some European states moved to found national institutions for marine insurance. In France, there was an unsuccessful attempt to promote a monopoly company for marine insurance in 1686.[8] Genoa, Copenhagen and Naples successfully established state monopoly companies between 1742 and 1751. Private companies undertaking both marine and fire insurance also appeared, beginning in Antwerp in 1756. Hamburg and Trieste also developed into major centres for private marine insurance companies. The first Trieste company was launched in 1766 and doubled as a credit bank for local merchants.[9] Like marine insurance, inland transport insurance was also essentially international. From the late 1760s Trieste fire and marine companies, for example, insured grain and tobacco in transit over land and on river from Hungary to the Adriatic port.[10]

Several points can be made about European marine insurance. First, there were multiple organizational forms at an early stage. There were individual underwriters, operating through brokers, as in Lloyd's, perhaps doing the bulk of the business before 1850. There were state monopoly insurers and quasi-monopoly private companies incorporated by the state. There were small private partnership companies and large private joint-stock companies and there were numerous private mutual insurance associations of shipowners. This mixture of organizational forms continued, with some variation in its composition, throughout the nineteenth and twentieth centuries, at least until the collapse of the traditional Lloyd's system of underwriting in the 1990s. The diversity and flexibility of form probably helped marine insurance deliver protection against losses at sea even when one or more particular types of organization were forced to contract or withdraw from the market, due to regulatory barriers or a lack of competitiveness. For example, when the two London chartered companies withdrew from the 'cross risk' business during the Napoleonic Wars, alarmed by the lack of information from overseas, underwriters at Lloyd's quickly moved in to supply that market. Second, in the Mediterranean ports, though less so in northern Europe, marine insurance, especially in its corporate forms, was closely associated with banking and the provision of commercial credit, and for this reason was encouraged by mercantilist states. This may, however, have added to the volatility of insurance markets in southern Europe and helps explain the high failure rate of marine companies there during the later eighteenth century, although further research is required to substantiate this. Third, regardless of the way it was organized, marine insurance – and other forms of transport insurance to a lesser extent – contributed greatly to the international diffusion of insurance practices. Merchants in eighteenth-century Trieste readily moved their insurances to underwriting centres abroad to obtain cheaper rates. Some of the early stock companies appointed agents or established subsidiaries outside their home territory. Fourth, marine insurance contributed little to actuarial techniques. The risks were non-standardized – by route, by composition of cargo, by type of ship – and underwriters worked largely by instinct, experience and rule of thumb, assisted, importantly, by an increasing flow of information about shipping risks. Some of this information was formally organized in *Lloyd's List* (1734) and *Lloyd's Register of Shipping* (1760), but much of it was passed by word of mouth on the floor of Lloyd's coffee house or among the communities of brokers in ports such as Liverpool, Bristol, Hamburg and Antwerp. This enhanced the problem of adverse selection that was faced by the two London marine insurance corporations in their unsuccessful struggle to compete with Lloyd's, as the corporations did not enjoy access to the same volume and quality of information.[11] By the beginning of the nineteenth century the corporations accounted for less than 5 per cent of the £137m estimated to be insured on marine risks in London.

The chartered monopolies of the two London corporations were finally repealed in 1824. During the 1860s new companies were formed in London and Liverpool that benefited from the huge transfer of American marine business to Britain during the American civil war. By the 1870s stock companies had acquired around 40 per cent of the UK marine insurance market. Lloyd's responded by diversifying into other lines, creating a host of new products and expanding others in general insurance, including burglary, loss of profits, credit, professional indemnity, boiler, engineering, bicycle, motor car and aviation insurance. In Britain the large fire insurance companies followed suit, taking over existing accident offices to create giant composite insurance enterprises.[12] Around 1850 there were just six lines of accident insurance available in Britain, Europe and North America. By 1914 this had risen to about fifty.[13] The benefits of the new types of insurance had to be explained to agents and vigorously sold to customers. In doing so, the level of inventiveness in marketing and product design rose to new heights. Personal accident insurance, for instance, was sold in Britain and America through slot machines placed at railway stations and hotels. In 1895 a Philadelphia company launched a 'perfection blanket policy', which covered within one contract employers' liability, public liability, steam boiler, elevator, sprinkler and team liability insurance.[14] Liability and accident cover was to become one of the huge growth areas of international insurance during the twentieth century.

Life Insurance

Long before the appearance of actuarial life insurance, the pooling of funds to provide compensation for the costs of death was widely practised. In the later Roman Empire burial societies provided a lump sum to the relatives of deceased members. Similar types of burial provision also occurred among the guilds and fraternities of medieval Europe and Tokugawa Japan, sometimes extended to include mutual protection against other hazards such as losses by fire, confiscation, capture, robbery and theft of cattle.[15] The medieval *Knappschaften*, for example, were formed to provide miners in Germany and Austria with sickness, accident and death benefits. By 1850 they had become compulsory in the German mining industry.[16] To same category belonged the growing number of widows' benefit societies in eighteenth-century Europe. These provided a widow and her children with a perpetual annuity upon the death of her husband, against the payment of regular contributions by him during his lifetime. In some places, the state not only authorized such ventures, but also participated directly in them, most notably in taking over the role of religious organizations in providing pensions and disability and infirmity allowances for certain groups of its key employees, beginning with soldiers.

The insurance of lives began in the fourteenth-century Mediterranean as a by-product of marine insurance when policies on ships and cargoes were extended to cover passengers or slaves on board. On *terra firma*, however, life insurance first appeared in the form of wagers on the lives of rulers and popes, a business that many states soon found morally and politically offensive. In Spain, insurance gambling, including all forms of life insurance, was suppressed by the Ordinances of Barcelona in 1435, the first codification of insurance law. Amsterdam, Middleburg and Rotterdam passed similar prohibitions between 1598 and 1604, Sweden did so in 1666 and France in 1681 (with the notable exception of ransom insurance sold to travellers planning to sail in pirate-infested seas).[17] By contrast in England, following half-hearted attempts by Elizabethan and early Stuart governments to regulate the business, life insurance came to operate entirely beyond the reach of state supervision. Wagers on lives were eventually banned in England under the 1774 Gambling Act.

Where there was the prospect of adding to the public treasury, however, governments were prepared to endorse life insurance in the form of tontines. The tontine was a contribution scheme in which annual payments were shared out among surviving members. The first tontine plan was devised by Lorenzo Tonti in 1652 to raise revenue for the French royal treasury. Some thirteen tontines were launched by Dutch towns in the 1670s as a means of increasing municipal revenue.[18] Tontines were used by the French state to generate revenue until they were finally banned for this purpose in 1763, but private tontine schemes quickly took their place. Similar tontines were found in other European countries. In Germany they were used to finance the military spending of many small states.

None of these schemes relied on *a priori* pricing, risk assessment or classification yet, despite their resemblance to speculative forms of insurance, private mutual schemes, such as contributionships, tontines and reversionary annuities, continued in England and parts of Europe throughout the eighteenth and nineteenth centuries. Between 1696 and 1721, for instance, some sixty mutual life insurance schemes – mostly short-lived – were launched in London. Life insurance in England was also sold on a premium basis from 1721 by the two new marine insurance corporations, the Royal Exchange Assurance and the London Assurance, both of whom acquired the right to sell fire and life insurance under additional charters.[19] These offered fixed fee and fixed benefit plans, in which, unlike the tontines, company profits were dependent on correctly predicting the future mortality of policyholders. This was a more risky business for underwriters than the older and simpler redistributive schemes, in which price was determined *a posteriori*. With just these two premium-based life insurance ventures in England, it was difficult to distribute risks widely enough to offset the uncertainties in accurately estimating the mortality of policyholders. Although eighteenth-century life insurance managers were sell aware of the various mortality tables in circulation, calculations of age-specific mortality remained highly problematic, not least because contemporary estimates of the underlying population were so varied. As a rule of thumb life insurers widely assumed that a fairly constant rate of mortality prevailed among younger and middle-aged adults, assumptions that persisted until the end of the century, notwithstanding the introduction of age-specific premiums by the Society for Equitable Insurances on Lives and Survivorships (1762).[20]

In sum, English life insurance initially developed on a non-premium non-actuarial basis, with variable or fixed contributions and benefits distributed according to mortality. At the end of the century, however, a number of new premium-based life assurance companies appeared, some funded mutually, some by joint-stock, and the industry began to take off. By 1850 some £150m was insured by 141 stock and 42 mutual offices. By 1914 £870m was insured in 94 offices, a growth rate that outstripped that of the UK population and national income.[21] By 1890 life assurance in the UK had become a mass market, with about 1m Britons holding ordinary life assurance policies, and a further 9.9m holding small industrial assurance policies, together about 30 per cent of the population.[22] Similar developments can be seen at this time in other major industrializing economies. In Germany, for example, life insurance premiums increased from RM 86m in the 1880s to RM 278m by the 1900s.[23]

Fire Insurance

The growth of different forms of financial protection and the expansion of public and private welfare provision in early modern Europe can be judged a major innovation, not in actuarial science or underwriting techniques, but at least in improved levels of security for private property and incomes. The same holds true for what became the largest branch of insurance. Fire insurance developed directly from the medieval tradition of 'briefs', official letters authorizing *post hoc* collections, sometimes compulsory, for the relief of victims of fires. In England the collections rapidly died out in the wake of the rise of private fire insurance at the end of the seventeenth century. In several European states they came to be regarded as an obstacle to the development of public fire insurance funds and were banned.[24]

Across central Europe from the early seventeenth century peasant insurance unions – so-called *Bauernassecuranz* – also became widespread, in which villagers helped their neighbours with materials, labour and money to rebuild their houses and farm buildings in the aftermath of fires. This was a mutual aid institution, similar in principle to the *turnahan* system in the Philippines noted above. During the nineteenth century, as estate property rose in value, the number of insurance unions grew. Local authorities began to worry about the flight of rural customers away from the public fire insurance associations that charged high rates for farmers' thatched and wooden buildings, towards the unions that operated with almost zero administrative costs. In Austria, for example, there were around 300 farmers' insurance unions with 320,000 members in the late 1880s, although numbers subsequently declined.[25]

In towns there developed public associations for the insurance of buildings. The first, and one of the most successful, was established in Hamburg in 1676, the Hamburger Feuercasse.[26] There was no compulsion on existing householders to join the fund – full compulsion was first introduced in 1817 – but whoever built a new house or bought or inherited a house was required to join within six months. In the event that the fund was insufficient to cover payments for losses, members were liable for further calls at rates proportionate to the sums they had insured. The fund was also used to pay the medical bills of citizens injured fighting fires or lifetime annuities to those rendered permanently disabled, and the burial costs of the victims of fires.[27] The Hamburger Feuerkasse provided a model for others to copy. Public buildings insurance associations were formed in nearby Harburg in 1677, in Magdeburg in 1685, in Berlin in 1718 and across the rest of Germany during the course of the eighteenth century.[28] In Copenhagen a public fire insurance association was started in 1731. In Stockholm the Brandförsäkringskontor was founded in 1746.[29] In Switzerland buildings insurance was organized by canton and by city, beginning with Zurich in 1782. Public buildings insurance associations were mostly local in scope, though sometimes they covered larger territories and, unlike Hamburg before 1817, insurance of buildings was usually compulsory except for a few privileged, often tax exempt, groups. They were essentially extensions of state bureaucracy and revenue systems, managed by civil servants. No actuarial calculations were involved. They mostly charged flat fees for all types of property, which were paid in same way as a tax, and they had no profit considerations.[30] Accumulated funds were used, first, to pay for the rebuilding of property destroyed by fire – there was often an obligatory rebuilding clause attached to policies – and, second, to supplement other public spending.

As cities expanded during the nineteenth century and the value of urban property grew, the public associations increasingly suffered from a lack of funds to cover their liabilities. There were concerted attempts to consolidate the many small associations into larger institutions, but as late as 1880 there were still 72 public fire insurance associations across Germany, many of them confined to individual towns. For these and other reasons, the market opportunities in Europe for private for-profit fire insurance increased quickly during the first half of the nineteenth century. With the growing influence of liberal reformers in *ancien régime* governments, traditional suspicions of private enterprise in fire insurance began to wane. In Prussia, a wave of company foundations commenced under the Stein-Hardenberg ministry with the Berliner Feuerversicherungsanstalt of 1812, followed by other stock and mutual companies in Leipzig, Elberfeld, Gotha, Aachen and Cologne between 1819 and 1839. In 1836 the requirement for property owners in the Prussian provinces to insure their buildings in the public societies was abolished. Most other German states eventually followed suit. In Russia the first private fire insurance company was authorized in St Petersburg in 1827. In France five new enterprises were founded for fire insurance between 1819 and 1829.[31] In Austria an imperial decree of 1819 established a more congenial environment for private fire insurance companies. Five stock companies were founded between 1822 and 1847. Private mutual societies were also founded in Vienna, Graz and Brünn.[32]

Progress was not smooth for this first generation of European private insurance companies. First, the level of state regulation and police supervision continued to be high in several states, which preferred to keep a close rein on their markets via obligatory licensing and reporting systems for companies and their local agents, fines for over-insurance, and a police approvals procedure for those wishing to take out an insurance policy. Second, inadequate risk classification remained typical. Where premium calculations were based on inadequate statistics, company reserves often proved insufficient to cope with large fire events, as the bankruptcies and financial crises in several early Austrian companies demonstrated. Third, the old banking and credit functions inherited from marine insurance remained in some areas of European fire insurance, which may have contributed to the volatility in the performance of the early companies. The 1812 constitution of Berliner Feuerversicherungsanstalt, for instance, stipulated that its share capital could be used to issue loans against good securities.[33]

Through to the end of the nineteenth century some states continued to support the public insurance associations, partly for ideological reasons. In several countries there was a persistent risk of the nationalization or the renationalization of individual branches of insurance, and in some places buildings insurance monopolies survived. In Germany from the 1860s the public fire insurance associations conducted something of a fight-back against the private sector as they formed new national associations to represent their interests and lobbied hard for the nationalization of the insurance industry, winning powerful supporters, notably Otto von Bismarck.[34]

The situation in central Europe stood in sharp contrast to Britain and Ireland, where the state played little other than a fiscal role in insurance, and to the United States, where the ease of incorporation facilitated a rapid increase in the numbers of private companies. There were 30 fire insurance companies in the UK by 1800. By 1850 the number had risen to 70, the great majority organized as joint stocks. The capital invested in English fire insurance offices accounted for 0.8 per cent of national income of England and Wales in 1800, but 2.4 per cent by 1850. Sums insured against fire rose from £206m to £730m, growth being especially rapid after 1815, helped by rising competition and a steep fall in premium rates.[35] In the US in 1850 there were some 99 companies writing fire, marine and inland transport insurance, earning cash premiums of $6m in 1850. By 1890 there were 827 such companies with a premium income of $157m.[36] During the first half of the nineteenth century most American companies remained local in scope, either insuring within their home state or extending their agencies cautiously to neighbouring states. This strategy facilitated the close personal monitoring of agents by the company's officers. There were also legal restrictions, such as hefty deposit requirements and high levels of taxation, in many eastern states, limiting the scope for insurers from out-of-state or abroad. This deterred British entry into the US until the great fire in New

York (1835) persuaded state legislators there to relax their punitive regulations on foreign insurers.[37]

As with marine and life insurance, the growth of fire insurance in Britain, Europe and North America led to a proliferation of organizational forms and widely varying market structures. In the markets dominated by private insurance, there was a fundamental line dividing the market between mutual and stock companies, a line that shifted over time partly as the result of fierce competition. Our data is far from complete but some examples illustrate the point. In France, where the state looked kindly on mutuals as not-for-profit organizations, there were 30 joint stock companies and 43 mutual societies underwriting fire insurance in 1878. The market share of the latter, however, was in decline for much of the second half of the century, falling from 27 per cent of net premiums in 1850 to just 9 per cent by 1889. In Finland in 1893, four mutual companies accounted for 57 per cent of sums insured against fire.[38] In Sweden, mutuals accounted for 38 per cent of fire insurance in both 1887 and 1913.[39] Within the mutual sector there were often also important differences between large regional or national companies and small and highly localized cooperative associations. In the Netherlands, there were 281 companies in the fire insurance market in 1910, including 72 national stock companies, 36 large mutuals, 21 provincial companies organized either as cooperatives or joint stocks, and 127 local associations, demonstrating how complex a European market could be, even where, as in the Netherlands, there were no state institutions competing.[40]

In countries with a large public fire insurance industry, the market structures were even more fractured. In Russia in 1885 there were 14 stock companies and 174 mutuals writing fire insurance. The later comprised 79 *gouvernement* institutes, 50 provincial associations and 45 municipal societies, plus several captive mutuals organized by industrial groups, such as the Kiev Union for the Insurance of Sugar Refineries. In 1890 the various types of public and private mutuals together accounted for 36 per cent of fire insurance premiums.[41] In 1878 in German fire insurance there were 28 stock companies, 20 private mutuals, 71 public mutual institutions (*öffentliche Anstalten*) and, in Prussia alone, some 247 local mutual unions (*Vereine* and *Verbände*), plus a small number of foreign companies.[42] The local mutual unions were very small, but the larger public and private mutuals together accounted for over 50 per cent of total premiums, and they managed to maintain most of this market share through to the First World War.[43]

In some places, the number of mutual organizations for fire insurance appears to have fallen during the second half of the nineteenth century, and sometimes this was accompanied by a collapse in market share. In New York state in 1859, 28 mutual companies accounted for 24 per cent of fire insurance premiums. By the early 1870s there were seven New York mutuals left, and they held only about 2 per cent of the market. Here the mutuals were squeezed by the growing competition from native stock companies and foreign corporations, and they also suffered from a tide of public criticism of mismanagement and fraud.[44] This, however, was not the case everywhere. In Upper Canada farmer's mutuals were first organized in the 1830s and seem to have gone from strength to strength. There were more than 150 mutuals in the Canadian market by 1900, some of them very small, others doing 'a considerable business'.[45] At present we can only discern such national trends from fragmented data. We are not yet in a position to explain them, but it is clear that there was no simple linear movement towards the dominance of fire insurance markets by private stock companies before 1914.

The Development of International Insurance in the Long Nineteenth Century

Outside the marine insurance market, the first insurance company to export abroad was the Phoenix Fire Office of London. This was founded as a joint-stock venture by a group of London sugar refiners in 1782 and immediately began to use its transatlantic and European trading connections to insure property overseas. Some of these risks were insured by their owners directly in London, for which purpose the Phoenix opened a 'home-foreign' department, but the company also established a network of overseas agencies. By 1815 the Phoenix had made 42 agency appointments in the Iberian peninsula, north-west Europe and the Baltic, in North America, the West Indies, Buenos Aires and the Cape. By the 1820s over half the Phoenix's total premiums came from abroad.[46] Other new British companies with overseas trading connections followed. The Imperial Fire Office set up agencies in the West Indies and also insured mercantile property around Europe from St Petersburg to Gibraltar. The Alliance Assurance, founded by the Rothschilds in 1824, tracked the *Phoenix* around the Caribbean and North America, and also benefited from its founders' powerful financial connections in Europe. By the early 1830s, 45 per cent of the Alliance's fire insurance premiums came from abroad.[47] As more and more of the domestic market was covered by insurance, companies looked to expand more rapidly overseas. By 1913 the home market accounted on average for only about one-third of UK companies' gross premiums from fire insurance.[48]

Although the British offices were its principal drivers, the early phase in the international diffusion of fire insurance, marked by agency and 'home-foreign' business, also witnessed cross-border operations by the new generation of private companies in Europe. Following its foundation in 1824, the First Austrian company of Vienna, for example, was quick to move across the borders of the Hapsburg Empire to do business in Bavaria, Saxony, Hanover, Mecklenburg, Bremen, Schleswig-Holstein and northern Italy.[49] The Riunione Adriatica di

Sicurta of Trieste was operating in Greece, Prussia and Switzerland within a year of its foundation in 1839.[50]

A third means of exporting fire insurance developed in the mid-1820s, when bilateral reinsurance treaties began to be struck between British insurers and some of the new German, French, Belgian and Russian companies.[51] From Europe, North America and the West Indies, fire insurance spread to British India, China and the Malay Peninsula during the 1830s and 1840s, largely through the agencies of British insurers, although local companies were also set up by colonial merchants in Bombay and Canton.[52] After 1850, led by the large British companies, fire insurance penetrated Australia, New Zealand, South Africa, Asia, Latin America, the Middle East, Spain and the Balkans. Joint ventures were sometimes organized between firms to share the risks of entry into a foreign market. More often, however, reinsurance was employed to operate in markets where it was difficult or illegal for foreign companies to insure directly. By the 1870s reinsurance constituted an important pillar of international fire insurance. For some offices it provided a means of generating revenue from foreign markets without the expense of establishing their own agency network, or of paying for the services of a general agency firm. In some markets, reinsurance supplied from abroad proved essential to local firms wishing to expand their underwriting capacity. In 1896, for example, 53 per cent of the fire insurance premiums earned by the eight Norwegian stock companies were reinsured. The comparative figure for Russian fire insurance companies in the 1870s was 60 per cent.[53] The reinsurance trade, however, was invariably reciprocal, so that companies from smaller insurance nations could become heavily involved, sometimes dangerously, in foreign risks without leaving their own shores. Commentators remarked with concern in 1904 that 35 per cent of the gross fire insurance premiums earned by Russia's thirteen stock companies came from accepting reinsurances from abroad, mostly from western Europe and the United States.[54]

A final phase in the international diffusion of fire insurance began around 1880 with the increasing establishment of subsidiary companies in overseas markets by British and European companies, and the growing number of acquisitions of native offices by foreign companies. These developments were stimulated by the need to circumvent the growing tide of protectionist legislation and taxation that discriminated against non-domiciled companies. The rising costs of doing business at a distance through brokers, commissioned agents or general agency firms was probably also a factor. As the above survey suggests, there was a wide range of methods by which insurance was sold across borders during the nineteenth century. Pearson and Lönnborg have identified at least ten different vehicles employed by companies to export fire insurance before the First World War.[55]

The range of nations involved in the export of fire insurance by the later nineteenth century was also remarkable. Although British exporters were most numerous almost everywhere, many markets experienced a diversity of foreign entrants. In 1879, for instance, there were 50 foreign fire and marine insurance companies operating in California, namely 22 British, 8 German, 5 Swiss, 5 Chinese, 4 New Zealand and 1 Austrian.[56] The share of national markets captured by foreign entrants varied considerably. Pearson and Lönnborg have compiled data for 21 markets in 12 countries during the period 1870 to 1914, covering fire, marine, inland transport, non-life or all branches of insurance as the sources allow. They found that these markets were divided almost equally between those characterized by low import penetration levels, such as Germany, Japan and Sweden, where less than 30 per cent of fire and marine insurance was done by foreign companies, and those, such as fire insurance in Canada, Finland and the Netherlands, where foreign insurers captured more than 30 per cent of the market. Only 3 of the 21 markets crossed the 30 per cent threshold during this period.[57]

Of course, import penetration was complete in developing economies without local firms or state monopolies, such as Romania before 1868, Japan before 1879, Turkey before 1893, Egypt before 1900, and much of Central America, the West Indies and south-east Asia before the First World War. Nevertheless, in the markets where native insurance companies were successfully established, the domination of foreign insurers generally diminished over time. In some places this was partly due to the hostility to foreign competitors taking premium revenue out of the country. In the Habsburg Empire, for instance, nationalist politicians were prominent in the foundation of the first native insurance companies in Hungary, the Czech lands and Rumania. The manifestation of Hungarian nationalism in insurance forced a response from the Austrian companies operating there. In 1857, for example, the Riunione Adriatica di Sicurta converted its Budapest agency into a Hungarian-speaking office at a time when the accepted language of business was German, issued its policies in Hungarian and appointed Hungarians to its sub-agencies.[58] We do not know much about the growth of native companies in emerging economies since the late nineteenth century, however, it is clear that early efforts were made by many of them to move into the export business. Four fire and marine insurance companies from New Zealand, for instance, set up operations in California between 1875 and 1882. In the latter year two of them also joined a syndicate with an Australian company to do business in the UK.[59]

As yet we have only limited data with which to compare the growth of property insurance across different markets and in relation to the development of national economies before 1914. Fire insurance premiums in England grew much faster than national income or population between 1760 and 1850,[60] and, as Tables I.1–2 show, the British fire insurance industry continued to outstrip demographic and economic growth during the second half of the nineteenth century, although this impressive performance owed much to the growing level of insurance exports. However, while *per caput* fire insurance increased in all the nations listed in Tables I.1–2, the insurance industry did fail to keep pace with economic growth in some of these countries when they were growing particularly rapidly, such as Germany and France before 1900 and the United States after 1900.

Table I.1: *Per caput* **Fire Insurance Premiums in Five Countries, 1850–1912 (US $ current).**[61]

Year	France	Germany	Britain	Japan	US
1850/1	0.15	0.27	0.35	–	0.26
1882	0.54	0.56	1.69	–	1.71
1900/2	0.62	0.78	2.43	0.04	2.40
1910/12	1.05	0.99	2.84	0.09	2.86

Table I.2: Net Fire Insurance Premiums as a Percentage of GDP.

Year	France	Germany	Britain	Japan	US
1850/1	0.20	0.62	0.23	–	0.23
1882	0.37	0.60	0.98	–	0.70
1900/2	0.37	0.55	1.14	0.14	0.97
1910/12	0.43	0.58	1.20	0.19	0.75

As the legal proscriptions on life insurance in Europe were gradually lifted during the early nineteenth century, this also became an export business, although to lesser extent than fire or marine insurance. Here too the British were pioneers. The Pelican Life Office, founded in 1797, insured British and foreign nationals residing abroad, and military personnel travelling overseas. The Gresham Life, founded in 1848, established branches and agencies in France, Belgium, Germany, Austria, Hungary and Spain, as well as Canada, Egypt, India and South Africa. Few British insurance companies, however, were formed as specialist life exporters. Large composites, such as the Royal and the Liverpool, London & Globe, captured overseas life insurance business through their network of fire insurance agencies, but the general pattern was one of early British entry followed by decline as local companies squeezed the British out. In the United States, competition from local mutuals and stricter regulation of foreign life insurers from the 1850s discouraged UK life offices. A dozen British offices established agencies there between 1844 and 1854, but their market share dropped from 7 per cent in 1855 to just 2 per cent ten years later.[62] In Canada, Australia and South Africa British life insurance fared better and acquired a large market share in the decades after 1850, but by 1914 that share had also declined with the rise of native offices.

During the nineteenth century, therefore, British life insurance never achieved the powerful foothold in world markets enjoyed by its fire and marine counterparts. The most vigorous exporters of life insurance before 1914 were undoubtedly three New York offices, the Equitable, the Mutual Life and the New York Life. During the 1870s and 1880s this trio pushed their way into Europe and Latin America with adventurous sales strategies and cheap tontine-type endowment products, supported by a flow of investment income from high interest funds and mortgages back home, but they were met with fierce hostility by the native offices and regulators in many of the countries they operated in.[63] They were eventually forced to wind up much of their overseas operations in the wake of the New York senate investigations of 1905 and the subsequent restrictions on their investment activities. They seem to have captured a significant share of some foreign markets, but by the First World War this had begun to decline. In 1914, for example, they earned less than £1m of the £31m total ordinary life premiums in the UK.[64]

As in fire insurance, the rise of native companies made the export of life insurance more difficult before the First World War. In Japan, for example, thirty native life offices were competing with five foreign insurers by 1911. The latter accounted for just 12 per cent of total life business in Japan.[65] Switzerland witnessed a huge growth in life insurance – by 1880 it had the second highest level of *per caput* insured of all the countries listed in Table I.3. This expansion, however, was accompanied by a decline in the foreign share of the market, from 57 per cent of premiums in 1886 to 45 per cent by 1912.[66]

Table I.3: Life Insurance in Twelve Countries, 1860–90 (£m insured).[67]

Country	1860	1890	Number Insured per 100,000 Inhabitants in 1880
UK	170.0	550.8	2659
USA	35.4	840.6	?
Germany	15.9	215.6	148
France	9.2	160.1	68
Austria	5.2	75.1	80
Russia	1.2	25.8	23
Belgium	0.9	3.0	213
Holland	0.5	11.4	?
Switzerland	0.3	11.2	1,313
Italy	0.1	5.2	30
Australia	–	40.0	–
Canada	–	24.8	–
Rest of world	0.7	28.4	–
World total	239.4	1992.0	–

Table I.3 charts the eight-fold increase in life insurance around the world during the late nineteenth century, but also indicates how uneven that process was between countries in terms of *per caput* coverage. In 1869 the US accounted for 44 per cent and the UK 37 per cent of the total sums insured on lives. These shares inevitably changed as national insurance industries grew at different rates. By 1925 the US had risen to two-thirds of global life insurance premiums, but the UK had fallen to just 10 per cent.[68] At the end of the twentieth century, the UK share of the world life insurance market remained almost the same, but the US share had fallen to 28 per cent, equal to the share held by Japan.[69]

What Factors Promoted or Obstructed the Global Diffusion of Insurance?

During the nineteenth and twentieth centuries innovations of different types both facilitated the spread of risk and also gave rise to new risks. Material innovations that helped reduce or eliminate hazards have been legion. These include the replacement of timber with brick, iron and steel in construction, the substitution of candles by gas and electric lighting, the introduction of traffic lights and road signs, and the development of antiseptics and antibiotics. Some of these were supported by state regulation, such as public health and factory inspection, building controls, and public welfare systems to provide support for citizens in times of sickness, unemployment and old age. Some materials and technologies, of course, have also increased risks or created new ones: the steam engine, electricity, the motor car, nuclear power and asbestos spring to mind.

Information innovations have also been important in reducing risk and facilitating the spread of insurance. There are countless examples of the interplay between information technologies, the reduction of the costs and risk associated with distance, and the growth of insurance. These include the telegram and telephone, weather stations, surveying and mapping, and modern data processing that has speeded up rating and loss adjustments and reduced insurers' costs.[70] Was international insurance, however, simply an offshoot of technological innovation, economic development and the expansion of world trade? Or did it possess its own dynamic and create its own markets? To address these questions we also need to examine the supply side: why do firms move insurance across borders? The theoretical literature on multinational enterprise (MNE) offers a variety of possible answers.[71] A firm may move abroad to avoid losing market share to another domestic competitor expanding abroad. There is support in the insurance evidence for this. The profits made by British and German fire insurance companies that had already crossed the Atlantic encouraged others to enter the United States in the 1880s and 1890s, leading contemporary observers to criticize the 'follow my leader' mentality.[72] Some firms adopt a market-seeking strategy, establishing businesses in areas without any direct relation to existing customers or competitors.[73] This was not true of the first British insurance exporters, who used their founders' existing trading connections to determine the initial pattern of their overseas business. A market-seeking strategy, however, became more attractive during the nineteenth century when transport and communications improvements provided greater access to new customers and greater managerial control over operations at a distance. Structural market failure has also been posited as an explanation for multinational enterprise.[74] Direct investment abroad was often the consequence of having to jump tariff barriers. Protectionism could both push and pull insurance companies across borders. Establishing a subsidiary from scratch in a foreign land, or purchasing a native office and then continuing to operate it under its own name, usually retaining the previous managers and staff, were devices motivated, at least in part, by fear of restrictive or burdensome regulation.[75] From the 1880s this was a common practice for foreign insurers operating in the United States, and to a lesser extent in Europe. State restrictions on direct underwriting by foreign companies, such as the legislation passed in Prussia in 1837 and in Russia ten years later, also encouraged the use of foreign reinsurance by native companies.

Local production also gave foreign companies a greater sensitivity to local tastes and enabled them to respond to local market needs more quickly. New firms lack information and experience, so their risky first ventures are usually into relatively familiar low-risk foreign environments. Bilateral affinities between home and foreign markets, such as language, culture or similar *per capita* income levels, may play a role in influencing locational decisions. Chain theory suggests that firms go through a sequential expansion process, the so-called 'establishment chain'. Due to 'psychic distance' and uncertainty, firms at the beginning of their foreign ventures will limit investment and stay close to their domestic market.[76] After gaining international experience, they will gradually invest further away (and on an increasing scale) from the domestic market. There are numerous examples of this establishment chain in insurance during the nineteenth century: Swiss companies underwriting first in France and Germany, the early presence of French companies in Spain, Austrian companies in Italy, Swedish companies in Norway, American companies in Canada, and Chinese companies insuring the property of Chinese communities in Singapore, the Philippines and California. Two qualifications, however, might be made. First, early mover advantages were important. Those companies that were first to enter a market from abroad, or indeed those that created a market from nothing, were invariably price makers and difficult to shift from pole position. Second, the size of a domestic market was often a factor in determining the timing and extent of its exports, especially before the 1860s when specialist reinsurance capacity had still to develop. Insurance companies moved abroad in the search for premium volume as much as profits. Foreign operations could help reduce income volatility and increase premium flow, but only if the market was large, hence the growing attraction of the United States after 1850.

Finally there were other factors that facilitated foreign ventures, notably the increased levels of business and scientific cooperation evident in the insurance industry towards the end of the nineteenth century, as well as the growing market for managers and actuaries that saw leading personnel move frequently between firms in different countries. International congresses functioned to facilitate the exchange of ideas and the standardization of underwriting technologies and business practices. Examples discussed in Martin Lengwiler's chapter below include the International Congress of Social Insurance (founded 1886), the International Congress of Actuaries (1895) and the International Congress on Life Assurance Medicine (1899).

The march towards internationalization, however, was not irreversible. There is unambiguous evidence that insurance markets around the world were becoming more protected and regulated before 1914, and some evidence too, though more conclusive for some markets than others, that insurance was becoming less international in scope. Peter Borscheid has estimated that the 'internationalization' quotient of the German insurance industry – measured as the sum of the foreign premiums of German insurers and the premiums of foreign insurers in Germany divided by total premium income in Germany – was already declining before 1914, ahead of its collapse in the inter-war years. The quotient, which was 12 per cent in 1901, dropped to just 2 per cent by 1938.[77] Elsewhere, Borscheid has charted the precipitous decline of foreign company participation in Switzerland – from 35 per cent of premiums in 1914 to less than 5 per cent by the late 1920s; in Japan – from 35 per cent of fire insurance premiums in 1917 to less than 5 per cent in 1939; and in Italy and Germany, where the premiums earned by foreign insurers fell by 27 and 30 per cent respectively during the 1930s. The large US life offices disposed of almost all their non-Canadian foreign business during the 1920s.[78] Other examples of insurance retreating behind borders include Spain, where the proportion of direct insurance written by foreign companies fell from 39 per cent in 1910 to 14 per cent by 1954.[79] In many countries the retreat worked in both directions. The number of foreign life insurance offices working in the Netherlands, for example, peaked at 51 in 1900, but fell to 19 by 1930, while Dutch life companies had 34 offices abroad in 1904, but just nine by 1927.[80]

Borscheid describes this trend as a 'globalisation backlash', and there were several causes. As noted above, the rise of native offices and growing public hostility to foreign insurers stirred up by the press, insurance lobby groups and by nationalist or populist politicians, contributed to this trend well before the First World War. Poor results in overseas markets, where monitoring problems were greatest, also forced companies to return home. Protectionist legislation, discriminatory regulation and taxation, however, were the principal forces behind the globalization backlash. The increasing rigour of state supervision from the 1890s raised the costs of operating in foreign markets and drove some companies out as well as encouraging others to establish domiciled subsidiaries.[81] There is no doubt the global regulatory environment for insurance exporters was becoming tougher before the First World War. The ultimate threat to the internationalization of insurance, however, was the growth of state-owned insurance, which between the 1920s and 1960s was associated in many places with economic nationalism. Where there was a powerful state institution, or where insurance was nationalized, private companies, including foreign ones, could find themselves effectively excluded. In several countries, particularly those where communist or nationalist governments came to power, or in newly independent colonies, various branches of insurance were transferred entirely to new state-owned institutions. Life insurance, for example, was nationalized in Italy in 1912 and in India in 1956. Turkey established a joint state-private reinsurance monopoly in 1929, while state monopolies were established for reinsurance in Chile and Uruguay in 1927 and in Argentina in 1952.[82] Accident insurance was nationalized in Spain in 1963, the culmination of a long policy of autarky that had begun with the dictatorship of Primo de Rivera 40 years earlier.[83] Between the wars these developments frequently occurred in states marked by political instability and financial crises. The widespread distrust of some regimes led to the operations of foreign companies being wound down. The instability of currencies between the wars also raised obstacles to the international trade in insurance. For example, foreign distrust of the Reichsmark after it collapsed in 1918 led some countries to respond with hostile legislation. Switzerland passed a law in 1919 requiring foreign life offices to keep three-quarters of their reserves there in Swiss francs. Due to the hyperinflation of the Reichsmark this was ruinous for German companies that could not afford to pay their claimants in Switzerland at current exchange rates. In this way 60,000 Swiss holders of German life insurance policies became indirect victims of the German currency crisis, which in turn encouraged more Swiss to insure at home than abroad. The market share of German life offices crumbled, as it did in Denmark and the Netherlands for similar reasons.[84]

The New Globalization of Insurance in the Late Twentieth Century

Not until the 1980s did German insurers begin to recover the international profile that they had lost so rapidly after 1918. There was renewed expansion overseas and acquisitions of foreign companies. The final quarter of the twentieth century and the first decade of the twenty-first century witnessed major changes in the structure of international insurance. This was the era of the second great globalization, when markets were being liberalized and multinational companies were expanding into all corners of the world economy. Paradoxically, the greatest insurance exporter of all, the UK, experienced a dramatic decline in the importance of its overseas business, especially in non-life lines. In 1961 foreign markets accounted for about two-thirds of UK companies' global net non-life premium income, about the same proportion as in 1914. By 2006, this proportion had fallen to just 22 per cent. Part of the decline was due to the nationalization of insurance markets in newly independent countries in Africa and Asia, and part was due to the high costs of entering some large European markets such as Germany, or to the restrictions on foreign entry imposed by some nations, notably Japan. The main factor, however, was the increasing difficulty of doing business in the US. Rising management and litigation costs, and heavy losses in motor, liability, property and casualty insurance caused, among other things, by hurricanes, riots and terrorist attacks, made the US a persistently unprofitable market for the big UK non-life companies from the 1960s. Only investment returns earned on companies' technical reserves held in the US, as well as the huge premium volumes generated, explain why the British persisted in America for so long.

By the 1980s many countries were beginning to relax their restrictions on foreign entry or deregulate their markets. India, Korea, Japan and China, for example, either denationalized their state insurance corporations or opened up their markets to foreign companies. Within the European Union the legal framework for a single market for life and non-life insurance was finally put into place between 1992 and 1994. Deregulation, however, remains incomplete, even in the EU. Areas such as health insurance in Germany bear witness to how difficult it is to overturn a century of protection barriers and exclusive behaviour.[85] Foreign penetration remains limited in many markets. Only 7 per cent of insurance premiums in Asia, for example, are accounted for by foreign firms. Moreover, the development of insurance remains stunted in many parts of the world. In 1992 just 22 per cent of South Africa's population had health insurance. In China *per caput* spending on insurance in 1999 averaged just $13, compared to $2,921 in the US. The combined insurance premiums of India and China were less than those of Switzerland.[86]

The Organization of this Book

As noted in the preface, there was but a general theme to the conference sessions from which the following chapters originate, and no common objective was set for their authors. The essays were selected in part to illustrate the breadth of geography and topics covered by current research on insurance history around the world. Part I below comprises four chapters on different aspects of non-life insurance in Europe and the Americas during the nineteenth and twentieth centuries. Manuel Llorca-Jaña attributes the decline in the insurance costs of the textile trade between Britain and the South American cone during the early nineteenth century to technical innovations in packaging and shipping. Based on the records of British merchant houses, he presents one of the first historical premium rate series for marine insurance, and also investigates the choices faced by merchants in selecting different insurance products. Christofer Stadlin describes the attempts at risk classification in accident insurance in nineteenth-century Europe, which were hampered by a lack of data and the difficulty of identifying relevant sample populations. Looking in detail at two Swiss firms, he argues that trial and error remained the basis of rating, and that premium tariffs, despite the illusion of actuarial precision, were first and foremost 'a marketing instrument to sell policies' (below, p. 60). Jerònia Pons Pons surveys the insurance market in Spain during the Franco era. Growth during the 1950s was accompanied by the gradual mechanization of back-office processes. However, mechanization, and the transition to computers that followed in the 1970s, brought its own problems, not least the shortage of skilled operators and the difficulties caused by strict controls on foreign exchange. Welf Werner examines the moves towards the multilateral liberalization of insurance markets after 1948, and identifies the constraints on that process, including the difficulties of monitoring the deregulation process in member states of the Organisation for European Economic Cooperation, the Organisation for Economic Cooperation and Development, the EU and the World Trade Organization. From the late 1980s the EU's Single Market Programme introduced an element of competition between states to provide the optimum conditions for insurance services, and this finally led to a leap forward in liberalization.

Part II comprises five chapters on life insurance and social insurance. Takau Yoneyama asks who bought life assurance in Meiji Japan and why. He finds differences in the target markets of first-mover and follower companies. The former focused on the demand from the western-oriented urban business and professional classes and used marketing strategies appropriate to these groups. The latter invested in a rural sales force and sold smaller policies as a vehicle for family savings. Liselotte Eriksson reports that the primary object of industrial life assurance in the UK and the US around 1900 was to cover the cost of burials and final medical bills, while in Europe endowment insurance with a primary savings element was the main characteristic of industrial assurance. The chief factor was the difference in the relative cost of funerals: higher in the US and the UK because the business was privatized and commercialized; lower in Europe because funerals were less commercialized and there was consequently less demand for burial insurance. Adrian Jitschin argues that the nationalization of life insurance in India in 1956 reduced the potential growth of that market by half. The original aim of the government was to seize control of insurance assets but, paradoxically, the state-owned Life Insurance Company of India subsequently presided over a fall in the proportion of its assets held in government securities and an increase in equities and loans for house-building. Grietjie Verhoef traces the development of life insurance in twentieth-century South Africa, and emphasizes the importance of the investment prescriptions required of companies there from 1943. Forced to invest in government securities, the funds of life insurance companies provided the South African state with a means to finance infrastructural and industrial projects, and helped stabilize the economy during the country's increasing political isolation between the 1960s and 1980s. Finally, Martin Lengwiler shows how the promotion of a mixed welfare system for social insurance was the consistent goal of the private insurance companies (though not their statutory counterparts) organized in the International Congress of Actuaries (ICA) from the 1900s to the 1950s. The ICA and other international expert bodies were influential in shaping what Lengwiler calls the 'epistemic framework' (below, p. 183) of welfare policies. He also finds, however, that the international convergence pursued by the ICA in this period was largely thwarted by national interest groups.

Although the chapters extend across a great variety of subjects, some common themes can be identified, which may form a basis for future comparative work on insurance history. First, several chapters focus upon the importance of national policy in shaping the structure and determining the direction of growth of insurance industries. This was most obvious in Franco's Spain (Pons Pons) and in Nehru's India (Jitschin), but that influence can also be detected in the different state policies towards the burial of the poor between Anglo-Saxon and European countries in the late nineteenth century (Eriksson). In his chapter Lengwiler outlines the interventionist (Swiss, German, Austrian) versus liberal (British) models of state supervision and the debates within the insurance industry about their relative merits. Regulation could block or stimulate the relationship between insurance and the growth of an economy. The chapters by Verhoef and Jitschin, on the role of life insurance investments in South Africa and India respectively, demonstrate this point well.

Second, the importance of cultural praxis in the international development of insurance also emerges from some chapters. Eriksson argues that cultural differences, alternatively emphasizing social welfare or market opportunity, help explain different attitudes towards funerals between Europe and the UK and US and thus the type of industrial assurance that developed there. Jitschin notes that the relative stagnation of foreign life insurance companies in India, when confronted with a rapid growth in native competition, was in part due to the cultural difficulties they faced in adapting to the Indian life market, for example, with regard to Hindu funeral practices. Arguably, the 'misconceived' determinism (below, p. 61) of nineteenth-century Swiss accident insurers that Stadlin describes, with their fixation on accident probabilities, may also have been culturally driven.

Third, several chapters point to external factors that have influenced the diffusion of insurance technologies. In Spain during the 1950s rising labour costs and the availability of finance stimulated the mechanization of back-office processes. The largest companies with the deepest pockets were the first to invest in this technology (Pons Pons). The different cost of funerals in the UK, the US and Europe helped determine the organizational forms taken by industrial life assurance in different countries (Eriksson). The availability of appropriate data for accident insurance tariffs in the late nineteenth century shaped the pricing strategy of firms in this field (Stadlin). The international transfer of insurance technology also hinged in places on the key role played by individuals and publicists, and on the process of imitation, so that German mathematicians were central to the pricing of accident insurance in Switzerland from the 1860s (Stadlin), and early Indian life assurance borrowed from UK models (Jitschin). At the beginning and again towards the end of the twentieth century transnational bodies and international networks of experts have played an increasing role in shaping, and to a limited extent standardizing, insurance technologies, insurance regulation and social welfare policies (Lengwiler, Werner). Some of these themes tap directly into the new body of research on modern business and professional networks and their influence in policymaking.[87] Such links between insurance history and more general themes and theories in business and economic history are certainly to be encouraged.

1 THE MARINE INSURANCE MARKET FOR BRITISH TEXTILE EXPORTS TO THE RIVER PLATE AND CHILE, *c.* 1810–50

Manuel Llorca-Jaña

Introduction

In the 1810s the River Plate and Chile gained independence after three centuries of Spanish dominion. From that point, British merchants opened for the very first time mercantile houses on the spot, marketing European manufactures in exchange for South American produce. During the first decades following independence, the main products imported by the new South American republics were textiles. These comprised over 80 per cent of British exports to the River Plate and Chile between 1815 and 1859 (see Figure 1.1).

Despite the predominance of textiles within British exports to these emergent markets, very little is known about the marketing chain of textile exports. This chapter sheds new light on this underexplored subject, by focusing on one aspect of this textile trade, namely, the marine insurance market in which British textile cargoes were insured before departing for the Southern Cone.[1]

This chapter relies heavily on the business correspondence of Huth & Co., a London-based mercantile house with branches in Liverpool, Valparaiso, Tacna, Arequipa and Lima, and which was very active in the marine insurance market. However, this firm was just one among over 250 British merchant houses trading with the Southern Cone during the first half of the nineteenth century. Therefore, further evidence was also obtained from other British houses involved in British textile exports to southern South America, namely Hodgson & Robinson (based in Buenos Aires), Hancock & Wylie (a Scottish house with branches at Bahia, Buenos Aires, Pernambuco and Rio de Janeiro), Dallas & Co. (also based in Buenos Aires) and Lupton & Co. (Leeds merchants exporting to the River Plate). Finally, the Chilean National Archives (Valparaiso Judicial Papers)

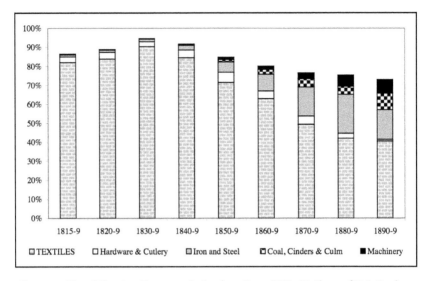

Figure 1.1: United Kingdom Exports to the Southern Cone, 1815–99: Shares of Main Product Categories (from declared value series).[2]

and British Foreign Office correspondence with consuls in the Southern Cone also proved useful.

The chapter is in four sections. After this short introduction, attention is focused on the structure of the British marine insurance market from the eighteenth to the mid-nineteenth century. The second section examines the costs of marine insurance for British textile cargoes to Chile and the River Plate. The third explains the different marine insurance policies available for British exporters, as well as the complexities derived from them. The final section discusses the growth of British textile exports to the Southern Cone from the 1810s to the 1850s, and points to the drastic reduction in the cost of marine insurances as one of the many variables behind this positive British export trade performance.

Marine Insurance: The Structure of the Market

As noted above, very little is known about marine insurances for British exports to the Southern Cone during the first half of the nineteenth century, and indeed for exports to any Latin American outlet during this period.[3] For this reason alone this chapter makes an important contribution to the field of insurance in history, particularly given that in the period 1815–49 Latin America received about a fifth of British exports.[4] Furthermore, as this chapter demonstrates, there is little doubt that marine insurances played a crucial role in facilitating the expansion of British trade to the Americas after the 1810s, a fact previously ignored by the historiography on Anglo–Latin American trade. First, however, we need to establish the general context in which British marine insurance developed during this period.

In eighteenth-century Britain, marine insurance was in the hands of private individuals, above all, those who met at Lloyd's coffee house. The first attempt to establish a marine assurance company was made in 1716 – the Public Assurance Office. Not surprisingly, there was great opposition from private underwriters, as well as from others interested in entering the market. When it appeared that the project had failed, a new scheme to create not one but two marine insurance companies was accepted, to silence the voices of those complaining about the inconvenience of having a single company monopoly.[5] Thus, in 1720, two companies were finally chartered, under the names of the London Assurance Corporation and the Royal Exchange Assurance Corporation, considered to be the 'first examples of corporate marine insurers in Europe'.[6]

For over 100 years, the British marine insurance market consisted of these two companies and the private underwriters operating mainly at Lloyd's. By law, no other corporation could enter the market. However, in spite of having a corporate monopoly, the Royal Exchange and the London Assurance had a small share of the market. Though originally chartered to operate in marine insurance only, after a few years the two companies were also allowed to effect both fire and life insurance, which soon became the main part of their business. The lion's share of the marine insurance market remained in the hands of Lloyd's until the mid-nineteenth century; Lloyd's became the foremost marine insurance centre in Europe.[7] Indeed, in time, it became clear that the main beneficiary of the 1720 charter was Lloyd's and, therefore, London. As stated by an 1810 British Parliamentary Committee, 'this exclusive privilege ... operates as monopoly, not merely to the companies, but to Lloyd's Coffee-House'.[8] Yet, in other British ports underwriters also operated. In 1802, for example, the Liverpool Underwriters' Association was created.[9] Private underwriters also signed policies at Bristol, Hull and Glasgow.[10]

The structure of the marine insurance market, thus, remained unchanged, despite the efforts made by the Globe Fire and Life Insurance Company from the late eighteenth century to enter the market. Freedom to establish new companies was not granted until 1824 when Nathan Rothschild's Alliance Marine Insurance Company was created as part of the repeal of the 1720 Act. In the same year, another company entered the market, the Indemnity Mutual, followed by others in subsequent years, of which the most successful were the Marine Insurance Company (1836), the General Maritime (1839) and the Neptune (1839). Many more subsequently entered the market, though without much success. By the mid-nineteenth century, few of the new companies had survived (e.g. the Marine Insurance Company), and the market remained highly concentrated. It can safely be stated that not until the late 1850s and early 1860s did a 'second generation' of successful companies appear in the marine market.[11]

This, then, in brief, was the market in which British cargoes of textiles heading to the Southern Cone were insured. But who effected the policies? Most of the insurance for such exports were effected by the British-based merchants handling the goods, particularly when advances on consignments were given. In the words of the London mercantile house of Huth & Co. to their northern England agent procuring consignments on their behalf: 'if we have to make advances, we must of course make ourselves the insurance'.[12] Alternatively, ship-brokers were often entrusted with effecting marine insurance for exports to South America, for which a commission was charged to the exporter.

The papers of Huth & Co. provide a rich source of information in this respect. Huth & Co. were in the habit of using mainly private underwriters to effect their insurances. Among the most frequently used were S. Boddington, R. Davis, G. Pearce, R. Ramsay and Mr Cruikshank. Huth & Co. also used the services of the London Assurance Corporation and the Royal Exchange Assurance Corporation and, from 1824, occasionally used the Marine Insurance and the Indemnity Mutual Marine Assurance companies.[13] In spite of having a Liverpool branch and most shipments leaving Britain from the Mersey, cargoes were insured by Huth at London. The standard brokerage commission charged by Huth & Co. to their textile suppliers for effecting marine insurances was 0.5 per cent of the invoice value of cargoes.[14]

Private underwriters took risks for as little as £50 for British textile cargoes to southern South America, which means that behind any given cargo there were a great number of individuals. The papers of a mixed Commission, established to investigate British claims against the government of the United Provinces of Rio de la Plata for losses suffered during a Brazilian blockade to the River Plate (1825–8) provide useful information in this respect.[15] These claims reveal that underwriters at Lloyd's in groups of up to 40 different 'names' might insure a single vessel, taking risks from £100 to £200 each.[16] Alternatively, the insurance of cargoes was shared, one-third taken by one of the incorporated insurance companies, and two-thirds by underwriters at Lloyd's.

In summary, when the market was highly concentrated in the hands of underwriters, who took little risk per ship, exporters needed to resort to a wide range of individuals to insure their cargoes. As a consequence, networks of contacts to guarantee the availability of as many underwriters as required were extremely important. The higher the risks in the shipments to distant markets, such as the Southern Cone, the lower the competition among underwriters. For exporters to Chile and the River Plate, the marine insurance market was very restricted and it was often difficult to obtain insurance, even for houses with the reputation of Huth & Co. It was not unusual for the pool of their underwriters to become exhausted. As stated to a Scottish supplier: 'we had great trouble in effecting the insurance per Zoe even at 80/pc, most of our underwriters being quite full upon her'.[17] Likewise, on another occasion the Liverpool branch was told that:

> you are not conversant with the manner in which insurances are effected here ... We have repeatedly explained to you that there are only one or two channels where we can place goods in tarpaulin @35 and that when they are full we are and shall be obliged to pay 40@, the premium that many of our competitors pay at all times. You must be aware that underwriters cannot be forced to take risks, and we need hardly add ... that we take the utmost pains with every order entrusted to us.[18]

In spite of these difficulties, London remained the most important marine insurance market of Europe for exporters to the Southern Cone. Even textiles exported from France to Chile were insured in London, though the cargoes never entered a British port.[19] Likewise, shipments from Antwerp to Valparaiso were also insured by Huth & Co. in London.[20] Furthermore, not only was insurance of British exports entrusted to London but also insurance of remittances from the Southern Cone, either Chilean silver and copper or Buenos Aires tallow and hides. Insuring shipments of Southern Cone produce in London was a generalized practice among local houses, as there was no insurance market on the spot. Dallas & Co., for instance, British merchants at Buenos Aires, were in the habit of requesting that their associated house in London insure hides shipped in Buenos Aires for England.[21] Likewise, David Campbell and George Faulkner (Hodgson's connections at Liverpool and Manchester, respectively) were also in the habit of effecting insurances of produce shipped from the River Plate to England.[22] Even cargoes of local produce shipped by British merchants in the Southern Cone to continental Europe and North America were insured in the London market.[23]

The Costs of Marine Insurance for British Textile Cargoes to the Southern Cone

Ocean freight rates for shipments from Liverpool to the River Plate during the 1810s–40s were most usually some 2 to 4 per cent of the invoice cost of cargoes, although moving within a wide range of between 1.5 and 6 per cent, according to the quality (therefore prices) of the fabrics or garments being shipped.[24] Likewise, packing costs were usually some 2 per cent of the invoice cost of cargoes, moving within a wide range of between 0.5 and 3.5 per cent, according to the quality of the packing used, as well as the price of the goods.[25] As with shipping freights and packing costs, marine insurance charges could also be a substantial addition to operational costs for those exporting to the Southern Cone. As already observed by Platt and Reber, during the early stages of direct legal trade between Britain and Latin America, insurance rates as high as between 6 and 12 per cent on the invoice value of cargoes were frequently seen, particularly during periods of warfare[26] and winter months, though rates were more usually 2 to 4 per cent (see Figure 1.2).[27]

As shown in Figure 1.2, in any given year there was a great dispersion in the premiums charged by underwriters. This was a result of many objective but also subjective factors. Indeed, the premium may be seen as a function, in which: premium charged $= f$ (packing used to protect against seawater damages;[28] seaworthiness and age of the vessel;[29] reputation of shippers; reputation of master and crew; nature of cargo; destination and route of voyage, accounting in particular for distance and the danger of seas;[30] season in which the trip was taken;[31] political situation;[32] reputation of the merchant taking the insurance; sums already covered by the underwriter in same vessel). Or, as stated by a contemporary:

> In life assurance, premiums are the result of the highest science brought to bear on data most laboriously collected. The production of marine premiums is practical, merely empirical, and unscientific in the last degree ... between the premiums of life and marine insurance there are real and organic differences. The event contemplated by every life policy is a certainty – the death of the assured. The contingent part of the transaction is the time for which that event may be deferred. The event insured against by a marine insurance ... is a mere contingency, one that may never happen at all ... Marine insurance premiums are an admixture of experience, tradition, and personal fancy. They fluctuate with seasons and states of a barometer; they are affected by locality, by a storm, and by political events; by prejudice, by the character of the assured or broker, by competition ... They are too uncertain to be tabulated, too unsettled even to be quoted in a price-current.[33]

Marine Insurance Policies

So far I have described the structure of the marine insurance market and given some idea of the costs of underwriting. However, a fundamental question remains to be answered: what sort of marine insurance policies were available? Policies could cover total loss of goods (general averages) as well as particular averages (e.g. seawater damage). Any policy covering both total loss and particular averages was called 'against all risks'. A policy covering only total loss was called 'free from particular averages' and was intended for goods especially susceptible to seawater damage, e.g. corn, fruit, sugar, salt, flour, although, on account of the great extent of seawater damage of cargoes sent to the Southern Cone, it was also extended to textiles (at least for the Anglo–Latin American trades).[34]

The exporter chose which policy to use. Fielden Brothers (merchants of Manchester), for instance, sometimes insured against both total loss and seawater damage, although at other times only against total loss or did not insure at all.[35] Owens & Son, also Manchester merchants, made 'it a rule not to insure

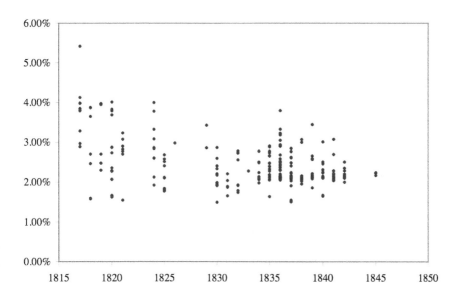

Figure 1.2: Marine Insurance as a Share of the Invoice Cost: A Sample of 271 Export Operations from Liverpool to the River Plate, 1817–45.[36]

against sea damage', while Crossley & Sons in general preferred not to insure at all.[37] Huth & Co., more cautious than any other, believed that 'we ought in the first instance look to perfect security, and next only to the terms upon which it can be obtained'.[38] It all depended on individual tolerance of or aversion to risk, as well as on the packing used. For example, a British merchant packing his textile cargoes for the Southern Cone in tarpaulin would be more inclined not to insure against particular averages, as tarpaulin provided a splendid protection against seawater damage. In the same vein, a merchant packing his textile cargoes in ordinary canvas – which provided little protection against water, would certainly prefer to insure against particular averages.

In turn, particular averages could be contracted for the whole cargo or for individual packages within a cargo. Likewise, different policies could be effected for each package insured. For instance, Thomas Walker wrote to Hodgson that 'I always insure my shipments [against] particular average on each package'.[39] These policies were called 'separate average' and were used because underwriters forced merchants to sell at public auctions all goods included in a given policy even if only few had been damaged.[40] When insuring individual packages, merchants sold at public auctions only the damaged bales; the sound ones being sold on the open market at higher prices. The only drawback of 'separate average' policies was that they were more expensive.[41]

Among policies there were other dividing lines: either to go for 'open policies'[42] or 'valued policies'.[43] In the first case, the price of the goods was not stated and to claim from the underwriter the invoice cost of the goods was required. In the second case, a quantity of goods was insured at a given price. To claim from the underwriters it was only necessary to prove that the stated quantity of goods were on board the ship, usually with a bill of lading. As explained by a Liverpool merchant:

> When insuring thus you are at liberty to value your property at any reasonable sum over the cost, without affecting the validity of the policy. But if I had insured any stated sum ... without describing the quantity or without valuing them, then this is what would be termed an open policy, and before I could recover I must produce an Invoice and Bill of Lading, and nothing over the Invoice amount could be recovered.[44]

Thus, merchants could insure for the actual cost of the goods or for something more. It was very common for merchants to effect insurances to cover not only the prime cost of goods but also freight charges, import duties and commissions. The purpose of this strategy was to assure that the trade operation was wholly covered. Thus, values insured were very often up to 40 per cent above the actual invoice costs.[45] Another alternative was for merchants to pay a higher premium, part of which (e.g. four-ninths) was returned by the underwriter once notice of goods being landed was received.[46]

In contrast with particular averages, general averages affected all who had interests in the ship or cargo. In the words of McCulloch, general average:

> comprehends all loss arising out of a voluntary sacrifice of a part of either vessel or cargo, made by the captain for the benefit of the whole. Thus, if a captain throw part of his cargo overboard, cut from an anchor and cable, or cut away his masts; the loss so sustained being voluntarily submitted to for the benefit of the whole, is distributed over the value of the whole ship and cargo, and is called 'general average'.[47]

In spite of the great impact general averages had on the business of those exporting textiles to the Southern Cone, there are no references in the related secondary literature, at least not to my knowledge.

But how exactly did general averages work? If a ship was chartered in sound condition[48] but during the voyage it was damaged by causes other than those which could be attributed to its captain (e.g. bad weather) so that it could not continue, instead having to anchor at the closest port to undertake repairs, then such damages were called 'general averages'.[49] Damage thus declared was the responsibility of the consignees, not the shipowners nor the ship's captain.

When, more typically, captains of damaged ships had no funds to pay for repairs, the solution was to sell part of the cargo, borrow money from merchants at the port where the ship was to be repaired, or both.[50] For this, captains had to mortgage the ship and possibly its contents, including cargoes, against loans extended. All these costs were paid by the consignees once the ship arrived at her final destination, by signing a bond of indemnity.[51] The liability each consignee bore had to be established, which was estimated according to their respective shares of the total invoice value of cargoes. If consignees refused to pay for their contributions, their cargoes were not unloaded.[52] Under this sort of legal regime, exporters were taking huge risks when shipping to the Southern Cone. The higher the share of an exporter in the total value of a cargo, the higher the risk of being liable for a great loss. In this context, the strategy of shipping regular and small quantities of bales in as many vessels as possible seems to have been better than chartering a whole vessel.

Growth of British Textile Exports and the Development of Marine Insurances

As can be seen in Figure 1.3, there was continuous and very high growth in the volume of British textile exports to the River Plate and Chile between the 1810s and the 1870s.[53] This was the result of many developments taking place during this period, including: improvements in packing of textiles (to protect against particular averages); falling costs of production in Britain for cottons, linens, worsteds and woollens; falling ocean freight rates; falling marine insurance rates (see below); introduction of free trade in Britain; dramatic improvements in communications; falling import duties on the spot; better port facilities; the difficulties faced by local craft industries; and the establishment of a more stable political system on the spot.

There is no space in this chapter to examine all these developments. However, as far as marine insurance is concerned, as a direct result of better packing and shipping improvements, insurance premiums fell significantly. Figures 1.4 and 1.5 provide convincing new evidence in this respect. If during 1822–4 premiums at Lloyd's for shipments to Valparaiso were 5 per cent of the value of the cargoes, in 1847 the rate had gone down to 1.63 per cent (see Figure 1.4).[54] The particular experience of Huth & Co. confirms this (Figure 1.5).[55] The historical literature, however, lacks any reference to this significant reduction in the cost of insurance, a material variable explaining the development of exports to the Southern Cone.

Improvements in the packing of textiles, which gave protection against damage from seawater and fresh water, were a positive development promoting exports, a point previously neglected by economic historians. During the early decades of commercial intercourse with the republics, a great deal of British textiles arrived soaked and had to be sacrificed at very low prices in public auctions. These were times when exporters packed their goods mostly in canvas or,

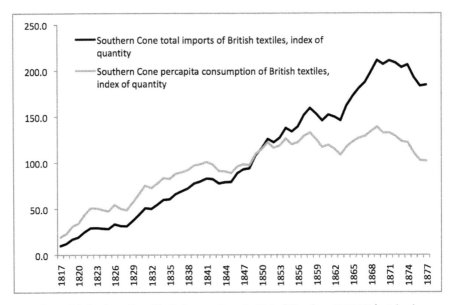

Figure 1.3: Southern Cone Textile Imports from the United Kingdom, 1817–77 (weighted indexes of total and *per capita* imports in volume; five-year moving averages of the series, 1850 = 100).[56]

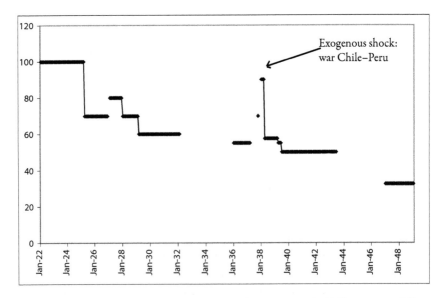

Figure 1.4: Premiums at Lloyd's for shipments to Valparaiso, 1822–49 (shillings per £100).[57]

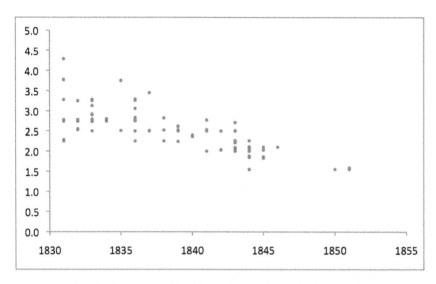

Figure 1.5: A Sample of Insurances Effected by Huth & Co. for Textile Shipments from Liverpool to Valparaiso, 1831–51 (percentage share of invoice costs; 118 operations).[58]

at best, in oil cloth. Thanks to the introduction of tarpaulin for packing textiles, the extent of seawater damage was dramatically reduced during the 1830s and 1840s. Thereafter, textiles bales were further protected through the introduction of iron vessels in the trade between Britain and the Southern Cone. Better packing and improved shipping reduced marine insurance premiums significantly, which was another important change that fostered British textile exports during the first half of the century.[59]

Conclusions

This is the first essay on the marine insurance market for British exports to South America following independence from Spain. Novelty itself does not necessarily lend any merit to a piece of writing. That said, for those interested in the history of marine insurance, this chapter sheds new light on the structure of the British marine insurance market, on the development of the costs of marine insurance for British textile cargoes to Chile and the River Plate, and on the different marine insurance policies available to British exporters. Finally, the chapter establishes a link between the growth of British textile exports to the Southern Cone from the 1810s to the 1850s and the drastic reduction in the cost of marine insurance. This is one of many variables behind the increase in British textile exports, an association so far neglected by historians. There is scope for much more research on the papers of other British merchants exporting to the Southern Cone, as well as on the business records of underwriters and marine insurance companies. I hope other researchers will join the train.

2 ACTUARIAL PRACTICE, PROBABILISTIC THINKING AND ACTUARIAL SCIENCE IN PRIVATE CASUALTY INSURANCE

Christofer Stadlin

Introduction

In 1997, Hans Bühlmann, one of the doyens of twentieth-century non-life actuarial science, gave a speech about the role of the actuarial profession. He stated that one of the oldest English life insurance companies, the Equitable Life Assurance Society, founded in 1762, 'managed to weather all storms in good shape, and flourished, because of the scientific methods it employed'.[1] Making the application of scientific methods the centrepiece of explaining the success of the life insurance industry raises a question about non-life insurance, particularly given that Bühlmann argued that actuarial science only first gained effective influence over non-life actuarial practice in the 1960s and 1970s.[2] The question is how did the different branches of non-life insurance manage to become successful insurance enterprises in the absence of scientific methods?

The cornerstones of the development of non-life actuarial science are known.[3] Much less is known about the actuarial practice of the non-life insurance companies.[4] In one of the first comprehensive textbooks on non-life actuarial practice, Max Gürtler noted in 1936 that most experts in non-life insurance had never seen a correct statistic during their career.[5] He also stressed that most premium rates were not so much derived from any calculations as from mere intuitions and practical experiences.[6] Keynes, for his part, famously poked fun at the seat-of-the-pants methods that most insurance companies used to calculate premiums.[7]

This chapter aims to shed light on this dark corner of insurance history. For this purpose, two Swiss casualty insurance companies are considered, namely the Zurich Accident, founded in 1872, and the Winterthur Accident, founded in 1875. After initial difficulties both companies grew to become among the largest casualty companies in Europe by 1900. In an article in 1927, the managing director of Winterthur associated the success of Swiss accident insurers to their technical mastery.[8] The main focus of this chapter is on the question of rate making and risk classification as documented in the insurance tariffs. The rating of risks is still considered today as one of the two core tasks of non-life actuarial practice.[9] The chapter also considers the deterministic conception of accident risk that was typically imposed upon it by nineteenth-century statistical science.[10]

To place casualty insurance in its broader context, the first section below traces the origins of casualty insurance in England around 1850, and examines the first French accident insurance company, founded in 1865, which provided the model for the German and Swiss accident insurance companies that followed. This section concludes with a discussion of key academic writings on accident insurance in the 1860s. The second and third sections focus on actuarial practice in the Zurich and Winterthur companies. The conclusion highlights the different means by which actuarial technologies were acquired by these companies and argues that, despite the increasing application of these technologies, actuarial practice in casualty insurance by the 1930s remained stuck somewhere in the borderland between deterministic and stochastic approaches.

The Origins of Accident Insurance and Early Actuarial Science, 1845–71

The first accident insurance schemes surfaced in life insurance companies in England during the 1840s.[11] Three types of coverage developed, namely a weekly payment of a fixed sum for a temporary period of time during a recovery from sickness or accident, including railway accidents; a pension that was returned in cases of permanent disability, including blindness, paralysis or insanity; and a fixed sum for death from an accident. These three types constituted the basis for the standard personal and collective accident insurance schemes, such as those offered by French, German and Swiss accident insurance companies founded in the 1860s and 1870s. The first English accident insurer, the Railway Passengers Assurance Company, incorporated in 1849, set premiums for train passengers according to the class of ticket, the sum insured and the duration of cover – policies were either for single journeys or annual. In 1852, however, the Railway Passengers Assurance obtained an Act extending its powers from underwriting railway accidents to general accidents. William Vian, its secretary, was given the task of working out premium rates. Using a table of fatal casualties for 1840, published by the Registrar General, Vian constructed three risk classes to classify occupations and specify insurance rates for the risks of accidental death. For class 1 he calculated 1*s.* per £100, class 2 2*s.* 6*d.* per £100, and class 3 was subject to application.[12] To calculate premiums for weekly allowances in the case of non-fatal injuries, Vian had no statistics to hand. General assumptions had to be made from the average recovery period from sickness. The company's own experience with regard to non-fatal railway accidents was also taken into consideration. Vian also suggested limiting the fixed weekly compensation to a period of twelve months, which marked a departure from the principle adopted for railway accidents. Between 1851 and 1870, sixteen further accident insurance companies were founded in the UK, which all adopted the schemes pioneered by the Railway Passenger Assurance, insuring fixed sums for accidental death and weekly payments for temporary disability.

The French company Sécurité Générale, one of the first accident insurance companies in Europe, was founded in 1865. Its charter explicitly stated that:

> By a series of studies, M. Besnier de la Pontoniere has demonstrated that the quantity and proportionality of accidents conform to mathematical laws; that, by carefully comparing these facts, one could determine both the scale of social liabilities and the tariffs appropriate for different categories of insurance. The dispositions drawn up in our statutes are the summation of these calculations.[13]

A table by de la Pontoniere, published by the Prussian statistician Ernst Engel in 1867, enumerated deadly accidents in France for the years between 1851 and 1860.[14] The accidents were grouped in thirteen causes of death, ranging from drowning, explosions of steam engines, railway accidents or falls from scaffolds to death by fire or thunderbolt. The table only displays certain regularities and trends between the annual number of casualties and the different causes. One would not call these mathematical laws, but they could be used as starting points to estimate claims costs and premiums to cover the *social liabilities* arising from deadly accidents.[15] This was only of use for the insurance of fatal accidents. However, Sécurité Générale also insured against permanent and temporary disability resulting from accidents. To specify premiums for these covers the statistics did not provide any sort of guidance. The coverage against permanent disability went beyond the English schemes. First, Sécurité Générale defined three basic categories of accident, which were obviously derived from the statistics of de la Pontoniere:

1. General accidents likely to happen to any person at any time, as for instance accidents in the water, on ice, accidents caused by extreme weather conditions, by fire, by free roaming or harnessed horses;
2. Work accidents occurring in mines, agriculture, construction, industrial premises of all kinds as well as chemical factories;
3. Railway accidents on moving trains.[16]

These categories were used in turn to define the concrete insurance coverages offered, namely personal and collective insurance against work and non-work related accidents, and personal railway accident insurance. The risk classification used to rate the covers conformed to the practice of the Railway Passengers Assurance. Apart from railway insurance, the insured were classified into three classes of occupations, exposed respectively to common, dangerous and highly dangerous risks. The former included lawyers and physicians, the latter included firemen and miners.[17]

According to Henri Jäggli, founder in 1883 of the statistical department at the Winterthur Insurance Company, two articles published by Ernst Engel, former head of the Royal Prussian Statistical Bureau, provided the basis for the establishment of accident insurance in the German-speaking part of Europe.[18] In his first article, Engel had noted that most of the small German mutual societies paying benefits in cases of disability caused by accident were not founded on mathematically sound principles.[19] Usually these companies were too small and localized, and suffered from too diverse types of risks. They offered pensions in cases of disability or old age, sickness benefits or capital payments for surviving dependents, but could never acquire the size and homogeneity of a portfolio necessary for some of these risks to start behaving with the regularity and constancy indispensable for insurance. In his second article about accident insurance, published a year later in the proceedings of the Prussian Statistical Bureau, Engel explored the statistical and mathematical methodologies of relevance for accident insurance.[20] To apply basic probability calculations, Engel argued, one must not only collect data on accidents, but also define the probabilistic frame of reference for calculation, i.e. the population at risk, the quantity of possible cases. Thus, fatal and non-fatal accidents in Prussian mining districts were referenced to the number of members of local miners' societies. Fatal and non-fatal accidents on German-Austrian railways were related to the total mileage travelled by passenger trains. The probability of such accidents was then calculated as accidents per number of miners or miles travelled. Engel detected a further problem in the selection of possible cases at risk. A sailor, who spent forty weeks a year on sea, for example, had less chance of becoming a victim of a railway accident than an engine driver, who travelled thousands of kilometres a year in his locomotive. The relation between the former and the distance travelled on trains was different from that of the latter. It was thus virtually impossible to determine a frame of reference that would enable the calculation of the overall accident risk of a sailor or an engine driver. Indeed, one had to substitute for the unidentifiable number of overall cases at risk the number of people working in certain occupations, the mileage travelled on railway lines, etc. That is why accident insurers had to work with risk classifications. The purpose of classifying risks was to get the best possible frame of reference required to apply the probability calculus.

For Engel, the main deficiency of contemporary accident statistics lay in the fact that most of them only covered fatal accidents. Only eight out of twenty-eight tables provided data on non-fatal accidents, even though the non-fatal ones were of greater importance for accident insurance. The few data available clearly confirmed the common assumption that non-fatal accidents by far outnumbered the fatal ones. From an insurance perspective, fatal accidents were already covered by the well-established life insurance business, thus, according to Engel, non-fatal accidents were the proper object of accident insurance. Engel concluded his article with some remarks about how to improve accident statistics. For every accident the following information should be registered: name of the casualty, gender, age, marital status, the existence of dependents, occupation or profession, type of accident, its cause, place and time. The record should also have a rubric for comments and the question whether the accident was a covered-up suicide. Such records could then be sent to the Statistical Bureau without further processing by the reporting institution. To view and tabulate this data would be possible without excessive work and expense, at least for a state like Prussia where only some 10,000 fatal accidents happened during a year. Engel also thought that this work and cost would not even have to be borne by the state. Engel believed that an accident insurance company would be more than happy to process such data at its own cost, because this would provide it in the shortest time possible with an insurance tariff of a precision that no other branch of insurance had at its disposal.

Another work cited in Jäggli's 1883 report to the Swiss Accident Insurance Company in Winterthur was Gustav Zeuner's 'Treatises on Mathematical Statistics', published in 1869. Zeuner, a Saxon, was professor of mechanics and machine design at the Swiss Federal Institute of Technology in Zurich from 1855 to 1871. Zeuner had first encountered questions of statistics and insurance in 1853 in the mining town of Freiberg in Saxony, where he had been commissioned with the revision of the Bergknappschaftskasse, the traditional mutual society of the local miners.[21] While in Zurich, Zeuner was employed by the Schweizerische Rentenanstalt between 1861 and 1864 to review its actuarial methods. Founded in 1857, the Schweizerische Rentenanstalt was the first modern life insurance operation in Switzerland. This work resulted in two reports that put the business of the Rentenanstalt finally on a scientific foundation.[22] From 1864 onwards, Zeuner audited the actuarial part of the company's financial statement. Later he was also a member of the Board of Directors and occasionally he lectured on the theory of life insurance at the Federal Institute.[23] This was the context from which his three treatises evolved, namely: the mathematical investigation of mortality, the mathematical investigation of invalidity and the mathematical foundations of accident insurance.

Zeuner's analysis of mortality required that mortality statistics had to focus on discerning the probability of members of an observed age group living at the end of one year (and then for the second successive year and so on) instead of calculating the probability of reaching a certain age, as in the tradition of Halley. Only with this new approach could error be minimized. This error derived from the fact that, from a strictly analytical perspective, age groups can only be defined in a contingent fashion.[24] In his second treatise, Zeuner applied the same analytical method to disability. Here too, the object was to calculate the probability of a person of a certain age becoming incapacitated during the next year and so on. The probability of disablement in general was calculated by simply adding the probabilities of the single years. Based on this analysis, Zeuner indicated how tables had to be designed to display the disability probabilities of any risk group in such a way that they could be used to calculate premiums rates for an insurance scheme.[25]

In his third treatise, using Engel's material, Zeuner calculated the probabilities of fatal accidents by age and gender for Bavaria and Belgium as well as England.[26] The probability of death by a fatal accident for the age groups between twenty and sixty – the target market for accident insurance – oscillated only within a small and constant margin, so Zeuner concluded that the probability of fatal accidents could be assumed to be nearly independent of age. As a result this could be kept as a constant. Zeuner's Accident Tabular Scheme a, shown as Table 2.1, gave the probability values for death, permanent disability and temporary disability.

In Tabular Scheme b, shown as Table 2.2, the actual case numbers would be calculated by simply multiplying the probability values with the members of the risk group or class (possible cases) for whom the data had been collected.

Zeuner freely admitted that the existing statistical material was insufficient to calculate probabilities of this completeness, especially with regard to non-fatal accidents.[27] Nevertheless, he developed formulae to calculate the net premiums necessary to insure the three accident risks. He also proposed formulae for short-term (up to a year) and long-term (greater than one year) insurances, and sketched formulae for the premiums for each of the three insurable risks. The net premium for an annual insurance against accidental death was deduced in the following way:[28]

- M stood for the number of persons who pay a premium of a_1; the insurance against accidental death for one year. So the premium income is Ma_1;
- Out of these M persons, Mr persons died during the following year through an accident. This results in the payment of the insured sum K. So the claims expenses are MrK;
- As the net premium has to cover the incurring claims, the two parameters equal, i.e. $Ma_1 = MrK$. This presents us with the formula to

Table 2.1: Zeuner's Accident Tabular Scheme a.

	Values of probabilities						
	1	2	3	4	5	6	7
Age in years	To live by year end	To die during the next year at all	To die during the next year by accident	To become permanently disabled by accident during year	To live at the end of next year and not become permanently disabled	To become temporarily disabled during year	Average duration of temporary disability in days
	p	$1-p$	r	q		s	t
m	p_1	$1-p_1$	r_1	q_1	w_1	s_1	t_1
$m+1$	p_2	$1-p_2$	r_2	q_2	w_2	s_2	t_2
$m+2$	p_3	$1-p_3$	r_3	q_3	w_3	s_3	t_3
...	...	...	...	...	...	...	...

Table 2.2: Zeuner's Accident Tabular Scheme b.

	1	2	3	4	5	6
Age in years	Living persons	During the next year to die at all	During the next year to die by accident	During the next year to be permanently disabled by accident	During the next year to be temporarily disabled by accident	Sick days consumed by the temporarily disabled during the next year
m	M	$M(1-p_1)$	Mr_1	Mq_1	Ms_1	Ms_1t_1
$m+1$	Mp_1	$Mp_1(1-p_2)$	Mp_1r_2	Mw_1q_2	Mw_1s_2	$Mw_1s_2t_2$
$m+2$	Mp_1p_2	$Mp_1p_2(1-p_3)$	$Mp_1p_2r_3$	$Mw_1w_2q_3$	$Mw_1w_2s_3$	$Mw_1w_2s_3t_3$
...	...	...	...	...	...	...

calculate the annual net premium to insure people (sharing the same probability r) against fatal accidents, i.e. $a_1 = rK$.

To calculate the income from a lifelong insurance against accidental death, Zeuner assumed that M persons paid the sum a when they took out an insurance.[29] After one year they paid the premium b. After a year not M but only Mp_1 persons would pay a premium, p_1 being the probability to live after one year. Thus, the premium income after one year is $Ma+Mp_1b$. At the end of the second year the premium is $Ma+Mp_1b+Mp_1p_2b$, and generalized for any period of time as $Ma+Mb(1+p_1+p_1p_2+p_1p_2p_3+ ... $ *to the end of the table)*. Under Zeuner's basic assumption that the necessary probability values were actually available, the bracket term could then be calculated for each age (m) with the help of the appropriate tables.

On the expenditure side, the expense in the first year is described as MrK.[30] Zeuner made two assumptions: first, that the premiums paid also included insurance against permanent disability; second, that people who became permanently disabled lost their entitlement to the sum insured on accidental death. The number of insured persons living at the end of the first year and not permanently disabled was therefore what had to be taken into account when calculating liabilities for the insurance of accidental death for the second year. That was denoted by Mw_1, where w_1 designates the probability of living after one year and not being permanently disabled. Out of these persons, Mw_1r was thought to die due to accidents during the second year, so that the expenditure for death claims at the end of the second year was Mw_1rK, and the end of the third year Mw_1w_2rK, and so on.

The work of Engel and Zeuner, however, did not inspire the foundation of accident insurance companies in Germany and Switzerland as the authors had hoped. In Germany it was the legislator who provided the decisive impulse. Partially intended as an answer to the 'social question', the Imperial Liability Law of 1871 made large areas of industry, including mining and railway companies, liable towards their workforces in the case of work accidents. Any compensation paid by an insurance company had to be calculated against the total compensation granted by a court, on the assumption that insurance would only cover part of an employer's legal liability.[31] That specific formulation indicates that the German legislators had knowledge of the accident insurance schemes established by private companies in other countries based on fixed sum payments. The idea was that the insured or her relatives would renounce litigation when compensated by such payments.

In 1871, at least two companies, as well as the insurance association of railway employees, took up the business in Germany. A year later, about 300,000 workers were insured with them.[32] The Zurich and Winterthur companies seem to have copied their first tariffs from the German companies. The Zurich probably copied that of the Magdeburger Allgemeine Versicherungs-AG, an accident insurance company that had been established as a subsidiary in 1871 by the Magdeburger Fire Insurance Company, founded in 1844. Unlike the tariff of the French Sécurité Générale that had just three risk classes, that of Winterthur had twelve and that of Zurich thirteen. Unfortunately, we do not know how these risk classifications were constructed. It is unclear whether they were based on statistical data or on commonsense estimations.

Actuarial Practice: The Zurich Insurance Company, 1875–1930

The Zurich was founded in 1872 as a subsidiary of the Schweiz-Marine-Insurance Company that had been established three years earlier. The Zurich's function was to absorb part of the reinsurance needs of the Schweiz and to build up its own marine portfolio. It quickly became clear, however, that the Schweiz was unable to generate enough reinsurance volume, and the Zurich began to explore opportunities for diversification. In August 1875, the Zurich commenced writing accident insurance. By the end of that year, apart from the Swiss offices, the company also had offices in Germany, Austria and Scandinavia. In 1877–8 branch offices were opened in Belgium and Paris. The international nature of the Zurich's early business was decisive for the distribution of its gross premiums. By 1881, 53 per cent came from Germany and 21 per cent from France. The home market, Switzerland, ranked only third at 19 per cent, Austria accounted for 4 per cent, Scandinavia 2 per cent and Belgium 1 per cent.

In 1880, following heavy marine losses and declining business, the Zurich abandoned marine underwriting and focused all its resources on accident insurance. The Zurich had four lines, three of which were accident insurance in the proper sense, namely collective (workmen's compensation), personal and travel accident insurance. The fourth line comprised third-party liability for industrial, railway and shipping companies. The following account of the development of the tariff focuses on personal accident insurance, which best illustrates contemporary actuarial practice at the Zurich.[33]

The basis of the personal accident insurance offered by the Zurich was the same as that of the Sécurité Générale, namely insurance against death, permanent and temporary disability. The compensations were also fundamentally the same. Unlike the French company, however, temporary disability was not insured on its own, but only in combination with either death or permanent disability, and the pension for permanent disability was not fixed to a certain amount but calculated on the insured sum against a pension table with conversion factors according to age. This table was based on mortality statistics, in 1876, for example, using those of the famous Belgian statistician Quetelet.

The personal accident insurance tariffs of the Zurich changed from 1876 to 1928 through four identifiable phases:

1. The years between 1876 and 1882 were the starting phase. It was marked by the use of a flat tariff that probably had been largely copied from German companies and was applied unaltered during this period. Occupations were grouped into thirteen risk classes and the rates per risk class to insure 1,000 francs included all three types of risk.

2. Between 1882 and 1891 there was an experimentation phase. This was marked by a rapid change in practically all parts of the tariff, from the basic rating principle (flat tariff for all insurable risks, establishment of two tariffs, separated for part and then for all risks, tariffs differentiated according to contracting period), the risk classification (number of risk classes, classification of professions / occupations) to the actual rates. For example, in 1882, besides the flat tariff (now tariff A), a second tariff (tariff B) was drawn up, differentiating two rates, one for death and permanent disability *pro mille* insured, and the other for temporary disability per franc daily allowances. The flat rate was finally abandoned in 1885. The number of risk classes was reduced to ten in 1885, then increased to eleven in 1888. There was a general increase in rates, especially for temporary disability policies under tariff B contracted for less than five years.

3. The phase between 1891 and 1910 was the first phase of continuity. The rating principle and risk classifications remained unchanged, at least with regard to the number of risk classes. The rates were changed only once, in 1898.

4. Between 1910 and 1928 there was a general overhaul and the second phase of continuity. The basic rating principle was changed again. Tariffs were discriminated according to the age of the insured instead of the contracting period. Risks of permanent and temporary disability were further differentiated by mode of compensation. The rate for permanent disability in tariff A was split into two: one rate for compensation in the form of a pension, and a higher rate for a one-time capital payment. The number of risk classes decreased. The rates were changed very substantially in 1910 and more moderately in 1912. The tariffs so modified then survived unchanged until 1928 and substantially even beyond that.

The changing tariffs are in themselves evidence that there was an actuarial practice at the Zurich. What can be said about the way these changes of tariff were actually effected? As there is no direct evidence, such as working papers or notes, secondary sources have to be consulted. Given the approach outlined by Engel and Zeuner, one would first look for accident statistics that could have been used to calculate accident probabilities for professions and occupations, which in turn would have provided the basis for a risk classification and the calculation of premium rates. The only traces of such statistics are to be found in the annual reports of the Zurich.

In the annual report of 1877, 598 adjusted claims were reported. Their composition was analysed by type of risk and by industry and occupation. In 1878, the breakdown by industry and occupation was extended to the cases of temporary disability, but the basic analysis of claims remained the same. In the report of 1882, the amounts paid for death and the two kinds of disabilities were added to the respective claims numbers. By 1887, the claims reporting took the form that it then retained until it was substituted by a simple total number of claims in 1917: namely a table that specified case numbers and payments by line of business for the three risks. What becomes clear is that with the number of claims factored by risk insured, industries and occupations, the basis was there for some kind of statistical investigation of different accident probabilities. However, no evidence has survived that points to investigations going beyond the numbers given in the annual reports. At most, the statistical claims data processed for the annual report were used as point of reference for risk classifications or rate making. There was a connection between statistics and the premium calculations of the Zurich, but only on a rhetorical level.[34]

Further insights about actuarial practice at the Zurich can be found in the Einzel-Berufs-Statisik (Individual Occupation Statistics; hereafter EBS), which were probably begun around 1890 and cover the years 1889–1902.[35] The striking thing about them is the way they were arranged. The data showed thirty-seven groups of occupations (Berufsarten) with no direct relation to the risk classifications in the tariff. Each group encompassed occupations that according to the tariff belong to different risk classes. The tables presented a kind of a profit and loss sheet for each group. Starting with gross premiums, four columns indicated the different expenditures: claims payments, commissions, expenses and claims reserves. A sixth column contained the total expenditure, which was subtracted from the gross premiums to give profit or loss figures in columns seven and eight. All these figures were given as gross and further down the table they were given net of reinsurance. In 1891, a second table was added that factored all the figures down to the single insured risks. Death was reported in black ink, permanent disability in green and temporary disability in blue. This was in accordance with the tariff of 1891, which, for the first time, gave rates for each insurable risk on its own.

What is completely absent from these statistics is any probabilistic frame of reference. One would have expected the policy or claims case numbers. Instead, there are only the money amounts gross and net of reinsurance, sliced and diced in the way described above. Such 'statistics' did not provide a statistical, but an accounting profit and loss view of the business. This is also astonishing from another point of view. The effort needed to put the EBS together must have been enormous. The only way to collect the data in the required detail was to extract it from the policy and claims registers at the level of single policies and claims. As this work had to be done anyway to put together the EBS, it would not have been a major additional effort to simply count policies and claims and add these counts to the statistics. Yet apparently this was not even considered. The Zurich people must not have thought in terms of possible and favourable cases and accident probabilities, but in terms of profits and losses. So what can be said about the way the EBS were used?

One possible use was in the revision of the personal accident insurance tariff in 1898. The statistics tables of 1897 reported the average profits or losses per group and insured type of risk from 1894 and 1891. On average, clear profits resulted from the insurance of death (30 per cent of gross premiums) and permanent disability (34 per cent), but the insurance of temporary disability showed clear and constant losses (minus –27 per cent). In this way the EBS provided some reference points to indicate which rates should be reduced or increased. Accordingly the 1898 tariff revision decreased rates for the profitable risks, death and permanent disability, up to risk class VII, and increased rates for temporary disability. Rates for the higher risk classes on the other hand were increased for all three types of risk, even though the EBS groups containing occupations in these classes were too small to be able to draw any conclusions about the incidence of death and permanent disability.

A closer look does indicate that occupations within some EBS groups were risk-related in the narrow sense. Group 28, for example, only included three different kinds of roof makers who all shared the risk of falling off high places. Group 13 encompassed general veterinaries, horse veterinaries as well as horse and cattle dealers, all exposed to the risks arising from close contact with livestock. Other EBS groups shared common social attributes, or a mixture of social attributes and work-related risks, such as the three groups embracing manual labourers, or group 2, which included only businessmen engaged in commercial activities together with agents, brokers, bankers, salesmen and white collar employees in general, or group 12, which comprised all kinds of medical professionals, physicians and doctors, nurses and midwifes. Measured by premium volume the largest part of the personal accident insurance portfolio of Zurich consisted of policies issued to those engaged in bourgeois occupations. EBS group 2 mentioned above generated an income of CHF 861,000 in 1897 and group 3 (professionals such as industrialists and manufacturers) CHF 402,000. None of the other groups each generated more than CHF 140,000 in gross premiums. Viewed from this perspective, the EBS may have been used to identify market segments in which to direct the company's sales effort.

A third possible use of the EBS was to test Zurich's underwriting assumptions. At least until the turn of the century, the Zurich's underwriting was controlled from the corporate centre, where each policy application was checked. Even though branch offices and agencies abroad underwrote and issued policies themselves, they had to send copies of all applications and policies to Zurich. If the assessment at headquarters deemed a risk to be unacceptable, the branch office was advised to cancel it as soon as possible.[36] Underwriting of workmen's compensation policies was even more tightly controlled due to the larger risk they carried for the company. As the process of underwriting such policies was naturally more information intensive, it reveals the strong reliance on common sense and practical experience. For example, before insuring construction workers engaged in building a church, the centre wanted to know the height of the planned steeple, what kind of basement was planned and whether there was a physician's practice near the building site or not.[37] This kind of common sense reasoning based on experience may be assumed to underlie the definition of groups of occupations in the EBS. One of the main objectives of the EBS may have been to test the correctness of such assumptions and whether the risk classification of the tariff was adequate, at least in so far as it led to profitable underwriting decisions or not.

A historical outline of the actuarial practice of the Zurich would be incomplete without reference to Jakob Zubler. When writing his memoirs in 1941, the former CEO and then chairman of the board, August Leonhard Tobler, who had joined the Zurich in 1900, called Zubler the best technician the company had ever had.[38] Zubler joined Zurich in the 1880s as an apprentice to the general agency Berne, and learned the casualty insurance business from scratch. In 1889 he went to the branch office in Paris where he stayed for about ten years. At the turn of the century he was promoted to executive rank. From that time, until his resignation due to health reasons in 1923, Zubler was responsible for the French and Belgian business units as well as handling all actuarial matters for the company.

To get an idea of Zubler's actuarial knowledge and application, one can turn to 'Zubler's rule', a methodology he devised for workmen's compensation.[39] When Zubler started working for the Zurich in the 1880s, it was standard procedure to send an executive from the corporate centre whenever a workmen's compensation portfolio of an agency or branch office became unprofitable. The executive then did a detailed portfolio review, comparing premium income with claims payments per policy. All policies showing a large loss were quickly cancelled. Witnessing this procedure in Berne and later in Paris, it appeared to Zubler to be very crude. He thought it was not very clever to cancel workmen's compensation policies in this way without discovering what exactly had caused the loss. In some cases, cancelling a policy that was normally highly profitable at the very moment when it had to carry an 'unusual, incidental' large loss (death or permanent disability) for which it had been purchased in the first place, meant not only taking losses, but also giving up the possibility of future profits.[40]

Zubler started to analyse the claims more closely. He drew up special registers, so-called policy rendements, listing for every policy net premiums as well as incurred claims by type (death, permanent disability or temporary disability). When Zurich experienced massive growth in its French workmen's compensation portfolio in 1898, due to new legislation making it compulsory for large parts of French industry, Zubler introduced so-called industry rendements at the branch office listing the same data as the policy rendements but classified by industry.[41] This work proved his basic assumption about large losses and profitability to be correct. Given that large claims in general made up only about 5 per cent of overall claims, Zubler concluded that only small claims caused by temporary disability needed to be examined in order to judge the quality of a workmen's policy. Such claims accounted for 95 per cent of total claims. Zubler used the small claims, with the help of the rendements, to check the sufficiency of net premium of respective policies. Whatever premium was left had to cover the large losses that were inevitable, and it was therefore this amount that provided the correct point of reference to judge profitability and the reasonableness of underwriting decisions. This amount turned out to be about 50 per cent of the net premiums, as Zubler was able to show over the years. Zubler summarized his methodology for workmen's compensation policies as two basic rules:

1. A workmen's compensation policy must be cancelled, or its premiums augmented, as soon as the small claims reported account for more than 50 per cent of the net premium.
2. A policy with a normal number of small claims must not be changed, even when carrying a loss due to large claims.[42]

Zubler faced resistance from the sales force when implementing this methodology. The application of the first rule could present them with the task of convincing customers to increase their premiums, or risk having their policies cancelled even though there was still a profit. For the sales force, this also threatened their commissions. Zubler noted that it was much easier to justify to both the sales force and customers a premium increase or cancellation for a policy running a loss. Nevertheless, Zubler's method seems to have prevailed within the company. Twenty-four years after officially retiring and five years after his death, Zubler was remembered as having provided a secure method to time and again check the ten thousands of risks making up the workmen's compensation book and to weed out the bad ones. Zubler's method has proven itself; thanks to it, Zurich's growth has remained sound.[43]

The Dangers and Benefits of a Scientific Approach: The Winterthur Insurance Company, 1875–1900

The Winterthur Insurance Company was founded in 1875 – the very year Zurich took up accident insurance. Like the Zurich company, the Winterthur quickly expanded internationally and by the end of 1875 was present in most German states and Scandinavia. France and Belgium followed. Germany was Winterthur's main market, accounting for about 40 per cent of total premium income in 1884. Switzerland came second with about 25 per cent, followed by France with around 23 per cent, while the remaining 12 per cent were written in Belgium and other countries including Egypt.[44]

The Winterthur's first personal accident insurance tariff was a flat tariff like that of the Zurich, in giving one rate for the three risks.[45] The twelve classes were not linked to occupations but instead organized into four categories: light, increased, high and highest accident risk. Occupations were then cited, more to provide examples than a comprehensive list. The actual rates, at least for the lower risk classes, were nearly the same as the ones that the Zurich offered under its personal accident insurance scheme. For higher risk classes, classification and rates differed widely. The Winterthur's personal accident tariffs were reviewed at a faster pace than those of the Zurich. Through 1881, when a tariff for whole life personal accident insurance was introduced, the personal accident insurance tariff was revised four times. Thirteen further revisions were made by the 1920s. Initially the changes were fundamental – involving basic rating criteria and number of risk classes – and then they became increasingly gradual, focusing mainly on the classification of individual occupations and rates.

The Winterthur's very first annual report published in 1877 suggests that the company started with a scientific mindset, for it quoted, without attribution, Zeuner's treatise on the 'Mathematical Foundations of Accident Insurance': 'The existing statistics as defective as they may be nevertheless unquestionably show that accidents repeat in a strange and intimidating regular fashion, that accidents in regard to frequency and type follow certain laws'.[46] In the same year a German expert, Wilhelm Lazarus, was engaged as technical consultant on the tariffs.[47] Lazarus was an expert in life insurance actuarial practice and one of the fathers of the German mortality tables published in 1883 and based on data collected from twenty-three German life insurance companies.[48]

What Lazarus concretely did for Winterthur is – at least as far as I know – not directly documented. But there are several traces that reveal his hand, such as the following excerpt from the 1879 annual report:

> Claims data indicates that the realm of accidents is only seemingly subject to pure hazard but governed by specific laws. Over time it will become possible to present these laws in the form of accident tables as it is the case with the mortality tables in life insurance. Tables which provide the latter with secure mathematical foundations. In this regard it would be desirable for the accident insurance companies to join forces to investigate together the unchangeable laws that rule their business instead of warring each other with contingent collections of numbers that can not be compared.[49]

The comparison of accident with life insurance, the basic notion that accidents are subject to similar laws as mortality, as well as the idea that companies should pool their data, which had worked so well with life insurers, echoed Lazarus's experience and his work on mortality tables in Germany. This is even more clearly the case with the tariff for whole life personal accident insurance that Winterthur published in 1881.

Preceding the rate tables and risk classification of this tariff was an unusually long introduction that set out the company's approach to the business.[50] It declared that it had always been the intention of Winterthur to adapt personal accident insurance better to address multiple needs, and to search for as reliable a statistical base as possible for the calculation of premium rates. It argued that the premium rates of the accident insurance companies were higher than the actual risk because they were derived in a merely empirical way, namely that rates were set by trial and error. The standard procedure for classifying applicants by occupation was challenged as more convenient than correct. Personal accident insurance, in contrast to workmen's compensation, also covered accidents outside of working hours, the risks of which converged for all people. As a consequence, classifying risk by occupation led to the exclusion of people from the benefits of personal accident insurance, even though it was possible to calculate correct rates for their accident risk. Death by accident was well researched and its frequency fairly well known. The tariff for whole life personal accident insurance had therefore been built on these statistics.

Rate tables were then given for two tariffs: one for whole life insurance with annual premium payments, and the other for whole life insurance with a single premium payment. Each tariff gave the rates to insure CHF 1,000 against death and permanent disability and CHF 1 daily allowance against temporary disability for eight age groups from ages twenty to sixty. The rates for all covers by age group were further differentiated by five risk classes, creating 120 tariff positions. The rates for all three risks in both tariffs increased by age group. This clearly indicates a life insurance mindset – the basic structure of a life insurance tariff to insure payment in case of death.

This Winterthur tariff for whole life personal accident insurance is astonishing. First, it is clear that with the statistical base they were using, only rates for the insurance of accidental death could have been calculated. To fix rates for permanent and temporary disability insurance, statistics on accidental death were of no use. The talk about rates being statistically sound was pure rhetoric. One might suppose that this would have been easily detectable for those familiar with Zeuner's treatise on accident insurance. Even assuming that the tariff evolved under the guidance of Wilhelm Lazarus, it is still strange that the Winterthur's management approved it. It does not seem that the scientific mindset went much beyond the basic conviction that accidents were subject to law-like behaviour. There was, however, a discursive aspect to this rhetoric that has to be taken into account. The introduction was primarily aimed at the agents of the company who would have to sell the insurance with the tariff at hand. The introduction could also be interpreted as a set of marketing arguments to which the company imagined its potential customers might be receptive. A certain unease of management with whole life insurance expressed itself in the request to agents to create as large as possible a portfolio in the shortest time. Only such a portfolio could bring to bear the law of large numbers so as to balance premiums and claims and justify the low rates.

The Winterthur's whole life accident insurance was an instant success. In 1881, 1,339 policies were sold, and in 1882 another 4,114 were added, accounting for two-thirds of total personal accident insurance sold in those years. The management's unease, however, seems to have been justified. The size of the portfolio did not allow the law of large numbers to compensate for low premiums, and in 1882 the tariff was completely overhauled. For the tariff with annual premium payments, age was immediately abolished as a rating criteria. The 120 tariff positions of 1881 collapsed to 15. The rates increased decisively for both this tariff and for single premium payments. Age remained a rating criteria for the latter. But the rate structure was inversed. Where previously the rates had increased with the age of the insured, they now decreased with it. And they started with much higher maximums than the tariff of 1881 had finished with.

Another 1,660 whole life accident policies were written with the new tariff of 1882. Notwithstanding this further sales success, by 1883 the product 'with its very low and totally unjustified rates' – as it was later expressed – was abandoned.[51] The run-off was not easy. Policies with annual payments could be cancelled by the company in case of a claim, but those with single payments could only be cancelled by the policyholder under the terms of the contract. Fortunately, most of the whole life policies had been written for annual premiums, thus the Winterthur reduced its portfolio from 6,630 policies in 1883 to 2,593 policies in 1890. Out of 297 whole life policies written on single-premium payments in 1883, seven years later 254 policies were still in force. One may imagine that the Winterthur continued to pay for claims on these well into the twentieth century.

In 1883, following two years of heavy losses that absorbed over 45 per cent of its share capital, the Winterthur reached a crisis point. The managing director, Carl Widmer, identified the absence of secure evidence on the nature and volume of accident risks as the main reason for the losses.[52] Other reasons given included the dire state of unlimited third-party liability cover; the explosion of claims costs for workmen's compensation; the poor performance of railway liability policies; an insufficient claims reserve; excessive dividend payments; and high expenses associated with the company's rapid international expansion. In his report of March 1883, having already announced a positive result for 1882, Widmer used the defective statistics argument to justify his position because he knew that it would strike a chord with the Board of Directors. In fact it did, but not for Widmer. On 15 April 1883 he decided to remove himself from the scene. He took securities worth about CHF 100,000 from the company's safe and fled via Basle to the United States. Two months later, a committee of the Board confirmed the necessity of a statistical department.[53] By the end of July 1883, its future head, Henri Jäggli, had delivered a preliminary report, outlining the objectives and tasks of the department.[54]

Jäggli began his report by rejecting existing accident statistics, like the ones published by Engel, with the exception of railway and mining accidents. He thought that it was *conditio sine qua non* for every accident insurance company, which wanted to construct an accurate tariff, to start investigating its own claims data, especially on non-fatal accidents. A preliminary review of the policy and claims registers for 1875 to 1882 had shown that during this period, about one million people (personal and collective workmen's business) had been insured with Winterthur. During this time the company had adjusted about 31,000 claims. Given the right methods of analysis, this sufficed to provide the company with the information required to calculate tariffs. The tariffs needed to reflect the accident risk of every profession and industry.

For Jäggli the main questions were the following: how was the total number of accidents distributed among fatal and non-fatal ones? How did the non-fatal accidents allocate to the three different grades of permanent disability and to temporary disability? What kind of accidents were observed? What caused them? What role did age play in accidents? All accidents had to be analysed by occupation (personal accident insurance) and by branch of industry (workmen's compensation). Jäggli's questions embraced nearly all of the types of data that Engel had argued were needed for a viable non-fatal accident insurance business. To process all the data back to 1875/6 six men would be needed for three years. To process the claims cards was a demanding job that could only be done by an experienced and trustworthy employee with knowledge of the business and policy conditions. Data quality was paramount if reliable statistics were to be derived. A major problem was the declaration of profession in the applications for personal insurances, where there were a lot of errors. Jäggli suggested that agents be reminded via a circular to fill in these forms with utmost attention and completeness. He also pointed to the fact that there were still many employees in the company who regarded statistical investigations as superfluous. He deplored that the company had disregarded these from the start of its operations. He was convinced that he could deliver 'incorruptible numbers, ending definitely the endless warring over facts'.[55]

Jäggli's department worked on the preparation of the data for workmen's compensation from 1875 to 1879, but this work was stopped when it became clear in 1884 that this line of business was to be nationalized in Germany. Assuming that the nationalization of workmen's compensation in other markets was only a question of time, the statistical department then focused its efforts solely on personal accident insurance.[56] Between 1886 and 1891, a total of three reports were released that together covered the period 1875–90. The reports have virtually the same structure. They first discuss general and methodological questions. Then they show various analyses of the personal accident business portfolio, its development and the claims incurred on it. The tables detail the policies in force by tariff, and also give the average premium rates per insured risk, the average sums insured per risk, and the age of the insured.

The data in these reports derived from a counting card methodology that is worth briefly describing.[57] Policy count cards were prepared for each personal insurance policy from policy registers or the policy application forms. All cards prepared for a business year were collected, making up the business written in that specific year. Then they were inserted into the overall stock of the policy cards and remained there until they were cancelled or expired. Once cancelled or expired, policies were immediately weeded out, so that the stock always represented the correct number of policies in force. On the policy count cards the following information was recorded: inception date, profession of the insured, sum insured and premiums factored by insured risk (death, permanent disability and temporary disability), duration and tariff of the policy, date of birth and place of domicile of the insured, and the producing agency. For each reported claim a claims count card was processed according to the notification form. After a claim was finally adjusted, the corresponding card was inserted into the stock of claims cards of the year the accident had occurred. The claim cards noted the duration of insurance, the sum insured and overall premium, the profession, gender, marital status and daily income of the insured, age of the insured when contracting the insurance and the time, date, place, cause of the accident, kind of injury, part of the body that was hurt, consequences of the accident and compensation, method of regulation (e.g. payment of insured sum, amicable settlement, litigation), and, in the case of temporary disability, the overall sick and compensated days.

The Winterthur intended to publish these data as a contribution to the science of accident insurance, however, the numbers for certain classes of occupations insured with the Winterthur were too small for statistical relevance. Other accident insurance companies did not follow the Winterthur's example and make their experience public. If only a few companies had worked together using uniform counting cards, a basis for a complete and correct risk classification of occupations could have been achieved, but the different policy conditions of the companies made this impossible in any case.

The statistical reports produced some interesting results.[58] The report of 1886, for instance, noted that the countries with the smallest policy values had the highest rates, because in those countries the insured on average worked in more dangerous occupations that belonged to the higher risk classes. This observation led to the formulation of the rule that the level of the premium rate was inversely proportional to the level of the insured sums. This rule reflected the social composition of the respective portfolios. In Belgium, for example, mostly people from a high social strata insured large sums at low premiums. This was due to their occupations, such as merchants, pensioners, civil servants or scientists, which fell into the lower risk classes. By contrast, policyholders in the Bavarian Palatinate, mainly craftsmen and labourers, insured relatively modest sums at high premiums, as their occupations ranked among the higher risks.

In 1889 it was reported that the overall net results per risk for the period between 1875/6 and 1888 showed a small loss on temporary disability. The profit margin on death insurance had declined. Only permanent disability had produced a profit. This led to the dramatic conclusion that it was in the best interests of the company to avoid insurance for temporary disability altogether. If it had to be written, it needed to be for small sums only and then ceded by the largest possible quota to reinsurers. The proposal to cease writing temporary disability insurance was abandoned in 1891, though the demand for the smallest possible policies and the largest possible reinsurance was maintained. Insurance against temporary disability still produced an overall loss but permanent disability insurance showed an increase in profitability, keeping the overall result across all risks positive.

The reports of 1889 and 1891 contained comments and statistics on claims per risk that reveal ambiguities in how the Winterthur conceived the factors governing the frequency of accidents. The number of accidents, especially non-fatal ones, was constantly growing, despite the development of better safeguards and protective devices by industrial and transportation companies. According to the 1889 report, the reason was to be found in the accelerating intensification of industrial production in general. The actual numbers, however, only partly supported this account. While the incidence of temporary disabilities was rising, claims for death and permanent disability fluctuated without a trend. In the 1891 report the increase in the former was attributed above all to less restrictive policy conditions regarding payments made for minor injuries, rather than to an intensification of production.

The occurrence of accidents was also analysed by day of the week and time of day. Assuming that accidents happening on Sundays as well as between 6 p.m. and 6 a.m. during workdays were non-work related, the Winterthur statisticians reported in 1886 that 11 per cent of all accidents registered between 1875 and 1885 happened on Sundays and 19 per cent occurred outside working hours. The reports of 1889 and 1891 suggested that these numbers were even too low because accidents reported without any indication of the time of day had most probably happened off work. This added another 9 per cent to the above figures. Even if accidents occurring on a Sunday were not counted, about a quarter to a third of all accidents in personal insurance were non-work related. This raised the question whether it was really justified to underwrite personal accident insurance based exclusively on a risk classification by occupation. The 1886 report concluded that the risk of accident, especially that leading to a temporary disability, grew continuously with age. The report of 1889 shared that conclusion and argued that it would be justified to classify by age alone or in combination with occupation. For reasons of competitive disadvantage, however, a single company could not make this change on its own. Concerted action would be necessary in association with other major accident insurance companies.

As it could not be expected that classification by age was to be introduced in the near future, the statisticians focused on the problem of improving the risk classification of occupations. The main difficulty here was that if each occupational title was investigated, the fragmentation of the data would be such as to make the results statistically insignificant for many occupations. Subsuming apparently similar occupations under generic terms could lead to confusion. However, to construct simple and reliable accident statistics the number of risk classes had to be as small as possible. This would also make underwriting easier, as minor variations in the job description would not necessarily result in a change of risk class.

In a paper of 1889 entitled 'Proposal for the Fixation of the Risk Classification of Occupations based on the Statistical Observations 1875–1888',[59] it was argued that in order to ascertain the risk classification of occupations, only the ratio of insured to compensated claims needed to be taken into account. The ratio of claim payments to premium income could not be used, for the premiums depended on the sums insured, which were chosen by the insured and therefore contingent. The method of calculation was as follows: first, the average total base rate was calculated, i.e. the sum of the rates to insure CHF 1,000 for death and permanent disability, and CHF 1 daily allowance for temporary disability. The objective was to establish the correct classification of occupations in regard to the tariff in force and the corresponding risk classification. The average total base rate for the four years, 1885–8, since the tariff had been in force turned out to be CHF 4.11. This was closest to the base rate for risk class II of the tariff (CHF 4). Hence, risk class II was identified as the average risk class of the portfolio.

In a second step, the so-called 'accident figures' for the insured risks were calculated from the overall policy and claims data of the preceding thirteen years. The figure for accidental death was simply the average number of cases per 10,000 insured. For permanent disability, the accident figure was calculated in the following way: first, the case numbers per 10,000 insured were identified for the three grades of permanent disability. These were multiplied with the average value of the corresponding case, expressed as a percentage of the insured sum. The resulting numbers were then added together to provide the accident figure for permanent disability. The accident figure for temporary disability was calculated as the average sick days per 10,000 insured. The calculation also took into account severe (long payments of allowances) and light (short payment period) cases of temporary disability, and the more costly cases regulated by litigation. The resulting accident figures for the three risks were then inserted as the upper limit of the average risk class II.

In a third step, the accident figures for all the other classes were calculated proportionally to the differences of the corresponding rates of the tariff in force. For example, the accident figure for accidental death set as the upper limit of class II had been found to be 4.8 per 10,000 insured. According to the tariff of 1885, the difference between the rates for accidental death for class II (CHF 0.9‰) and the next lower class, Ia (CHF 0.65‰), was CHF 0.25. By calculating the relative difference on 4.8 proportionally to 0.25, the result was 3.6. This was then set as the lower limit of risk class II. The death case figures for class II were established to be between 3.6 and 4.8. That meant that per 10,000 insured under risk class II an average of 3.6 to 4.8 fatal accidents occurred. The lower limit, 3.6, was taken as the upper limit of the next lower risk class (Ia). The upper limit, 4.8, was considered the lower limit of the next higher (IIa). The corresponding lower and upper limits were calculated in the same way as for class II. The same procedure was followed for permanent and temporary disability.

The classification of the occupations was executed in the following way: The data for a single profession was analysed in the same way as for the single risks and then scaled to 10,000. The resulting figures for the three risks were then compared with the tables to see in which class they fell. The rates according to the tariff were finally added together to give a total base rate for the profession.

By comparing this total base rate with the total base rates of the risk classes of the tariff, it was then determined how the occupations needed to be classified. Employing exactly the same method the various accident figures were again calculated in 1901,[60] this time for three periods, 1875–1900, 1895–1900 and 1890–1900.

In sum, two points may be noted:

1. The methodology described above was primarily designed to assign occupations to the correct position in an existing rating structure. It was not designed to construct a tariff rating structure from scratch.

2. At the core of the methodology, were the so called 'accident figures'. As they related to accidental deaths, the accident figures were the equivalent of the average probabilities of becoming a victim of a deadly accident. They included the overall population and professional groups insured with the company. With regard to permanent disability, the probabilities differentiated by grades of disability were only part of the accident figures. The average claims payments per case were added to the accident figures for permanent disability. This can be interpreted as an effort to bring these figures closer to the concrete claims experience. Such an effort became even more tangible in the calculation of the accident figures for temporary disability.

Conclusions

This chapter shows that life insurance really provided the 'historical matrix', as Daniel Defert has called it, on which commercial accident insurance developed:[61]

1. The first commercial accident insurance schemes emerged in (English) life insurance companies. Even though it is unknown whether any policies were written, this is significant.

2. Most experts who were involved in accident insurance had an established background in life insurance.

3. The first statistics used in accident insurance were statistics of fatal accidents. These were a subset of mortality statistics on which calculations in life insurance were based. According to the paradigm of 'social physics' introduced by the Belgian statistician Quetelet, the statistical sciences of the nineteenth century interpreted mortality statistics as revealing the laws of mortality.[62] By means of accidental death statistics, this deterministic concept influenced the perception of accidents. It became natural to view accidents as social facts

governed by laws. These laws were thought to be discovered by investigating accident probabilities.

4. On the practical side, it was the basic underwriting principle of life insurance to insure against fixed premium rates on fixed sums.

When the Winterthur and Zurich entered the accident insurance business in 1875, they only needed to adopt an already well-developed insurance technique. Both companies simply copied the tariffs of German accident insurance companies. Any further know-how needed to set up an accident insurance operation was also imported from Germany. The Winterthur immediately refined the technical basis. The accident tariffs were revised after just a year. Three further revisions followed shortly after. An additional German specialist was hired with the task of advising on tariff questions. The Zurich adhered to its initial tariffs for six years. The reason for this probably lies in the fact that the Zurich was still active in marine insurance until 1880. In the four decades that followed, both companies changed their personal accident insurance tariffs at regular intervals. In the beginning the changes were quite fundamental. As time passed they became more gradual.

In the case of the Zurich, there is little direct evidence left of an actuarial practice related to the changes documented in the tariff booklets. There were statistics that would have provided data to calculate probabilities in the way Engel and Zeuner proposed, but they were not used for tariff revisions. Other statistics that probably were used for this end only reported financial figures. They provided an accounting profit and loss view, but not a probabilistic one. The Zurich did not base its tariffs on statistical analysis and calculation. It made use of a trial and error method, underwriting experience and commonsense. This conclusion is supported by the fact that underwriting control at the Zurich was executed at the level of individual policies. In the company history, written on the occasion of the fiftieth anniversary in 1923, this practice was described in the following way:

> Everywhere, the business had to be guided by one mindset, which is the guarantee for sustained success. This was the spirit of strict self-discipline, not dazzled by the shine of the moment, instead checking the potential of each insurance contract and rejecting everything that, given context and experience, promised damage and not profit. It was a spirit of precision and thoroughness.[63]

Under this perspective, the tariffs have to be seen as guidelines for premium rates. Tariffs were a marketing instrument to sell policies, while the statistics provided tools to check whether the experience and commonsense applied to underwriting generated profitable business.

Some actuarial practice is tangible at the Zurich, namely the rule of thumb that was developed for the review of workmen's compensation portfolios. This rule could be called a 'probabilistic heuristic'. On the one hand, it was based on a correct assumption about the statistical significance of temporary disability claims. On the other hand, it could be worked out only by investigating claims ratios. Probabilities, apart from being tacitly present in the basic assumption, did not play any significant role. With regard to the development of non-life actuarial practice, it is important to note that the deterministic perception of the accident risk was largely resolved once the statistical investigation was focused on the claims expenses. This was done with the help of so-called 'claims tables', which finally contributed to the modelling of accidents as stochastic processes.[64]

The case of the Winterthur insurance company is significantly different from that of the Zurich. There is plenty of evidence that the Winterthur followed the concepts and methodologies outlined by Engel and Zeuner. However, it took eight years and a near catastrophe for the company to understand them correctly. The tariff for whole life accident insurance suggested by the Winterthur in 1881 can be seen as a typical example of how misconceived mathematical knowledge and methodologies, especially when they are state of the art, can create havoc in insurance and financial services.[65] The fact that the fundamental misconstruction of the whole life accident tariff was discovered relatively quickly is an indication that a correct understanding was already present at the Winterthur. It may well be, however, that this understanding was not present at the right place in the corporate hierarchy. Thereafter, Winterthur began to analyse its own business as proposed by Engel and Zeuner. In three consecutive reports, 1886, 1889 and 1891, the resulting statistical material was analysed under various perspectives. The following points can be drawn from these:

1. Contrary to Engel's and Zeuner's beliefs, collecting statistical data on accidents turned out to be a very ambitious task. They had ignored the fact that insurance companies first needed to sell policies to get possession of such data. This was the typical theorist fallacy. The reports emphasize repeatedly that the Winterthur's own data was too limited to determine certain accident probabilities. In particular, the Winterthur lacked the data on individual occupations. This was crucial to classify them correctly. The unwillingness of other companies to share their data has often been remarked.

2. All three reports repeatedly recommended that any kind of method to classify and rate by profession should be abolished for personal accident insurance. Instead, it was agreed that the insured should be rated on the basis of age. This is interesting, because occupation remains the core rating criteria for accident insurance to the present day.

3. Nevertheless, a methodology was developed to check whether occupations were correctly attributed to the risk classes of the tariff. This

methodology was based on the specific accident probabilities that occurred in the different occupations. In terms of tariff revisions, this was the most important result of the statistical work.

4. The deterministic perception of accident risk persisted at least in principle, even though the statistical investigations revealed observations that could have put such a view in a different perspective (e.g. the influence of contract conditions on accident probabilities; the non-correlation of accident probability and claims expense in temporary disability). The methodology for checking risk classifications remained somewhere on the borderline between a deterministic and a stochastic view. The methodology clearly worked with accident probabilities, yet it also tried to model claims expenses, at least for permanent and temporary disability insurance, as realistically as possible.

3 THE DIFFICULTIES OF SPANISH INSURANCE COMPANIES TO MODERNIZE DURING THE FRANCO YEARS: THE MECHANIZATION OF ADMINISTRATIVE TASKS AND THE INTRODUCTION OF THE FIRST COMPUTERS, 1950–70

Jerònia Pons Pons

The end of the Spanish Civil War paved the way for a new regime in Spain, where autarky, interventionism and isolation from the international market were the most significant characteristics of economic policy.[1] During the 1940s there was a fall in the standard of living of the Spanish population and in levels of national income. The 1935 *per caput* income was not recovered until the 1950s.[2] Autarky also meant that the Spanish economy was isolated from abroad, with the entry of foreign capital denied.[3] The Spanish Institute for Exchange Control (IEME) was created, which controlled the buying and selling of foreign currency.[4] Any international transaction and payment had to have the Institute's authorization and concession of the corresponding foreign currency. By the late 1940s the autarkic model had collapsed, Spain's economic situation had become unsustainable and was further aggravated by international isolation. This situation started to undergo modifications in 1947 with changes in international policy, the start of the Cold War and the American administration's interest in having closer relations with the Franco regime. Changes to the policy of autarky began with a government reshuffle in 1951 and with the signing of the Treaty of Madrid with the US in 1953.

As far as the insurance sector was concerned, and in fact all other economic sectors as well, the end of the Civil War and the establishment of the Franco dictatorship led to significant changes.[5] First of all, from an institutional perspective, all the associations, unions and cartels that had been developed in the insurance sector since the end of the nineteenth century were abolished.[6] Within the new state organization, the different interest groups in the insurance world (employers and workers, insurance companies and mutuals, agents, etc.) were obliged to join the Sindicato Nacional del Seguro (National Insurance Syndicate).[7] The decree of 6 December 1941 recognized this 'trade union' as a Public Law Corporation.[8] In its second article, the National Insurance Syndicate was considered 'to be the only organisation with sufficient personality to represent and discipline the production interests in this Branch of the Economy'.[9] This institutional framework continued throughout the dictatorship although, with time, and especially from the 1960s onwards, different associations and groups emerged to develop and organize the diverse interests of commercial companies, insurance mutuals and social benefit institutions.[10]

Not much is known about the insurance business during this period and very little historical work has been produced on the subject.[11] In this chapter, first of all, the most significant changes which took place during the Franco regime will be analysed, along with the persistence of problems inherited from the previous stage which were aggravated by the government's interventionist policy, the influence of economic nationalism on the sector and the isolation from foreign markets. Second, insurers' attempts to modernize the sector after more than a decade of autarky by introducing, in an initial phase, the mechanization of administrative tasks will be studied, along with the bureaucratic difficulties that hampered this process during the 1950s. Finally, an analysis will be made of how the regime's greater permissiveness with regard to the creation of associations increased demand and how a greater relaxation of foreign trade in the 1960s allowed the spread of mechanization and, in a second phase, the introduction of computers.

Basic Characteristics of the Insurance Sector during the Franco Regime, 1940–75

During this stage, a series of characteristics of the Spanish insurance market can be highlighted. First, there was a large number of companies operating in some branches, which resulted in a very fragmented market. Second, there was considerable state intervention, which was apparent in such aspects as the attempt to control reinsurance, the prohibition of professional associations outside the National Insurance Syndicate or the nationalization of social insurance. Third, strident economic nationalism meant that the Spanish market was isolated from abroad during the autarkic period and there was a reduction of foreign capital in Spanish insurance.

As in other sectors of the Spanish economy, there was a clear sluggishness which showed itself in the slow growth in premiums throughout the autarkic period. There was no obvious change until 1953, when a notable increase in business began, especially in the branches of industrial accidents and automobiles (see Figure 3.1). This process was linked to the evolution of the Spanish economy, which clearly stagnated during the years of autarky, followed by a vigorous expansion initiated during the 1950s. From then on, industry became the motor of the Spanish economy, growing at an annual rate of 6.7 per cent between 1950 and 1960, driven by substantial investment. The rate of gross fixed capital formation from 1950 to 1958 was 9.8 per cent. Likewise, private consumption changed from the 1950s onwards. Private national consumption grew 4.9 per cent from 1950 to 1958 whereas it had only grown at an annual rate of 1.2 per cent between 1939 and 1949.[12] The growth in internal demand favoured the reactivation of the insurance sector.

The excessive number of companies operating in the Spanish market was one of the main problems inherited from the previous stage, and this situation persisted and even worsened during the dictatorship. There were 668 institutions authorized to operate in the Spanish insurance market in 1957, comprising 372 Spanish companies, 222 mutuals and 74 foreign companies. In the same year Italy had 135, Switzerland 86, England 412 and only France surpassed Spain with 686.[13] One of the main factors which explained the existence of an excessive number of companies in some branches was the scant requirements for reserves and deposits.[14] The government modified the capital, deposits and reserves required of different institutions through the law of 18 March 1944.[15] This law established a minimum share capital of 25 million pesetas with a paid-up capital of 50 per cent for Spanish companies operating in the principal branches (e.g. life, fire). However, only 1 million pesetas were required, with a minimum of 50 per cent paid up, for companies operating in the branches of sickness and burials, and 3 million with 50 per cent paid up for those operating in the branches of plate glass, hail, theft and livestock.[16] Similar differences also applied to deposits and reserves. As far as deposits were concerned, mutual societies received special treatment, requiring only 10 per cent of that demanded from stock companies. This special treatment for the mutuals, together with all the companies operating in branches such as sickness, plate glass, livestock, etc., led to a very large total number of companies in the Spanish market, with an important proportion of mutuals in relation to commercial companies (Table 3.1).[17] The law of 16 December 1954 increased the amounts demanded, but prolonged the differences of capital, deposits and reserves required of different types of institutions.

This different fiscal treatment, with varying administrative and guarantee requirements, had a historical origin. The historical legacy was further developed by other factors, derived from the autarkic policy of the regime, which facilitated the creation of national insurance companies, thereby increasing the number of institutions in the sector. Numerous national commercial companies were created in the period up to 1947, especially between the end of the war and 1942.[18] This growth took place within the context of a generalized increase in the number of companies in all economic sectors. Torres Villanueva emphasizes

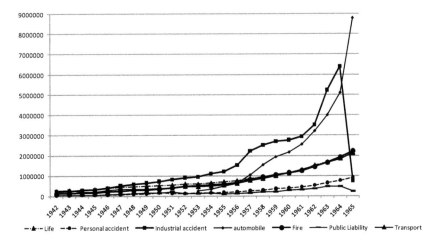

Figure 3.1: Spanish Premiums by Branches, 1942–65 (in thousands of pesetas).[19]

the re-registration of companies already existing before the Civil War under new legal forms, and the proliferation of small firms under autarkic policy and import substitution, as primary causes.[20] Both of these can be confirmed in the case of the insurance sector. On the one hand, many mutuals became stock companies, and on the other, the regime promoted the creation of national companies in all branches, and especially in the reinsurance sector.

With regard to the re-registration under new legal forms, there were legislative changes after the Civil War which encouraged mutuals to become commercial companies.[21] The law on mutual societies passed on 6 December 1941 established state intervention, through the Ministry of Labour, in the field of social insurance. It also abolished some of the privileges that mutuals enjoyed over commercial companies, and above all limited their participation in profit-making activities. The mutuals reacted to this law with different strategies. The first strategy was conversion into stock insurance companies. After this law, some mutuals with substantial profits, many of them founded for industrial accident insurance, became joint-stock commercial companies. This was the case with the Mare Nostrum, the Comercio, Industria, Agricultura (CIA) and the Hermes, three companies constituted in 1942 which were the successors of industrial accident mutuals.[22] New conversions took place in the following years such as the creation of the Galicia, SA in 1944 as a continuation of the Mutualidad Gallega de Seguros, founded in La Coruña in 1901.

Table 3.1: Number of Companies by Branch and Total Number of Authorized Companies, 1920–70.[23]

Branches	1920	1930	1942	1950	1960	1970
Life	23	31	49	80	89	110
Industrial accidents	31	51	164	222	288	–
Personal accidents	22	42	62	122	143	172
Public Liability	–	–	58	115	100	134
Automobile	–	–	–	–	133	–
Compulsory	–	–	–	–	–	159
Voluntary	–	–	–	–	–	161
Fire	60	87	118	169	203	227
Transport	–	51	61	89	108	127
Sickness	61	76	69	121	183	347
Burials	–	–	–	–	126	194
Theft	2	15	38	77	101	128
Plate glass	12	18	23	52	72	105
Livestock	11	8	13	21	28	–
Hail	3	4	14	21	35	49
Other branches	3	6	16	34	50	80
Cinematography	–	–	–	–	–	35
Machinery breakdown	–	–	–	–	–	34
Aviation	–	–	–	–	–	30
Legal Defence	–	–	–	–	–	12
Total authorized institutions	–	–	–	511	596	666
Reinsurance	2	4	10	13	–	–

Alternatively, other mutuals opted for a second strategy based on the acquisition or creation of related companies. This was the case of the Campo, SA, for example, created by some directors and executives of the MAPFRE to carry out insurance activity forbidden to mutuals. In many cases during the 1940s and 1950s mutuals acquired small commercial companies to this end. These companies were not linked to the mutuals by the direct purchase of shares, but rather by directors of the mutuals acquiring shares individually. These companies functioned under the effective management of the mutuals and in some cases did not even have their own administrative infrastructure or network of agents, sharing with the mutual. While the mutual company covered the majority of the costs, the profits, if there were any, in the form of dividends or from the sale of shares, went, to a large extent, to the directors.[24]

As regards the effects of autarkic policy on the insurance sector, and the fostering of small-scale national companies which substituted imports, this policy became a reality above all in reinsurance. The foreign dependence of reinsurance before 1940 presented serious problems in the postwar period with the introduction of an autarkic economic policy. The initial solution was to take control of reinsurance, creating the obligation to reinsure in Spain, with a drive to create national reinsurance companies. The first provisions in this sense were initiated with the decree of 13 March 1942, which dealt with the insurance and reinsurance of ship hulls registered in Spain, obliging insurance with those institutions enrolled in a special insurance register created by the first article of the law of 14 May 1908. In October 1942, the government elaborated a study on the basis of information furnished by insurance companies, and from this calculated that reinsurance moved around 1,200 million pesetas in 1943.[25] Subsequently, the decree of 29 September 1944 was passed in which reinsurance operations were subjected to the law of 14 May 1908. Furthermore, the only institutions allowed to reinsure in Spain were those registered in the same branches as they were authorized to practice direct insurance in, those authorized in the practice of reinsurance in general, or some foreign companies given special authorization by the Dirección General de Seguros (Directorate General of Insurance). On the basis of this decree, companies practising direct insurance would not be authorized to register for reinsurance in general. When the authorizations issued applied to branches other than those where the company practised direct insurance, they would expire within a fixed period (seven years for the life branch, three years in other branches). The main effects of the law were to create new national reinsurance companies, and also to arouse the interest of important direct insurance companies in buying those already in existence. Prior to 1940 there were only two authorized national reinsurance companies: La Garantía[26] and La Equitativa, Fundación Rosillo. Yet by 1945 there were fifteen authorized reinsurers operating, the majority of them national (see Table 3.2). Many of these, however, were hardly viable as they concentrated their reinsurance in institutions linked to their insurance group and had scant capital.[27] Many of them in reality acted as commission agents, as in the majority of cases they finally transferred the reinsurance abroad.

In 1948 there was an increase in the number of companies and a reduction in average premiums per company compared with 1947. A similar situation had also occurred in some branches between 1942 and 1944 (Figure 3.2). In view of this, the government decided to pass a law suspending the admission of new operators to the sector for a period of three years. On passing the law of July 1949, the government explained that a comparative analysis of Spain with similar markets showed a much lower ratio between companies and premiums collected than in other countries. From this moment on, new admissions were suspended, as was the entry of existing companies to new branches. The initial suspension was for three years, after which the authorization of new licenses would be studied 'when there has been an average increase in the collection of premiums per institution and year for three consecutive years'.[28] The three-year period was subsequently extended to 31 December 1952, due to

the importance of this problem for the future of Spanish Insurance, which requires a careful study, as well as the advice of the most authoritative consultative body in this matter, the Insurance Consultation Board, reorganised by the law of 7 April of this year.[29]

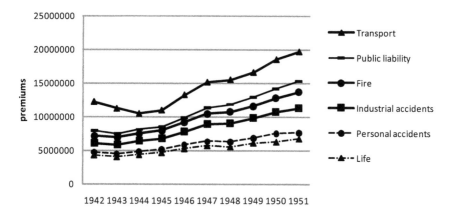

Figure 3.2: Average Premiums per Company (in pesetas).[30]

Table 3.2: Reinsurance Companies Not Working in Direct Insurance, 1945.[31]

Companies	Date of Constitution	Location
Agripina		Madrid
Compañía Española de Reaseguros, SA CER	January 1941	Madrid
Compañía General de Reaseguros, SA	21 April 1942	Barcelona
Compañía Mediterránea de Seguros y Reaseguros	9 April 1942	Madrid
Consorcio Español de Reaseguradores, Sociedad Anónima CERSA	4 October 1939	Seville
Continental, SA, Compañía Española de Seguros y Reaseguros	21 April 1942	Madrid
Cresa, Compañía Anónima de Seguros y Reaseguros	13 July 1942	Barcelona
La Equitativa (Fundación Rosillo), Compañía Anónima de Reaseguros		Madrid
La Equitativa Hispano-Americana		Madrid
Garantía, Sociedad Anónima de Reaseguros		Bilbao
Guipúzcoa Reaseguros, SA	15 June 1940	San Sebastián
Nacional de Reaseguros, SA NACREA	11 February 1939	Madrid
Nervión Reaseguros, SA	13 September 1940	Bilbao
Reaseguradota Española, SA RESA	5 February 1940	Bilbao
Wimtemburguesa y Badense, Compañía Reunidas de Seguros		Barcelona

In spite of this intervention, the number of companies continued to increase, growing from the 511 companies operating in the market in 1950 to 596 in 1960 and 666 in 1970. In fact, this situation was to be a constant factor of the Spanish insurance market until the concentration process of the 1980s and

1990s. The greatest number of companies were concentrated in the branches with fewer requirements and smaller deposits, such as sickness, death, fire and industrial accident insurance, where there were many mutuals operating on a local and provincial scale.

The growth in the number of companies, however, was not homogeneous, but rather depended on the type and nationality of the company. The number of national commercial companies increased while the number of foreign companies and mutuals decreased (Table 3.3). The case of the mutuals has already been explained, and the reduction in foreign companies was due to the fact that foreign investment was severely limited in all sectors of the national economy during the autarkic period, including the insurance sector.[32] There were special circumstances, however, in the case of German companies.[33] One of the most important restrictions for foreign insurers was the prohibition on transferring the profits and interest from their activity in Spain abroad.[34] With these limitations, the Spanish insurance market remained isolated from international business. The reduction in the number of foreign companies and of their market share, a process which had already begun after the First World War, accelerated after the Civil War, especially during the 1940s and 1950s (Table 3.3). There were 71 foreign companies operating in Spain in 1950, accounting for almost 16 per cent of the premiums collected, but this fell to 12 per cent in the following decades. By 1970 there were only 51 foreign companies operating with 12.6 per cent of total premiums. The activities of Spanish insurers abroad were also very limited, with exceptional cases such as La Unión y El Fénix, which continued operating in Latin America and Europe during the Franco period.[35]

Table 3.3: Premiums (P) per Company according to Type and Nationality.[36]

Year	National Companies			Foreign Companies			Mutuals			Total		
	No.	P	%	No.	P	%	No.	P	%	No.	P	%
1950	184	1,501	63.14	71	358	15.97	256	480	20.89	511	2,340	100
1960	–	6,468	68.08	–	1,087	11.44	–	1,949	20.48	596	9,504	100
1970	465	30,034	76.22	51	4,967	12.62	150	4,397	11.16	666	39,399	100

Meanwhile, there were notable changes with respect to the weight of each branch in the total premiums of the sector. One of the most significant phenomena was the reduced weight of life premiums due to the drastic fall in the living standards of the Spanish population.[37] In 1950 life insurance accounted for 21 per cent of premiums in the sector, whereas by 1960 it was little more than 10 per cent (Table 3.4).

Table 3.4: Premiums (P) Collected by Insurers by Branch, 1950–70.[38]

Branch	1950		1960		1970	
	P	%	P	%	P	%
Industrial accidents	650	27.8	2,758	29.01	–	–
Life	492	21.02	1,026	10.79	4,330	10.99
Transport	343	14.67	1,082	11.38	3,772	9.57
Fire	297	12.73	1,032	10.85	4,177	10.6
Voluntary sickness insurance	244	10.44	594	6.25	3,232	8.2
Automobile third party and combined	137	5.89	1,612	16.96	–	–
Compulsory auto-mobile	–	–	–	–	4,815	16.19
Voluntary automobile	–	–	–	–	11,265	28.59
Personal accidents	85	3.67	354	3.72	2,731	6.93
Theft	18	0.78	43	0.45	216	0.54
Livestock	16	0.71	9	0.09	–	–
Hail	11	0.5	43	0.45	144	0.36
Public liability	10	0.44	133	1.39	579	1.46
Other branches	8	0.36	107	1.12	177	0.45
Plate glass	7	0.3	25	0.26	133	0.33
Breakdown of machines	4	0.21	–	–	599	0.19
Cinematography	2	0.11	8	0.08	–	–
Burials	–	–	678	7.13	2,025	5.14
Aviation	–	–	–	–	157	0.46
Total	2,340	100	9,504	100	39,399	100

On the other hand, industrial accident insurance became the most important branch of the sector up to 1965. In 1940 it was the third most important branch, after transport and life, but by 1950 it had moved into first place with 27 per cent of premiums, a percentage which grew to 29 per cent by 1960. State intervention in 1963 through the passage of the Basic Law of Social Security altered this situation by establishing the transfer of industrial accident insurance management to the public authorities, a process which was actually put into practice in 1966. The industrial accident branch was the one which took the largest percentage of total premiums. The loss of this branch, in the hands of private insurance since 1900, was a serious blow to many insurance institutions which lost an important part of their production. However, this business was quickly substituted by the branch of compulsory automobile insurance, which had been approved in 1962 although its implementation was delayed until 1965. The coincidence in the timing of both phenomena makes it appear that the regime was compensating the sector for the loss of industrial accident business.[39] The coexistence of both phenomena, whether fortuitous or forced, allowed the loss of premiums from

industrial accident business to be substituted by the branch that was to experience the greatest expansion in the following decades.[40] Automobile insurance
went from accounting for 17.0 per cent of total premiums in 1960 to 44.8 per
cent (voluntary and compulsory automobile insurance combined) in 1970.[41]

Changes in Private Insurance in the 1950s: Interest in Increasing Productivity and the First Stage of Mechanization

During the 1940s, at the height of autarky, the dictatorship had opted for an
intensive labour model. Labour was abundant and cheap and it remained that
way during a good part of the Franco regime. The dictatorship, through the sup-
pression of the rights of workers and trade unions, maintained a tight control over
wages. The real wages of Spanish workers in the industrial sector continued falling until 1955, with an improvement from then on, although labour costs were
always below European levels throughout the entire dictatorship.[42] Within this
context, the insurance sector maintained the same intensive labour model with a
large number of non-specialized workers involved in administrative tasks. Difficulties in importing equipment, including the electro-mechanical punched-card
tabulating equipment used in the insurance sector, due to the sanctions applied
to the Spanish economy and due to the policy of autarky, also contributed to this
situation.[43] Nevertheless, the Spanish economy started to experience significant
changes from 1951 onwards, tending towards fewer restrictions and with the government showing more interest in increasing productivity, essentially in industry,
but which had an effect on other sectors including the insurance sector.[44] In this
year the National Commission of Industrial Productivity (CNPI) was created
to promote industrial productivity. This commission was eventually constituted
as a permanent body assigned to the Ministry of Industry in 1958 by a decree
of 5 September.[45] These changes instigated by the government were reflected in
the insurance sector by a greater concern for the question of productivity. In
this sense, the regime started to anticipate possible changes in the labour market
due to technological developments. In 1954, for example, a national insurance
fund known as the Caja Nacional del Seguro de Paro Tecnológico was created,
with the aim of solving possible displacements of the labour force as a result of
the introduction of new methods and techniques of rationalization in the workplace.[46] A revitalization of the purchase of equipment and machines appeared in
the balance of trade. The entry of machinery and equipment was decisive for the
increase in productivity and the modernization of the productive sector.[47]

No data is available about the number of workers in the insurance sector
per year, so it is difficult to make calculations about productivity in different
branches of insurance. According to sources of La Estrella, in 1957, there were
about 20,000 people working in the sector, of whom only 4,000 carried out spe-

cialized tasks. For the same year, a report by this company, with data from the National Insurance Syndicate, estimated that there was one employee in productive tasks for each 321,957 pesetas of premiums produced by all of the companies in the sector. The average cost of an employee was 62,776 pesetas, which signified a productivity of 19.4 per cent. The average productivity had been 14.4 per cent between 1952 and 1957, but productivity dropped in the latter year due to significant salary increases.[48]

It has been possible, however, to make calculations about the expense ratio. The data for administration costs include, basically, the cost of commissions, agency expenses and labour costs (wages and social charges). The behaviour of the expense ratio curve varied in each branch although the trend was similar (Figure 3.3). The trend from 1942 onwards was an increase in the expense ratio in all branches except life insurance. In this branch, the expense ratio remained around 20 per cent and then from 1949 started to fall until it reached 15 per cent in 1957, a percentage which continued until 1960. On the other hand, the expense ratio in fire, personal accidents and public liability increased notably up until 1951, reaching levels such as 38 per cent in the case of personal accidents, 36 per cent in the fire branch or 37 per cent in the public liability branch. From 1951 onwards there was a generalized, although slight, descent. In the branches of personal accident, public liability and fire, the expense ratio remained around 35 per cent, while for the transport branch it stayed at around 20 per cent, closer to the level of the life insurance branch. The factors behind these trends are difficult to analyse although some may be noted: the reorganization of production, with the creation of branch offices with their own staff who substituted some of the external agents, and the introduction of mechanization in administrative tasks.

The change in attitude of the regime with regard to productivity encouraged the National Insurance Syndicate to favour European meetings in Spain to facilitate foreign contacts for Spanish companies. During the 1950s, a meeting of the European Insurance Committee was held, which led to the creation of a productivity group. On an international level, the Comité d'Accion pour la productivité dans l'Assurance (CAPA) was created in 1952, with the participation of some representatives of Spanish companies.[49] Its president, Jean-Raymond Fouchet, was in Spain in 1953.[50]

By 1953, the following Spanish firms had mechanized systems for their administrative tasks: RENFE, Compañía Telefónica Nacional, Banesto, Catalana de Gas y Electricidad, Compañía de Tranvías, Maquinista Terrestre y Marítima and ENASA. Materiales y Construcciones, Banco Español de Crédito de Barcelona and the company Dr Andreu had theirs on order. Besides these companies, some ministries and public authorities were mechanized to some extent.[51] In the insurance sector, La Unión y El Fénix had machines installed, the Banco de Vitalicio de España was in the process of installing machines and

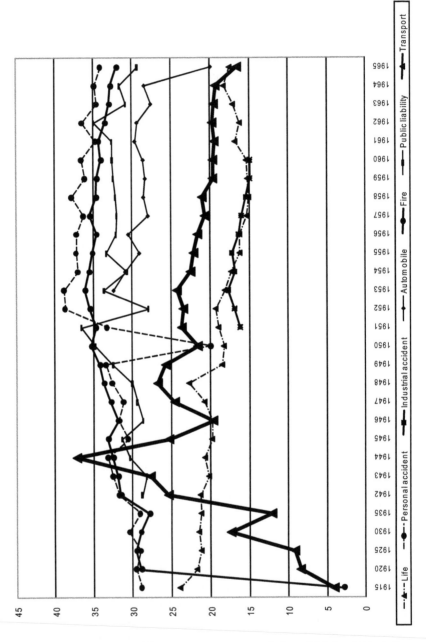

Figure 3.3: Expense Ratios of the Insurance Companies in the Spanish Market, 1915–65.[52]

the Mutualidades y Montepíos Laborales and the branch of the French company L'Abeille had applied to import machinery.[53] Insurance companies were starting to show an interest in the mechanization of administrative tasks, principally for the issue of receipts which required a great deal of largely unskilled labour. In the life insurance branch, the expense ratio (including commissions as well as administration costs) of the companies operating in Spain was stable at about 20 per cent until 1948. In the following years there was a process of reducing expenses, down to 15 per cent by 1957. This percentage was maintained from 1957 to 1960, then it started to increase again in the 1960s. According to the sector's own sources, the excessive number of workers created high costs and companies were very sensitive to wage increases. For example, the pay rise agreed in 1956–7 made the total administration costs of all companies operating in Spain rise from 884 million to 1,263 million pesetas. Despite this employers' perspective, it must be remembered that workers' real wages fell by about 60 per cent between 1942 and 1955, and that they had suffered a progressive loss of purchasing power while company profits had grown.[54] High inflation and the rigidity of the system of wages eroded workers' purchasing capacity and led to a certain protest movement. In view of this situation, the government decided to decree pay rises in 1951 and 1954 and with the decree of 8 June 1956 opened up the possibility of setting wages higher than those established in the regulations.[55] In spite of the low wages maintained during the first stage of the Francoist regime, insurance company managers considered the increase to be excessive and thus an incentive to introduce the first stage of mechanization:

> This leads towards mechanisation, the inevitable path, in the future, of insurance companies, although they encounter obstacles to this, not only in the natural resistance of labour to cutbacks, but also in the few units operated on, which could make the employment of machinery to substitute manpower barely profitable.[56]

Part of the gradual reduction in administration costs from the mid-fifties was due to the introduction of mechanization in the administrative tasks of insurance companies. Nevertheless, the small scale and scant capitalization of a significant part of Spanish insurance companies did not favour the introduction of machinery which was expensive to purchase or hire.

The demand in the Spanish market for machinery for the mechanization of administrative tasks in the 1940s was so small that a single company held a monopoly. This was International Business Machines (IBM), which had doubts about whether to increase its presence in Spain, in contrast to what was happening elsewhere. During the period 1940–50, the firm Máquinas Comerciales Watson, a subsidiary of IBM, had set up in Madrid and Barcelona in order to sell tabulating machines, electric typewriters and clocks. Business was slack, however, and the situation was aggravated by bureaucratic and financial obstacles. During autarky there were numerous impediments to the normal importation of machinery, as well as other problems such as the lack of sufficiently high-quality paper to make the perforated cards. There were not only serious obstacles to trading in machinery in particular, but on top of these were the restrictions imposed by the monetary policy of Franco's government, which distorted real exchange rates and hindered the transfer of capital.[57] Following the 1953 agreements with the US, the first computers were introduced into Spain as part of the process of American aid.[58] Small and medium-sized businesses did not start to hire mechanical tabulators until 1955.[59] The banking sector was the first private sector to see the introduction of tabulating machinery, which occurred to a lesser extent in the insurance sector. This first mechanization came with the use of punched-card tabulating equipment. In the US most insurance companies had been using punched-card machines since the beginning of the 1940s.[60] However, autarky and economic sanctions impeded their use in Spain at first. One of the first companies to mechanize was the Mutua General de Seguros, leader of the industrial accident branch and second in the overall ranking of insurance institutions with premiums to the value of 102 million pesetas in 1950. The leading company was La Unión y El Fénix Español, which dominated the Spanish market with 202 million pesetas of premiums collected during the same year. The Mutua General de Seguros had increased its personnel costs, especially since 1944 when it had reached an agreement with the Instituto Nacional de Previsión (INP, National Insurance Institute) to manage compulsory sickness insurance. By 1956, the section of compulsory sickness insurance alone had reached a total of 747 workers and annual costs of 18 million pesetas. The mutual company's process of increasing its staff had already been causing it financial problems since 1947. Apart from decisions about short-term reorganization, the Mutua General de Seguros opted to start modernizing its administrative management with the aim of reducing administration costs. The intention was to initiate the mechanization of the issue of receipts, payroll preparation and statistics. This goal did not materialize until 1953 when it was decided to rent nine machines from IBM at a cost of 390,000 pesetas a year, plus 10 céntimos (0.1 pesetas) for the price of the cards (between 700,000 and 800,000). The process of acquiring this machinery was not easy as an import licence was required, then once attained the licence was ceded to IBM so that this company could buy the foreign currency necessary to pay for the equipment. By July 1953 the Ministry of Trade had authorized the import licence, and by March 1954 the actual mechanization of offices had begun.

By the late 1950s, even the National Insurance Syndicate was backing attempts to improve the productivity of Spanish insurance companies. In a meeting in Madrid, the European Insurance Committee was formed, which later established a productivity committee. In 1958, the president of the productivity committee, Georges Tattevín, gave a talk on the subject, promoted by the National Syndicate.[61] In his address, he insisted on making changes to labour organization, not only through the use of machinery but also in the field of personnel training. He also explained that it was not a matter of implementing pure American methods, but rather that these had been modified with elements used by French companies. With regard to internal organization, Tattevín insisted on basic improvements, on simplifications which could be applied without the use of electronic machines and computers. As far as external organization was concerned, he insisted on the training of agents and inspectors. Finally, Tattevín advocated the association of insurance companies in order to study these questions and exchange information. On a broader scale, he recommended that European companies join CAPA.

The spread of mechanization in most industrialized countries was promoted by professional or actuarial associations.[62] In the case of Spain, however, the obstacles to association established by the dictatorial regime, apart from the National Insurance Syndicate, fomented private meetings between companies in order to improve the mechanization process which was taking place at the time. This mechanization was on the basis of punched-card equipment. Its introduction caused profound modifications in the organization of insurance companies, both at their head offices and in agencies. Its use led to a simplification of administrative tasks. Punched-card machines had great possibilities because they could mechanize not only the issue of receipts but also agents' accounts, general accounting, the evaluation of and reserves for outstanding claims, the financial portfolio, the payroll, the state of the treasury and securities, interests and dividends, portfolio movements, the profit and loss accounts for agents and reinsurance. In the life branch, they could be used for managing annuities, actuarial reserves and profit-sharing among the insured.[63] However, in the late 1950s, the punched-card equipment installed in Spanish companies was underused (Table 3.5). In 1958, a meeting was held at the head office of the Compañía General Española de Seguros, with the participation of representatives of this company and of the Cervantes, SA, the Bilbao SA, the Occidente, SA and the Mutua General de Seguros. The meeting was also attended by actuaries and the managers of the IBM equipment, basically punched-card tabulators, possessed by these five companies. The aims of the meeting were, first of all, to study the IBM system for the issue of receipts for premiums and commissions in the life branch, employed by the Cervantes, SA, and also for the calculation of the actuarial reserves for life insurance, also employed by the Cervantes, SA with the use of IBM machines. From the report prepared by the Mutua General de Seguros representative for company executives it can be gathered that only the receipts for premiums and commissions had been mechanized in a generalized fashion, and many tasks still needed mechanizing. One of the obstacles to the spread of mechanization was posed by the fraction of the peseta, although this was being overcome through rounding.[64] By 1958, this practice had already been adopted by the Cervantes, the Winterthur and the Hispania-Zurich, as it saved a series of spaces in the punched card and an equal number of columns in the tabulator.

Table 3.5: Mechanization of Administrative Tasks in Four Spanish Companies, 1958.[65]

Mechanized Tasks	General Española de Seguros	Cervantes, SA	Bilbao, SA	Occidente, SA
Payroll	Yes	Yes	Yes	Yes
Receipts for premiums and commissions	Life	All branches	Only two branches	All branches
Reserves for claims	In process in auto-mobiles of the public liability branch	No	No	No
Results of policies	No	No	No	No
Banda Ormig (Duplicator)	Has a machine but does not use it	In all branches except life	No	In the issue of policies
Photocopies	No	No	No	No
Work in circuits	No	No	No	No
Accounts	No	No	No	Yes

According to a CAPA report, the minimum equipment to deal with 10,000 receipts a month should consist of at least one tabulator, two sorters, one collator, three punches and two verifiers. The initial outlay plus rental meant a monthly expenditure of 250,000 francs.[66] Besides the high cost, the great problem in Spain during the 1950s was the difficulty of importation. The Mutua General de Seguros mechanized most tasks with its punched-card equipment introduced in 1954, which served until the introduction of an IBM 604 electronic calculator in January 1961.[67] The decision to acquire this calculator was taken at the end of 1959, but nevertheless the bureaucratic and administrative hurdles to importation maintained by the interventionist system of the first stage of the Franco regime prevented its installation before 1961.[68] In 1963, the Mutua General de Seguros had the following machines (Table 3.6):

Table 3.6: Machines Available at Mutua General de Seguros and their Cost, 1963.[69]

Number	Machine	Function	Regime
1	Calculator		Annual rent of 650,880 pesetas
1	Duplicator	From card to card	
1	Collator		
1	Interpreter	Translates the perforations (numbers/letters) of card	
2	Tabulators	Card–paper transfer	
3	Verifiers	Controls punching	Owned; 7,134,072 pesetas paid
1	Sorter	1,000 cm	
1	Summary punch	Connected to tabulator and reproduces general totals	
6	Punches		

Annual maintenance and cleaning of the property: 285,072 pesetas
Total annual expenditure: 935,952 pesetas
All property paid

One of the main arguments used by managers in favour of mechanization was the savings in the number of workers and in wages. However, the introduction of mechanization actually created the need to substitute unskilled workers with skilled workers, who were lacking in the Spanish labour market due to Francoist educational policies.[70] This paucity of qualified personnel was evident, for example, in the increased demand for fast typists for punching cards and, above all, for skilled technicians to control the machines. Generally speaking, it was IBM's own employees, or those of another company that had supplied the equipment, who took charge of training the workers of the company that acquired the machinery. This explains why at times a short period of instruction led to the underuse of the equipment.[71] The expense of specific staff training, therefore, had to be added to the high cost of the equipment.[72] The incorporation of mechanization would thus only lead to reduced administrative costs in the medium term.

The Second Stage of Mechanization: The Introduction of Electronic Computers, 1960–70

The application of the Franco regime's stabilization plan gave rise to numerous reflections within the insurance sector about the repercussions of the plan and the need for a number of changes in the structure of the Spanish insurance market.[73] A tentative process of concentration was undertaken in an attempt to solve the problem of the large number of small-scale companies operating in the market. During this decade some mergers took place in the most fragmented branches, such as industrial accident insurance. An order of 26 June 1962 approved the merger of the Mutua de la Asociación de Patronos del Ramo de la Madera de Manresa (Barcelona) with the Mutua Manresana de Seguros Sociales from the same area.[74] Likewise, the merger of the Mutua Carcax del Seguro contra Accidentes del Trabajo en la Industria Carcagente and the Mutualidad Patronal del Seguro contra Accidentes del Trabajo en la Agricultura de Carcagentes in Valencia was approved by an order of 23 December 1963.[75] There were also various mergers in the branch of sickness insurance. For example, a takeover merger was approved by an order of 23 September 1966 between the Interprovincial Española de Seguros, SA (INTESA), the acquirer, and La Equitativa Ibérica, SA, the Policlínica Manresana, SA and the Gremial Médico Quirúrgica, SA, the target companies.[76] There were also cases involving general insurance companies, such as the merger of La Mundial, SA with La Estrella SA de Seguros approved by an order of 30 December 1966.[77] Mergers also took place among mutual societies, such as the one authorized on 12 December 1963 between the Mutua Regional Gallega de Seguros and the Sociedad Aseguradora Automovilística de Vigo.[78] One of the most outstanding cases, due to the age of the target company, was the takeover of the Centro de Navieros Aseguradores, founded in 1879, by the Hispano Americana de Seguros y Reaseguros.[79]

During the 1960s changes were finally made that allowed other professional associations apart from the National Insurance Syndicate. Governmental permissiveness in the creation of professional and employers' associations increased during this decade, with technical objectives that articulated the interests of the different business sectors in the world of insurance. The Association for the Protection of Accidents, or APA, was created on 2 June 1960 on the initiative of various accident mutuals. This was the first registered technical association related to the prevention of industrial accidents and professional illnesses.[80] On 1 February 1963, ICEA (Investigación Cooperativa entre Entidades Aseguradoras) was created with the participation of the most important insurance companies in the sector.[81] This association supported studies of markets, products and prevention and distribution networks and promoted training courses and seminars.[82] The majority of studies of mechanization in insurance were thanks to this association. These studies laid the emphasis on elements of change, although enormous problems persisted. The excessive number of insurance institutions continued to be an outstanding factor. One of the significant changes highlighted by these contemporary articles was the effort made by various companies to mechanize and install electronic equipment.[83] The principal problems continued to be the importation difficulties and the price of the product. At the start of the 1960s, a large computer cost 75 million pesetas, a medium-sized one between 25 and 50 million and a small one between 5 and 25 million.[84] According to data supplied by De Diego, there was a total of 21 computers installed in Spain by 1962, with a total value of 462 million pesetas.[85] However, the number grew rapidly and by 1965 there were 129 (with a combined value of 0.28 per cent of GDP), and in 1969 the total had reached 748 (representing 0.88 per cent of GDP).[86]

In the early 1960s, in a new context of accelerated economic growth, and with the backing of these professional associations, many insurance companies studied the possibility of introducing computerized equipment.[87] The demand for computers grew notably from the private sector, especially banking.[88] Supply was also increased with a greater diversity of models, ranging from the IBM 360 to the BULL-GE 400, the UNIVAC 9000, the Siemens 4000 and the NCR Century.[89] In Spain, companies had the option to choose between computers supplied by the French company Bull or the American IBM. The Catalana Occidente group chose to incorporate an IBM 1401 electronic computer in 1962.[90] Activities such as portfolio issue, statistics and the issue of policies were simplified with this computer. The Mutua General de Seguros considered introducing the same model from 1961 onwards in order to achieve the total integration of work in a circuit which would enable risk selection and premium calculation as well as issuing policies and receipts and recording all information. However, in the end no computers were introduced until January 1968 when the installation of an IBM 360/20 electronic computer substituted previous equipment. The MAPFRE decided to introduce Bull equipment, starting in 1962 with a system of punched cards. By the end of 1963 this company had mechanized all of its branches and had monthly balances. It can be gathered from the ICEA survey published in 1969 that the most popular computer models used by insurance companies in Spain in the 1960s were the IBM 360/20 and the 360/30 (Table 3.7).[91]

Table 3.7: Stock of Computers Installed in 14 Insurance Companies Operating in Spain, 1969 (according to ICEA survey).[92]

Make	Model	Memory	Reader	Punch	Printer (L/M)	No. Characters	No. Tapes	No. Disks
BULL	GE–55	5	150	30	200	64	–	–
IBM	1401	16	800	250	600	132	6	–
	360/20	–	600	180	600	132	4	–
	360/20	8	1,000	500	600	132	–	–
	360/20	8	600	100	350	120	–	–
	360/20	8	600	250	450	56	–	–
	360/20	8	500	100	350	144	–	–
	360/20	12	600	–	350	120	4	–
	360/30	16	600	120	600	132	4	–
	360/30	16	1,000	300	1,100	132	4	–
	360/30	32	650	90	1,100	132	4	–
	360/30	32	1,000	300	1,100	132	4	–
	360/30	32	1,100	300	600	132	4	–
UNIVAC	–	–	450	150	600	130	–	–

It is clear from this report that of the 43 insurance companies surveyed, 14 had computers. Only two had acquired computers before 1966, then four more in 1967, four in 1968 and three in 1969 (Table 3.8). A third of the 43 companies surveyed, however, still used punched-card machines, now referred to as classic machines. In general, computers were first introduced in those companies where a process of mechanization already existed on the basis of punched-card machines and tabulators.[93]

Table 3.8: Equipment Used in 43 Spanish Insurance Institutions, 1969.[94]

Equipment	No.	%
Classic machines	14	32.56
Computer centre	12	27.90
Only computer	9	20.93
Classic machines and computer centre	3	6.96
Classic machines and computer	5	11.63

Ten years later, in 1979, of 72 insurance institutions surveyed (whose combined volume of premiums was 123,490 million pesetas, which represented 56.8 per cent of the sector total), 69 used computers. Of these 69 institutions, 33 (45.8 per cent) had small and medium-sized computers, 3 used microcomputers and 36 (50 per cent) had their own or external computer centres. There was a considerable increase in collaboration between companies in the use of computer centres to share costs due to a large extent to the proliferation of small and medium-sized companies that could not meet the expense of computer equipment on their own.[95]

In spite of attempts at transformation during the 1960s, with some cases of improved productivity or mergers, the Spanish insurance market underwent few changes that affected the composition of the rankings of the fifteen leading companies in 1950, 1960 and 1970. La Unión y El Fénix Español, the Mutua General de Seguros, the Banco Vitalicio de España, El Ocaso, SA, the Plus Ultra, the Bilbao and the Sociedad Catalana de Seguros were to be found in all of these rankings. In 1960 only the Federación de Mutualidades de Cataluña, La Vasco Navarra, La Caja de Previsión y Socorro and the Hispania failed to appear. The largest Spanish insurers continued to lead in 1970, including the Mutua General de Seguros, the major Spanish insurance business. Certain changes can be discerned due to the incorporation and growth of some companies specializing in funeral insurance, such as the Santa Lucía, SA, or companies that grew rapidly during the 1960s in automobile insurance, such as the Mutua Madrileña Automovilística. Also noteworthy was the rise of the MAPFRE and the appearance of the recently created Mutua del Instituto Nacional de Industria, or Musini. Mechanization took place first of all in the largest companies, which had a greater volume of premiums, so the introduction of punched-card tabulating equipment and, later, computers was not a determinant factor in the modification of these rankings.

Conclusion

During the first stage of the Francoist regime, the Spanish government established an economic policy of autarky and interventionism and was subject to strict international isolation. Within this context, Spanish insurance companies employed large numbers of unskilled workers. As labour costs were very low, an intensive labour model was used. However, in the early 1950s, changes in the government, agreements with the US and the end of economic sanctions led to a tentative interest in increasing productivity. In the case of the insurance industry, pay rises from 1954 onwards made employers in the sector began to think about mechanization. In spite of tentative changes, obstacles to the importation of equipment continued in Spain. There were impediments when it came to obtaining an import licence and, above all, strict controls continued in force on the foreign currency needed to pay for imports. For this reason, the first punched-card tabulating equipment did not enter Spain until the late 1950s. The mechanization of administrative tasks gradually progressed in the following years, but this process was hindered by the lack of skilled workers. This shortage was due to the Franco regime's educational policy, which obliged companies to provide training at their own expense, and on many occasions the machines were underused.

In the 1960s, with the end of autarky, and with significant economic growth thanks to an extensive process of industrialization, the insurance sector started to grow due to an increase in demand. The government finally allowed the creation of professional associations which, in the case of insurance, promoted collaboration in research and in the spread of computer technology linked to the mechanization of administrative tasks. The first computers were introduced in the early 1960s although, in contrast with other sectors such as banking, their number was fairly limited. This was due to a large extent to the small scale of Spanish insurance companies. For this reason many of them opted for the joint creation of companies providing computer services or the shared use of computer centres. Administration costs started to fall, although very gradually, from 1953 onwards, thanks to a greater rationalization of processes and also due to mechanization. This reduction in costs gained momentum after 1963 owing to the introduction of computers. Nevertheless, the abundance of small-scale companies explains why computers were initially only employed by those larger companies that collected a significant volume of premiums and that had already mechanized with classic machinery.

4 MULTILATERAL INSURANCE
LIBERALIZATION, 1948–2008

Welf Werner

Whereas it is generally implied in the literature that financial markets are global markets in every respect at the beginning of the twenty-first century, a different picture emerges upon closer examination of the insurance industry. Attempts by insurance companies to offer services abroad from their home base or to establish branches and subsidiaries in a foreign country face quite a few regulatory barriers. Most of these barriers originate from national prudential regulation, the main purpose of which is to protect safety and soundness, that is to limit the risk-taking of insurance companies, to guarantee the stability of national markets and to provide a safety net for domestic policyholders. The protectionist effects of prudential regulation result not only from the challenges of compliance with requirements that differ significantly from one country to another but also from the fact that international activities of insurance companies have been treated by national regulators with reservations if not outright hostility as they represent the biggest challenge to the control of domestic insurance markets.

In particular the cross-border supply of insurance services is severely restricted. However, the delivery of insurance services by a foreign company operating in the home country of foreign customers is also complicated by numerous regulatory obstacles. Attempts at establishing a commercial presence abroad face restrictions on foreign equity ownership, the number of foreign service providers, the type of legal entity required (for example branches or subsidiaries) and needs tests, among others. Companies which are not discouraged from international activities by such limitations to *market access* are often confronted with an infringement of the *national treatment* principle, that is they find themselves at a disadvantage in comparison with domestic competitors in their business activities in the host country. Foreign-owned insurance companies are, for example, restricted to certain lines of business, to specific regions of a country and to transactions in a specific currency. In addition, they are often restricted in their trans-border investment of assets.[1]

Traditionally, states have taken action against such restrictions on market access and national treatment by means of bilateral trade negotiations and agreements. In the second half of the twentieth century, however, they increasingly made attempts at multilateral trade liberalization of international insurance trade.[2] In fact, quite a few of the most prominent international organizations in this field have, at one point or another, included insurance services in their trade negotiations. Among them are the World Trade Organization (WTO), the European Union (EU) and the Organisation for Economic Cooperation and Development (OECD) as well as their predecessor organizations the General Agreement on Tariffs and Trade (GATT), the European Economic Community (EEC) and the Organisation for European Economic Cooperation (OEEC). Unlike bilateral agreements, accords agreed upon by these organizations contain general rules concerning liberalization objectives, liberalization procedures, standards of conduct and dispute settlement. International agreements are designed to prevent backsliding regarding the level of liberalization already achieved and to promote a process of progressive liberalization in the future. By means of the principle of unconditional most-favoured nation treatment (MFN), they extend the reach of individual liberalization commitments to all signatories in the same way, producing a level playing field in which international trade is much less influenced by the many different regulatory barriers of individual countries that exist in a world dominated by bilateral agreements.

Through the activities of international organizations, international insurance trade became subject to the most fundamental change in international trade policy in the twentieth century.[3] The question, however, is to what extent the liberalization of international insurance trade has made progress similar to that of trade in goods, which has been at the centre of modern trade agreements for the last sixty years. The standard of comparison set by agreements on trade in goods is very high. Duties on industrial manufactures were reduced through multilateral agreements from an average of 44 per cent in 1948 to 4 per cent in 1994. In Western Europe progress came even more quickly. Initiatives by the OEEC and the EEC already led to an elimination of quantitative restrictions and tariffs in the late 1960s.

Besides the question of how much progress has been made in the elimination of trade barriers for international insurance trade through multilateral agreements, another question is that of the liberalization concepts employed in these agreements. More specifically: How have these concepts developed over time? Has their growth been influenced by the development of trade policy agendas in the more conventional field of international trade in goods? Have they profited from the expansion of multilateral trade policy into new fields such as foreign direct investment (FDI), behind-the-borders barriers and services trade?

OEEC and OECD

The OEEC was the first organization that engaged in multilateral liberalization of insurance services. In the literature it is well known for other activities: its role in the management of the funds of the European Recovery Program (ERP) and its engagement in the early liberalization of trade in goods in Western Europe. Regarding the integration of goods markets, the Paris-based organization had two closely connected objectives in the 1950s: the reduction of quantitative restrictions on trade and the restoration of currency convertibility. The latter goal was achieved through the European Payments Union (EPU), formed in 1950, and the European Monetary Agreement (EMA), concluded in 1958.

After it had become clear that with the establishment of the EEC in 1957 responsibilities for the liberalization of trade in goods would be transferred to this new organization, the role of the OEEC in trade diplomacy shrunk considerably. Plans to convert the organization into a free trade area – which would have comprised the six founding members of the EEC and the eleven remaining OEEC member states – were not adopted.[4] When the OEEC was finally replaced by the OECD in 1961, it was charged with very broad but somewhat blurry responsibilities that still characterize the organization's activities today. With the exception of the fields of culture, sports and defence the OECD addressed practically all major economic policy issues of national relevance without, however, initiating any important binding agreements. The OECD became the debating society of the industrialized nations, or, to put it more positively, their academic think tank. Apart from a few low key and generally unsuccessful attempts at liberalizing FDI and financial services in later years, the organization has not engaged in international trade policy activities since its foundation in 1961.

A closer look at the beginnings of the OEEC's attempts at trade liberalization in the late 1940s and early 1950s shows that its jurisdiction over international insurance trade derived directly from its initiatives to liberalize trade in goods. Initiatives to reduce quantitative restrictions on trade in goods, which the OEEC had begun right after its foundation in April 1948, led in 1951 to the enactment of the Code of Liberalisation of Trade and Invisible Transactions. The title of this Code already indicates that the OEEC was not only engaged in the liberalization of goods but also in the liberalization of 'invisible transactions', or, in other words, international services trade. This part of the liberalization agenda addressed among other services those of insurance and banking industries, even though it did so to a very limited degree so that these activities have been largely overlooked in the literature.[5] The drafters of the Code had by no means intended to create an extensive liberalization programme for the entire insurance or banking industry, let alone for the entire service sector. Only in the 1980s did liberalization of insurance trade gravitate towards the centre of multilateral trade policy initiatives, notably with the EU's Single Market programme and the General Agreement on Trade in Services (GATS). Both initiatives covered the great majority of service industries as well as all four modes of international service supply, specifically: 1. cross-border supply of services; 2. operations of foreign insurers; 3. service consumption abroad by an individual; and 4. service provision abroad by an individual.[6]

In the post-war years the OEEC dealt only with a very few of these many different dimensions of international trade in insurance. The main motive for the liberalization of selected trans-border activities was to support the development of international trade in goods which was high up on the list of economic policy priorities of Western European countries in the post-war years. The main motive for inclusion of 'invisibles' in the Code of 1951 was that trade in goods could not function smoothly without the efficient international provision of specific services such as transport services, trade credit or specific insurance services such as transport insurance. Narrow limits were set to these liberalization efforts by the general shortage of foreign exchange, which restricted the entire cross-border exchange of goods and services. Initiatives to liberalize services were further limited by the specific shortages of the post-war economies in many areas of the 'real economy'. These shortages suggested a concentration on liberalization of trade in goods and left little room for manoeuvre in other fields.

The liberalization obligations that the OEEC introduced to the insurance trade were listed in an Annex of the Code of Liberalisation of Trade and Invisible Transactions. Three chapters covered direct insurance, reinsurance and operations of foreign insurance companies. The chapter on direct insurance comprised liberalization obligations concerning transport insurance, property insurance, life insurance and capacity shortages, that is, situations in which domestic insurance companies were not able to cover all domestic risks. For transport insurance, which was particularly important for international trade in goods, obligations were comparatively far-reaching even though only cargo insurance, i.e. the insurance of goods in transit, was considered and not hull insurance, i.e. the insurance of the means of transport. Since 1954 obligations for cargo insurance had referred both to 'transfers', that is restrictions on foreign exchange, which were at the centre of the entire liberalization programme of the OEEC, and to 'transactions', that is limitations on the conclusion of individual insurance contracts, the majority of which derived from prudential regulation.

Apart from the support of international trade in goods, the OEEC had further motives for focusing on international insurance trade. Liberalization of life insurance, which made only little progress in later years in the EEC and the EU, was included because of strong international migration that had emerged right after the end of the Second World War. These movements necessitated cross-border payments of life insurance policies in large quantities. The liberalization obligations consequently focused on trans-border payments to migrants, and did not include other trans-border activities such as the signing of new contracts, the licensing of foreign-owned insurance companies or the ongoing activities of already established foreign firms. Moreover, there were strict limits on the total amount of trans-border payments that could be made under life insurance policies.

The consideration of international reinsurance activities in the Annex of the Code can be interpreted as an effort to return to the level of liberalization that had already been achieved in many countries before the Second World War. Reinsurance has had a strong international orientation right from the start.[7] Consequently, for reinsurance as well, comparatively far-reaching measures were taken. Besides transport insurance, reinsurance was the only other insurance service for which the OEEC did not only address barriers to transfers but also to transactions.

Reinsurance and transport insurance had something else in common. Liberalization efforts were actively supported by industry representatives.[8] The case that was made by them for free international transport insurance was straightforward. Cargo insurance had always been international in scope and domestic regulation had never been very strong in this field. Representatives of reinsurance companies successfully argued that insurance companies, the recipients of reinsurance services, were experienced enough to buy insurance policies in sophisticated international markets without any oversight from domestic regulators. Moreover, they pointed out that their business was particularly dependent on the international sharing of risk so as to ensure a balance of their risk portfolios. Representatives from other fields of insurance were notably less enthusiastic about the prospect of liberalization; for many decades to come, high growth rates in national insurance markets provided most insurance companies with plenty of business opportunities in their home markets. An ever-extending web of national prudential regulations protected them not only from international competition but, in the majority of member states, also from unfettered free-market competition at home.[9]

The strict limits to the OEEC's liberalization measures in the insurance sector are best described with respect to liberalization obligations on property insurance, the operations of foreign insurers and shortages of insurance capacity. As in the field of life insurance, obligations on property insurance focused only on existing contracts. Provisions aimed at shortages of insurance capacity were of little practical relevance, since it had already been common practice of supervisory authorities in the past to admit foreign insurers to the domestic market in such situations. Obligations upon the operations of foreign insurers covered only specific international transfers of foreign subsidiaries and branches with their parent companies. Neither restrictions on market access, for example the restrictive licensing of foreign insurance companies that had emerged in practically all member states on the basis of more or less arbitrary needs tests, nor the national treatment principle, i.e. the equal treatment of foreign subsidiaries *vis-à-vis* domestically owned companies under national prudential regulations, were addressed.

Even though the progress that the OEEC achieved in the liberalization of insurance markets was by today's standards extremely limited, it is important to recognize that by focusing on some particularly pressing issues the organization met the special needs of the post-war years. More importantly, as limited as the reach of these early measures was regarding lines of business and modes of international service supply, they already contained all the essential elements of modern multilateral trade policy, such as: 1. the principle of progressive liberalization; 2. a catalogue of concrete liberalization obligations (listed in the Code's Annex); 3. the principle of unconditional most-favoured nation treatment; and 4. institutions and procedures to monitor compliance. In 1954 an insurance sub-committee was established to observe the progress of the programme. This sub-committee was to support the Committee on Invisible Transactions which was responsible for all service transactions covered under the Code. In addition, multilateral rules for the insurance sector comprised a number of derogations and reservations, allowing sufficient scope for member states to move towards the agreed-upon objectives at varying speeds and according to specific national economic circumstances.

Taking all these instruments together, there is no doubt that the introduction of the Code of Liberalisation of Trade and Invisible Transactions in 1951 represented the first step towards a treaty-based multilateral approach to liberalization of insurance in the history of international insurance markets. There was a crucial aspect, however, in which the liberalization concept applied to insurance trade did not meet the standards of that applied to trade in goods. The provision for insurance trade did not make use of the 'percentage method', which guaranteed for trade in goods that all countries made similar progress in their liberalization efforts despite differences in the treatment of individual classes of goods. Balance of payments statistics did not provide enough information on 'invisible trade' to make this method applicable to trade in services. Thus an efficient monitoring of the overall liberalization achievements of member countries was not possible in the case of insurance services and other services. Surveillance had to rely solely on peer pressure and on a case-by-case evaluation of liberalization commitments. Neither a formal dispute settlement procedure nor sanctions were available and the liberalization process was much less transparent.

By far the most important conceptual weakness of the insurance programme was, however, the little attention paid to the many obstacles that existed in the form of domestic regulation and specifically to prudential regulation.[10] These obstacles were addressed only in the cases of transport insurance and reinsurance, that is, in fields in which domestic regulation was not very stringent to begin with. As in the case of liberalization of trade in goods, the liberalization of the insurance trade was concerned mainly with transfers, and not with transactions and the many ways in which they were limited. Domestic regulation had, on the other hand, much more serious consequences for international trade in financial services, which were among the most highly regulated industries in the post-war era. The harmonization of national prudential regulations in the wake of liberalization initiatives, although every now and then touched upon by the OEEC, was not a realistic policy option in the 1950s. Such initiatives in fact remained fruitless in Europe for many years to come. While the EEC and the EU approached domestic regulation in their liberalization efforts in the 1960s, 1970s and early 1980s in a more systematic way, only the Single European Market programme came to grips with these challenges with a double strategy of minimum harmonization and mutual recognition.

While the time was not ripe to include in the multilateral trade negotiations of the 1950s barriers to trade resulting from differences in domestic regulation, this was even less the case with the prudential regulation of the insurance and banking industries, the main purpose of which was to guarantee safety and soundness. In the Bretton Woods era, this area of regulation was commonly regarded as the sole domain of national economic policy. Broad and far-reaching intervention in prudential regulation, which the Single Market programme introduced quite a few years after the demise of this system, was still unthinkable. The concentration on liberalization of trade in goods rather than trade in financial services in the OEEC was firmly grounded in a monetary system that was designed to keep activities in international financial markets to a minimum. The Bretton Woods system granted independent national monetary policy and fixed exchange rates at the expense of free short-term capital movements. However, it was not only short-term capital movements that were restricted but activities in international financial markets generally.[11]

The lack of political support for addressing domestic regulation in the OEEC can best be seen in provisions of the Code which explicitly stated that a member state may take action to deny foreign insurance firms access to their domestic markets through prudential regulation. Even modest steps towards harmonization, for example the introduction of a standardized system of classification for the different lines of insurance business, failed in the Council of Ministers. However, the nearly complete lack of progress had also a positive side to it. While the OEEC was far from developing a broad-based liberalization programme for insurance or any other service, discussions in the organizations had at least led to the firm belief that the major challenge to any broad-based insurance liberalization programme, if it was ever to be undertaken, was the difference in national prudential regulations and the fact that the trade-distorting effects of these differences can only be overcome through harmonization. To that effect the OEEC and the OECD commissioned the first systematic stocktaking of national regulatory systems in the insurance industry in 1956 and 1963.[12] Although these studies showed significant differences in national prudential regulations and their negative effects on trans-border activities, no further action was taken.

Not only the OEEC but later on also the OECD became active in the liberalization of insurance trade. This resulted largely from discussions about the future of the OEEC in the years 1956–8. At the request of the US, the OECD, which replaced the OEEC in 1961, was not to take over any responsibilities for trade liberalization. The overriding goal of the Americans was to keep trade policy initiatives outside the GATT to a minimum. The only exception that was made in the era of the Cold War for political reasons was the EEC. After its re-establishment in 1961, the organization was consequently stripped of the main part of its trade policy agenda, the liberalization of international trade in goods. The organization remained, however, responsible for 'invisibles', a component of the trade policy of its predecessor organization that was obviously not taken seriously enough by the US to come into conflict with its demands to end the organization's involvement in international trade policy. On the occasion of the establishment of the OECD in 1961, the Code of Liberalisation of Trade and Invisible Transactions was not completely resolved but transformed into a Code of Liberalisation of Current Invisible Operations. The organization was to keep its responsibility for trade in services.

Another Code of the OEEC, the Code of Liberalisation of Capital Movements, was also carried over into the new organization. This Code had originally been introduced in 1959. It was not aimed at short- or medium-term capital movements, which were off-limits in the Bretton Woods era as they would have threatened the stability of fixed exchange rates, but at long-term movements and especially at foreign direct investment. With these two Codes the OECD was equipped with a surprisingly modern trade policy agenda in 1961. The field covered by the two Codes – international services trade and FDI – only became the focus of the Single Market programme much later. If the political will had been sufficient, and the Codes had been developed in any serious way, they could have brought progress to financial services similar to that introduced by the Single Market programme. In its further development, however, the OECD made progress neither in the field of international insurance trade nor in other fields of international trade diplomacy. All efforts to develop a modern trade policy agenda, which includes services liberalization as well as capital account liberalization, were indeed focused on the EEC and the EU. Interestingly though, the OECD never formally gave up on the work on their two liberalization codes. In 1976 the organization introduced a National Treatment Instrument that for the first time and somewhat belatedly acknowledged that a foreign subsidiary should not be treated less favourably than domestic companies.[13] This instrument was, however, not legally binding. The same was true for the results of a more broad-based overhaul of the two Codes that began in 1979, with financial services now officially at the centre of the initiative. Although quite a few papers were produced and new rules drafted, political support was once again inadequate to give this initiative any relevance for markets. Among other problems, there was once again no support for harmonization of prudential regulation.[14] In other words, with regard to the two Codes and their development, the OECD remained, as in other areas, a think tank whose actions were of little consequence.

EEC and EU

The European Economic Community, which began its involvement in European economic integration almost ten years later than the OEEC, started out with a remarkably far-sighted trade policy agenda in 1957. Paragraph three of the Treaty of Rome laid out goals for progressive liberalization not only for trade in goods, but also for trade in services, capital movements and the free movement of workers. The treaty also addressed the problems of domestic regulation, which was to be harmonized as far as this was necessary for the integration of the national economies into a Common Market. Even though there was no doubt that this endorsement was to be interpreted to cover prudential regulation, liberalization in the field of financial services turned out to be a painstakingly slow and inefficient process until the implementation of the Single Market programme in the late 1980s and early 1990s. As before in the OEEC, the liberalization of trade in goods had priority over other more challenging trade policy agendas. After the OEEC had focused on quantitative restrictions on trade in goods, the EEC turned its attention to tariffs. In 1957 the six founding members of the European Economic Community had committed themselves to creating a customs union by 1968. The community set to work so diligently that it reached this goal a year earlier.

Although little progress was made in the liberalization of insurance services and other financial services until the introduction of the Single Market programme, quite a few efforts were made in this area. In the 1960s and 1970s representatives from national regulatory agencies, financial ministers and central banks engaged in intense discussions of this topic. In the first half of the 1960s the first liberalization measures were introduced in areas in which the OEEC had already been active. The first liberalization directive that was introduced in 1964 for the international insurance trade addressed reinsurance and co-insurance.

Further liberalization directives were agreed upon only in 1973 and 1979. They were directives on life insurance and non-life insurance. The most important objective of all these first-generation measures was the freedom of establishment, which was to be accomplished for subsidiaries as well as for branches and agencies. The liberalization commitments introduced lacked, however, a broad-based commitment to the principles of market access and national treatment.

Numerous second-generation directives were introduced in the late 1980s and therefore coincided with the preparations for the implementation of the Single Market programme. They were, in particular, the non-life insurance directive of 1988, the automobile liability directive of 1990 and a life insurance directive that was also agreed upon in 1990. The objective of this second generation of directives was to make progress towards the liberalization of cross-border supply of services, or, in the terminology used by the EEC, the 'free movement of services'. In the absence of any meaningful harmonization of national prudential regulations, the effectiveness of these directives was, however, limited. In order to compensate for the lack of harmonization, provisions for life insurance, for example, included specific customer protection requirements. The signing of life insurance contracts with insurance companies of other member states was only permitted if the foreign company had not actively solicited business, for example through advertisements or sales representatives. Access to foreign markets was only granted on the basis of a so-called 'passive freedom' to provide services. The signing of a contract had to be initiated by the customer, a scenario that was so rare as to be insignificant if not completely irrelevant in the markets. For private non-life insurance, member states were granted the right to make market access dependent on a test of insurance tariffs of the foreign insurance company, a complex procedure for which no clear guidelines existed. All member states except the Netherlands and Great Britain made such tests mandatory. Insurance companies attempting to serve the Common Market thus had to receive permission for each and every insurance tariff in all member states (except in the Netherlands and Great Britain). Understandably very few insurance companies found this to be an attractive option so that the liberalization of cross-border supply of insurance services remained ineffective in the case of private non-life insurance as well. The second-generation measures brought progress only in the field of substandard risks for which mutual recognition of national prudential regulations was introduced, a principle of the Single Market programme that was fully applied to international insurance trade only with the introduction of a third generation of insurance directives in the 1990s.

In the years before the Single Market programme was systematically applied to all lines of business, attempts at harmonizing prudential regulations had been made rule by rule and member country by member country. Under the guidance of national regulatory agencies, whose main responsibility was to protect safety and soundness and not to open up national markets to foreign competition, the European liberalization process had turned into an ineffective piecemeal approach to harmonization. The most important innovation introduced to the liberalization process through the Single Market programme was that by far not all rules of the complex national regulatory systems had to be addressed in the harmonization process but, through a process of minimum harmonization, only a very few significant ones. Only regulations that were regarded as indispensable for guaranteeing safety and soundness were subject to harmonization efforts in the new programme. The focus of the third generation of directives was specifically on crucial regulatory standards such as solvency. The great majority of domestic regulations were not harmonized but became subject to mutual recognition, the other one of the two main principles of the Single Market programme. Countries had to recognize rules from other member countries as being equivalent to their own. In other words, an insurance company signing a contract with a customer from another member country could do so on the basis of: 1. core rules of prudential regulation harmonized on the basis of the principle of minimum harmonization; and 2. individual domestic regulations that had to be acknowledged by other member states as equivalent.

The new approach to liberalization, comprising the two key elements of minimum harmonization and mutual recognition, had the advantage that quite a few differences in the complex national regulatory systems did not have to be dealt with on the EU level but only in the member countries, which could decide individually whether to leave them as they were or whether to engage in a process of deregulation. Of course, with the increasing cross-border competition that the Single Market programme was finally to introduce to insurance markets, it was in the best interests of member countries to keep a critical eye on regulations that would unnecessarily burden domestic insurance companies *vis-à-vis* competitors from other countries. The introduction of minimum harmonization and mutual recognition to the liberalization process resulted in a situation in which not only companies but also – to a certain degree – regulatory agencies had to compete with each other in providing favourable conditions for an efficient provision of insurance services. The Single Market programme thus gave an important impetus not only to liberalization but also to deregulation on the national level. At the same time minimum harmonization prevented member states from engaging in a destructive race to the bottom.

The new liberalization principles applied to the insurance industry through the Single Market programme were not geared specifically towards this industry but towards broad and partly overlapping trade policy agendas for services, FDI and behind-the-border barriers to trade. The principle of mutual recognition, for example, which was first introduced by the Supreme Court, was originally applied to a case in the field of international trade in goods. In the case of Cassis de Dijon the judges had ruled in 1979 that the Federal Republic of Germany could not reject the import of a French currant liqueur on the basis of national foodstuffs regulation, which stipulated that liqueurs have to have a specific alcohol content that the French beverage failed to meet. The court emphasized in its judgement that goods that were legally produced and sold in one of the member states could also be sold in other member states. Only in 1986 was the concept of mutual recognition applied by the Court to trade in insurance services. Taken together, the decisions of 1979 and 1986 provided a basis for introducing the principle of mutual recognition to a broad field of industries in the service and manufacturing sectors.

For the insurance industry the Single Market principles were applied in the third generation of directives to all fields. Broad-based directives for life and non-life insurance, both of which came into effect in 1994, granted a single licence to all insurance companies based on minimum harmonization and mutual recognition. As for banks, this licence made it possible for insurance companies to offer their services in all member states through the trans-border supply of services and also through branches.[15] Subsidiaries, on the other hand, remained subject to the regulation of the host countries in which they were licensed.

Although the EU's efforts to liberalize insurance trade remained a remarkably tedious process, even after the introduction of the Single Market programme, this programme has undoubtedly the most advanced concept of any multilateral liberalization programme on insurance trade developed until today. The European programme represents so far the only successful attempt at tackling the challenges of prudential regulation. It is the only programme that integrates the two main functions that any multilateral regime for international financial markets will eventually have to tackle: safety and soundness on the one hand, and the openness of markets and progressive liberalization on the other. Moreover, liberalization measures undertaken in the Single Market programme cover all four modes of international service supply and all major fields of insurance, indicating that free international insurance trade was no longer regarded as merely supporting trade in goods, as it had been in the OEEC during the post-war years, but as a trade policy agenda in its own right. Many factors contributed to this development, among others the demise of the Bretton Woods system and a general broadening of multilateral trade policy initiatives into areas such as trade in services, FDI and behind-the-border barriers. As the breadth of the Single Market programme indicates, the insurance industry was only one of many industries which profited from a general broadening of multilateral trade policy.

Remarkably, all the progress made regarding liberalization concepts with the Single Market programme does not mean that insurance markets were as integrated as goods markets twenty years after the introduction of the first liberalization measures of this programme. A first systematic study of the effects of the Single Market programme, which was published in the Single Market Review in 1998, already indicated that the development of the trans-border delivery of insurance services had by far not kept pace with the development of the operations of foreign insurance companies, which experienced a considerable boost through the introduction of the Single Market programme.[16] Moreover, while almost all branches of industrial insurance profited from the liberalization programme, private insurance remained largely a domain for established domestic insurance companies. Later studies came up with similar results.[17] Consequently a period of fine-tuning of the Single Market programme began. The negative effects of tax-, company- and contract law, which had already been addressed in earlier years, received more attention. However, the slow growth in the trans-border delivery of insurance services and in private insurance was certainly also the result of a group of factors that were not tackled in multilateral liberalization efforts: cultural barriers.

GATT and WTO

In the GATT, the international insurance trade became subject to negotiations for the first time during the Uruguay Round (1968–94) as part of an effort systematically to liberalize the many different service industries. When the GATS came into effect on 1 January 1995, financial services were not covered because of controversies over the strength of liberalization commitments. As a consequence, negotiations on insurance and banking had to be carried on after the official completion of the Uruguay Round. They led to an agreement in December 1997, which will be in effect until a new negotiating round has been successfully completed. Since the Doha negotiations stalled in 2008, there are currently no expectations that the agreements reached in 1995 and 1997 will be developed further in the near future. Unlike the EU, which is making continuous efforts to fine-tune the Single Market programme, the WTO cannot alter agreements unless it officially enters into a new trade round.

The impulse for including services in the Uruguay Round had originally come from the US, where financial firms such as Citicorp and American Express had lobbied for such an initiative for quite some time.[18] Developing countries and the majority of Western European countries were at first not particularly interested in pursuing this topic. The overall perception of services negotiations in developing countries was that they are a defensive trade policy issue or, in other words, that there would be little to gain from such negotiations. Europeans, on the other hand, had a preference for a narrower agenda for the Uruguay Round than the Americans. According to their view, complex issues such as services liberalization jeopardized the outcome of the whole negotiating round. Another reason for Europe's reluctance to engage in services negotiations was bad timing. When the Uruguay Round was officially launched in 1986 the EU had just taken its first steps with the Single European Market programme. The Commission had introduced its proposal finally to complete the internal market with the publication of the White Book in 1985. Taking on two extremely ambitious trade policy projects at the same time might have simply overburdened the EU.

There was, moreover, no doubt that liberalizing services would turn out to be far more difficult in the WTO than in the EU. The most obvious difference between service liberalization in the Single Market programme and in the GATS is that WTO agreements are not confined to a comparatively small number of like-minded countries. The WTO that emerged from the GATT in 1995 currently has 153 members representing not only all industrialized countries but also transition and developing countries, the great majority of which had to participate in the service negotiations if they were to be concluded successfully.

The large number of potential signatories is at the same time the biggest advantage and the most significant disadvantage of any WTO agreement. An obvious advantage of this large number is the much wider reach of the MFN principle. Although regional initiatives such as the Single Market programme have a clear advantage when it comes to finding common ground for new and complex trade policy agendas, any agreement reached will exclude – and probably actively discriminate against – the great majority of countries worldwide. In other words, only the WTO offers the basis for agreements which provide a level playing field on a global basis.

On the other hand, the large number of potential signatories makes it very difficult for the WTO to reach a meaningful consensus, especially with regard to the many new and complex trade policy issues that emerged worldwide once quantitative barriers and tariffs were successfully removed. Member states of the WTO show, for example, dramatic differences regarding their levels of and philosophies for prudential regulation and their willingness to open financial markets to foreign competition. Although the great majority of developing countries gave up on protectionist strategies of import substitution a long time ago, and quite a few of them have also pursued the cautious opening of their financial service sectors, their policy regimes in these sectors are in no way comparable to those of industrialized countries.[19] Opening up financial services markets is one of the key challenges to development policies. Because of a comparatively low level of development of financial institutions and regulatory agencies, and an unstable macroeconomic environment, limits to liberalization are manifold. Financial liberalization carries not only a high risk of destabilization for these countries, but also offers significant welfare gains given the central role that financial services play in the development process.

How did the drafters of the GATS cope with this difficult situation? First and foremost, the WTO framework agreement was not aimed at full reciprocity, that is at reaching the same absolute level of liberalization commitments for all signatories, but at first-difference reciprocity, i.e. at moving towards the common goal of progressive liberalization with approximately the same speed. The two crucial liberalization obligations of the agreement – market access and national treatment – are not general but specific obligations. Signatories are free to choose to what extent they want to take on such specific obligations – with respect to the different fields of insurance and other services and regarding the four modes of international service supply described above. A single liberalization commitment, for example a commitment for any narrowly defined insurance service in any one of the four modes of supply, is already sufficient for a WTO member country officially to become a signatory to the GATS and thus to have access to the specific liberalization commitments of other member countries under the MFN principle, which is one of the general obligations of the agreement.

The *à-la-carte* approach to liberalization commitments was undoubtedly a necessary condition to reach an agreement on trade in services among the very diverse membership of the WTO. This approach meant, however, that it was very difficult to arrive at meaningful liberalization commitments in the trade negotiations between member states once the framework agreement was drafted. The great freedom offered to signatories left the negotiating process without much orientation as to what commitments to expect from individual member countries. The main reason for the prolongation of the financial services negotiations beyond the official conclusion of the Uruguay Round was that quite a few countries – especially in Asia – had not even come close to offering the *status quo* of their unilateral liberalization process in crucial fields of financial service industries.[20]

The other notable effect that the large and heterogeneous group of signatories had on the GATS framework agreement was in the area of domestic regulation. The main emphasis of the relevant provisions of the framework agreement (Article VI, GATS) is on guaranteeing signatories the greatest possible freedom to pursue independent regulatory policies. This goes back to a demand of developing countries that made sovereignty over regulatory policies a prerequisite for their participation in the GATS negotiations right at the beginning of the Uruguay Round. As in the case of liberalization commitments, this freedom was undoubtedly another necessary condition for reaching an agreement on trade in services. There was no way that the WTO could have dealt with the vast differences in domestic regulations of many service industries of member countries, neither through traditional harmonization, i.e. rule by rule, nor through minimum harmonization and mutual recognition. This is even clearer with respect to insurance services, for which sovereignty over domestic regulation is emphatically ensured in sector-specific provisions of an Annex on Financial Services in its so-called prudential carve-out. Both provisions, article VI, GATS and the sector-specific prudential carve-out, leave wide open the question of to what extent changes in prudential regulation may be used as an excuse for protectionist backsliding and to what extent liberalization commitments may limit countries making *necessary* adjustments in their domestic regulation.

In spite of all these obvious weaknesses the GATS has been regarded as one of the more promising results of the Uruguay Round.[21] It was, for example, argued that the fact that such a broad agreement could be formed under the auspices of the WTO is in itself a remarkable achievement and that the GATS marks a first and necessary step towards a more meaningful agreement. For financial services this conclusion is, however, questionable. There is no perspective in the framework agreement and the Annex on Financial Services regarding how to integrate in the future the two main functions of an international regime for financial markets: providing for safety and soundness on the one hand, and for openness of markets and progressive liberalization on the other. Because the framework agreement leaves the responsibility for prudential regulation firmly in the hands of individual member states, there is no strategy for coping with the many conflicts that come from different regulatory systems in a more globalized insurance sector.

Summary and Outlook

Has the multilateral liberalization of international insurance trade made similar progress over the last sixty years as the liberalization of trade in goods? The answer to this question depends on where we look – towards the European integration process or the global level. Attempts by the WTO to liberalize trade in insurance have been quite limited so far. In its first initiative to bring international insurance trade under the discipline of a global agreement, the organization has been struggling to reach the *status quo* of the unilateral liberalization process of its member states. From a historical point of view these limited results are not surprising. The GATS can indeed only be seen as a first and somewhat provisional step in the direction of a multilateral agreement with a global reach. The greatest weakness of the GATS is that it does not tackle the challenges of prudential regulation adequately. The attempt of the WTO at keeping domestic regulation out of liberalization negotiations is reminiscent of early initiatives in the OEEC, even though these initiatives were different in an important respect. In view of the fact that regulatory hurdles could not be overcome by the OEEC in the 1950s, the organization confined its activities to a very few narrowly defined key areas of the international insurance trade that were of great importance to the functioning of international goods markets in the post-war years. Such modesty is absent from the WTO approach to insurance liberalization and to services liberalization in general. The GATS framework agreement does not tackle domestic regulation but still opens the doors wide to liberalization in all service industries and to all modes of international service supply.

The stark difference between the WTO and the OEEC initiatives reflects a fundamental change in economic policy philosophies between now and then. In the Bretton Woods era, which was characterized not only by strict limits on short-term capital flows but by an overall distrust of the many different activities of international financial markets, multilateral trade policy initiatives for insurance were not developed to their full potential. The most obvious example of this is the very limited progress made for the treatment of foreign operations of insurers. The introduction of the national treatment principle was not considered in the OEEC and later in the EEC even though this principle – treating foreign subsidiaries no less favourably than domestic insurance companies – would have in no way endangered the monetary system of fixed exchange rates. The GATS on the other hand reflects an economic policy philosophy of a late and somewhat troublesome stage of the post-Bretton Woods era, in which the liberalization of financial services, whether on a unilateral or on the multilateral level, is seen by major players in the WTO, such as the US, as desirable – even if no adequate concepts for prudential regulation are available.

The only programme that adequately integrates liberalization measures with concepts for safety and soundness is the Single Market programme. This programme has undoubtedly made the greatest progress in the liberalization of international trade in insurance – despite the many weaknesses that have remained after the implementation of the main measures of the programme in the 1990s. The achievements of the EU can be understood against the background of exceptionally strong intergovernmental institutions and a learning process that started long before the formulation of the White Book in 1985. While early initiatives in the OEEC and the EEC only made progress in specific, narrowly defined areas, they introduced multilateral rules to insurance trade for the first time and raised awareness among policymakers of the extraordinary challenges that would await them if they were ever to make a serious attempt at broadening and deepening this branch of modern trade policy.

The Single Market programme provides other regions of the world with a blueprint of a liberalization concept consisting of mutual recognition and minimum harmonization, which undoubtedly means a great deal of delegation of regulatory powers. With some modifications, this programme has already worked well for central and eastern European accession countries. Other small groups of like-minded countries may copy this model in the future. For agreements with a more global reach, crucial developments may come in time from multilateral initiatives to improve safety and soundness, although institutions that have taken up such responsibilities in the past, such as the Basle committee of the Bank for International Settlements, are more advanced in banking than in insurance.

5 POLICYHOLDERS IN THE EARLY BUSINESS OF JAPANESE LIFE ASSURANCE: A DEMAND-SIDE STUDY

Takau Yoneyama

Introduction and Research Background

It is commonly said that the Old Equitable of England (established 1762) was the first life assurance company that sold a modern life assurance product. However, if we examine life assurance from the demand side, we may reconsider this. It cannot in fact be claimed that the Old Equitable was a typical modern life assurance company, because its customers were richer than those of modern life assurance companies.[1]

Victorian ideology that emphasized the responsibility of the master of the house for his surviving family had a great impact on the modernization of life assurance products in that it helped to popularize life assurance. Life assurance companies revised their sales channels, sales techniques and life products in the face of the demand for death indemnity from family breadwinners. In this context, therefore, not the Old Equitable but the Prudential (1848) best resembles a modern assurance company.[2]

Most current studies of life assurance history have been written from the perspective of the insurers. By contrast, only a small number of studies examine the demands of the assured.[3] This is unsurprising. The explanation lies in the fact that, while there is a comparatively large quantity of historical documents in insurance business archives, it remains difficult for historians to obtain information about policyholders.

In 1997 the organizers of the insurance history session at the World Economic History Congress in Madrid, Alain Plessis and André Straus, asked the participants 'who bought insurance and for what?' It is a very important question, but I have not yet been able to answer it with regard to Japanese insurance history. Indeed, I do not think that any insurance historians have yet arrived at an adequate answer.[4]

This is the context for this chapter. My research question is very simple. It is to clarify who bought modern life assurance. It is curious that there is no study of early policyholders in Japan.[5] Although the data are certainly fragmentary, we can obtain some information about early policyholders. Some company histories help us, and an insurance manuscript that I discovered in an auction market is also useful. Furthermore, in order to deepen this demand-side study, we have utilized not only historical documents from libraries and company archives, but also neglected insurance documents and pamphlets that libraries did not collect.

In this chapter, we will discuss three first-movers and one follower in addition to pioneering projects in Japanese life assurance.[6] Who bought their life products, products previously unimagined in Japan?

The Assured before Modern Life Assurance: The Kyosai 500

Before the birth of the modern life assurance company, there were two important projects in the Japanese life assurance business. One was the unsuccessful project of Nitto life assurance, and another was the successful foundation of an assessment insurance association. The former was the first life assurance project in Japan, whose central figure was Norikazu Wakayama. He became a member of the Iwakura Mission to the West,[7] and his function there was to study public finance in America. Upon returning to Japan, he hoped to create a modern life insurance company taking American life assurance as a model. However, he failed to raise money for the business, and abandoned the project just after its foundation. The latter was the Kyosai 500, whose membership was limited to 500 people. The association was established in 1880 and promised to pay 1,000 yen to the surviving family when a member passed away. The association paid the insurance money by collecting assessments from the other members. In other words it was a mutual relief fund for widows and orphans. In fact, there were plenty of associations like this at that time, but the Kyosai 500 was the only one that enjoyed a comparatively long life. Moreover, in 1894 it evolved into a new organization that became a modern life assurance company, the Kyosai Life. This association was more important than the previous unsuccessful projects in Japanese life assurance history, and we discuss its membership and its characteristics below.

The names of all the members of the Kyosai 500 have been ascertained and most of their occupations identified. From this analysis it appears that the membership came together by way of the personal network of the founder, Zenjiro Yasuda, an influential banker who later built up a strong financial combine that became one of the big four Zaibatsu. The office of the Kyosai 500 was established in the main building of the Third Bank, whose president was Zenjiro Yasuda.

The bank employees bore the association's operation and management costs, and thus there was no expense loading on the insurance enterprise. This helps explain why the association enjoyed a longer life than others.

Table 5.1 shows about 50 distinguished people from various fields who were members of the Kyosai 500. They include ex-Samurai from the Meiji revolution, journalists, scholars, cultural and religious figures, military officers and medical doctors. Most of these people were men of independence and self-supporting, with few high-ranking government officials.[8] There were no government leaders. On the contrary, the Kyosai membership included former vassals of the Tokugawa shogun. The financial condition of these individuals became riskier than it had been in the era before the Meiji Restoration, and they probably needed a mutual support network.

Table 5.1: Famous Figures in the Membership of the Kyosai 500.[9] The founders are underlined; members of the board of directors are shown in italics.

Occupation	Members
Ex-Samurai in the Meiji revolution	T. Yamaoka, H. Nakai, H. Hijikata, M. Kusumoto, *T. Ginbayashi*, K. Nagamatu, Y. Murakami
Journalists	<u>R. Narushima</u>, S. Suehiro, *S. Koyasu*, *K. Katou*
Scholars	K. Mishima, T. Kawada, F. Otsuki, S. Tsuda, S. Tsuji, S. Koizumi,
Cultured men	T. Kusakabe, O. Iwaya, M. Yoda, K. Onoe
Religious figures	S. Ouchi, M. Shimachi, *K. Suzuki*
Military officers	K. Nakamuta, H. Totake
Medical doctors	R. Takamatsu, S. Kumakawa, S. Nagayo, K. Takayama
Businessmen	<u>Z. Yasuda</u>, *H. Kawasaki*, *S. Kawasaki*, H. Shoda, M. Asada, S. Matsuo, I. Morimura, M. Okura, M. Shimizu, I. Kiya, J. Morita, K. Ono, *K. Kajima*, *K. Hasegawa*, *K. Ichikawa*

It is interesting that a famous Kabuki actor was to be found among the membership.[10] Kabuki is a traditional form of drama and music performed by male actors. This actor was probably patronized by the founder Yasuda. There was also a comparatively large number of medical doctors. At that time in Japan serious conflicts persisted between Western and Oriental medicine, and the doctors among the members all practiced Western medicine. Most medical doctors owned their own clinics and opened their businesses in their home town or village. Such doctors operated their businesses at their own risk, so they had a need for death cover for their surviving family members. A few doctors belonged to the university hospital or to the Ministry of Home Affairs that was responsible for public health. Dr Sensai Nagayo, famous for his major contribution to the improvement of Japanese public health, was the very last member, that is to say the 500th member of the association.[11]

Those joining the Kyosai 500 clearly worried about what would happen to their surviving families when they died, and were wealthy enough to pay about 2 yen when any other member passed away. The benefit of 1,000 yen was a comparatively large sum for a family at that time. The members, therefore, were not common people. By comparison, for example, even the Meiji Life, whose clientele were generally wealthier than those of other first-mover life insurance companies, had some policyholders whose insurance was for sums less than 500 yen.

It is significant that these members came to have a connection with life assurance business in the early Meiji period. Some took out policies with modern life assurance companies, and others bought modern life assurance companies' stocks. Most medical doctors became 'Revisionsärzten' or commissioned doctors.[12] Although the association was an old fashioned assessment insurance type of organization, it exerted a great influence on the introduction of modern life assurance in Japan.

An Analysis of Policyholders in Japanese Life Assurance Business: The Early Life Market and its First-Movers

While the first-mover in Japanese marine insurance, the Tokio Marine, was established in 1879, the Meiji Life started its life business in 1881.[13] The Teikoku Life and the Nippon Life followed.[14] Generally speaking, these three first-movers strongly invested in life assurance business, and in doing so helped raise the public profile of the 'new intellectuals' in the urban community. The 'new intellectuals' were those who had learned Western culture and science. Traditional knowledge based on Oriental culture and science became obsolete just after the Meiji Restoration in 1867. For example, Oriental medicine had been in control of medical science for a long time, but the new Meiji government suddenly introduced Western medicine into official medical education.

Many new projects and companies challenged these three first-movers, but successful companies were rare. Of these challengers only seven companies survived more than thirty years.[15] These were the Nagoya Life,[16] the Kyodo Life,[17] the Kyosai Life,[18] the Yurin Life,[19] the Sogo Life,[20] the Jinjyu Life[21] and the Kyoho Life.[22] These companies, with the exception of the Sogo Life, successfully built up their businesses as medium-sized life assurance companies.

Table 5.2 shows the new business of three first-movers and the follower companies. Of the latter, three major companies have been selected. By 1900 the Nippon Life had moved ahead of all other life companies. At the same time, among the follower companies the new business of the Yurin Life was growing steadily. The data only gives new business so the table does not necessarily show the overall performance of these companies. As discussed below, new business was not an important indicator of the solidity and performance of these companies because of the different life products they sold. It does, however, reveal something of the competitive situation prevailing at the time in life assurance.

Table 5.2: New Business of the Three First-Movers and Three Followers, 1881–1900 (in yen).[23]

	Meiji	Teikoku	Nippon	Nagoya	Kyosai	Yurin
1881	485,300	–	–	–	–	–
1882	431,900	–	–	–	–	–
1883	253,500	–	–	–	–	–
1884	466,500	–	–	–	–	–
1885	213,400	–	–	–	–	–
1886	400,600	–	–	–	–	–
1887	500800	–	–	–	–	–
1888	690,300	500,900	–	–	–	–
1889	1,170,400	996,500	225,800	–	–	–
1890	1,322,000	775,400	1,790,900	–	–	–
1891	1,276,700	1,426,500	2,125,520	–	–	–
1892	1,375,700	2,498,600	1,436,680	–	–	–
1893	1,482,600	3,651,800	1,789,430	60,400	–	–
1894	1,879,600	3,237,200	2,331,220	100,200	1,408,000	320,400
1895	2,269800	3,986,600	2,700,740	101,600	2,433,300	1,741,040
1896	1,926,100	4,745,300	3,251,430	287,600	3,048,700	3,321,410
1897	1,903,300	4,425,300	5,317,470	498,700	2,586,900	3,749,010
1898	2,100,500	4,024,200	5,912,010	553,900	2,290,700	2,525,590
1899	3,024,700	3,843,400	6,176,480	666,100	1,962,300	3,253,330
1900	4,028,400	5,107,500	6,294,370	625,500	2,501,000	4,010,300

The Policyholders of the First Modern Life Assurance Company in Japan

The Meiji Life was the first modern life assurance company in Japan. It was promoted by Yukichi Fukuzawa and his pupils. Fukuzawa was an important intellectual in the movement to introduce Western civilization into Japan, and was one of the first Japanese to introduce Western insurance systems to the country.[24] He was also the principal of a private school – which later developed into Keio University – that sent many Western-influenced graduates into business. Fukuzawa pupils founded Meiji Life in 1881 and one of them, Taizo Abe, became its first president.

At first, Abe faced great difficulties in selling life assurance because he had to explain, customer by customer, how it would benefit them in the future. In 1908 Abe recollected those experiences as follows:

> Japanese people couldn't understand what is insurance and knowledge about insurance had never been diffused in Japanese society. So it was very difficult for us to get new life assurance business. If we used ordinary sales techniques, we were unable to get it. As a result, I had no option but to access so-called new intellectuals, a prefectural governor, a civil servant, a justice, a teacher, a banker.

I hoped that new business would be promoted by religious circles, but the plan failed. Mr. Atsumi, who was a leader of the Higashi-Honganji Temple, added his name to the list of promoters, and I hoped that we would get the new business of many religious believers. However, a critical conflict occurred between this religious group and other groups, so the Higashi-Honganji Temple sect parted from our company.[25]

The Meiji Life proposed cooperation with friendly industrial companies like Mitsubishi for the purpose of selling new life business. The experience of Saburo Utsunomiya, Abe's early supporter, was as follows:

At first I asked Yataro Iwasaki's approval of life assurance, and also if he could recommend directors of the Iwasaki family and top managers of his companies to buy life assurance. But he didn't give me a clear answer, and said that I could not force them to buy life assurance because no one could interfere with their free choice for life assurance. Utsunomiya replied to Iwasaki that if your directors and top managers would buy life assurance, they would work with peace of mind.[26]

Many graduates of Keio Gijyuku School were recruited to companies related to Mitsubishi and the Iwasaki family. For that reason, the Meiji Life obtained considerable new business from the salaried men of such companies. It appears, therefore, that the first prospective clients of the Meiji Life were new intellectuals, including the top and middle managers of modern companies.

We now know all those who assured during the first month of business, and we can partially identify their occupations (data summarized in Table 5.3). We can identify policyholder occupations for up to 25.2 per cent of all new business. It is interesting that the Yokohama Specie Bank provided more policyholders than the Mitsubishi Company. Altogether, 6.5 per cent of new business came from the Bank and Mitsubishi connections. Civil servants were the most important group, accounting for 6.9 per cent of policyholders. If we look in detail at the civil servants, we find that there were no new government leaders and a comparatively small number of high-ranking officials. Businessmen included a newspaper owner, a trading merchant and a silk merchant. Scholars and teachers included a professor of Tokyo University and scholars of British studies, besides teachers at Keio Gijyuku. Most new policyholders who identified their occupations were members of Kojyunsha.[27] Sixty members of Kojyunsha bought new life assurance during the first month after the opening of the Meiji Life.

For the Meiji Life there is also a list of those assured from 1881 to 1897 whose policy values were over 500 yen. In general, the numbers of medical doctors and influential people who were not Kojyunsha members were gradually increasing. One month after opening for business, the Meiji Life Assurance had contracted 291 policies.[28] The promoters had close connections with the early policyholders. The promoters' council consisted of ten members, six of whom were graduates from the Keio Gijyuku School. Of the promoters, both Nobukichi Koizumi[29] and

Table 5.3: Occupations of the Assured who Contracted during the First Month of the Meiji Life.[30]

Occupation Identified	No.	%	Details
Civil servants	17	6.9	Ministry of Finance, etc.
Businessmen	13	5.3	Journalist, trading merchant, etc.
Scholars and teachers	10	4.1	Teacher of Keio, etc.
Yokohama Specie Bank	9	3.7	President, directors, officers
Mitsubishi Company	7	2.8	Directors, officers
Meiji Life	2	0.8	President, director
Kojyunsha officers	2	0.8	
Medical doctors and dentists	2	0.8	
Total identified	62	25.2	
Not identified	184	74.8	
All life assurance contracts	246	100.0	

Tokujiro Obata became the presidents of Keio Gijyuku, and the others had some connection with Fukuzawa, the founder of the school. Moreover, Heigoro Shoda and Eiji Asabuki[31] became members of the Mitsubishi Company. Consequently, it is easy to recognize the importance of the Keio and Mitsubishi connections among the early policyholders.

Having said that, a careful reading of the membership list reveals not only the Mitsubishi and Keio connections, but also policyholders with no connection to either organization. In general the Meiji Life attracted the custom of the so-called 'new intellectuals' in urban areas. This can be illustrated by examining more closely the company's earliest contracts. The Meiji Life sold five types of life products at the outset. These were whole life insurance, whole life with a limited term payment, endowment insurance, term insurance and savings assurance for children. The first whole life policy was contracted by Saburo Utsunomiya, a high-ranked officer and a technical expert in the Ministry of Industry. The value of the policy was 1,000 yen. The first whole life insurance with limited term payment was contracted by Otami Amano, a judge of the Yokohama Court. His insurance benefit was 500 yen, and the term of premiums payment was ten years. The first endowment policy was purchased by a member of the Mitsubishi Company. Its value was only 100 yen and its term was twenty-five years. An official of the Ministry of Agriculture and Commerce bought the first term insurance. The Meiji Life insured this for 500 yen for seven years. Finally, the first savings insurance for children was bought by a commoner, and its insurance benefit was 200 yen. The policy matured when the assured reached the age of fourteen years old.

Policyholders in the Second First-Mover: The Teikoku Life

The Teikoku Life was established in 1886. The founder was an obscure former serviceman named Tameshige Kato, and the company had unusual origins. Kato entered the new School of Army Paymasters in 1875 as one of its first students. Most graduates were appointed to the army as a paymaster and Kato also became an officer in Army Paymaster Corps together with his friends. However, at one point Kato and his friends were imprisoned for disobeying the orders of their superior officer. In jail they decided that they would work together to establish an insurance company when they were freed at the expiration of their sentence. After leaving prison, despite shedding his friends, Kato continued to promote the Teikoku Life, and he eventually found some influential supporters to back him, including Arinobu Fukuhara, a founder of Shiseido, one of the largest cosmetics makers in Japan. It may be said that not many companies emerge from an idea hatched behind bars. Once the Teikoku Life started to do business, the company strongly invested in marketing channels and became the second first-mover company in the Japanese life insurance market. Its competitiveness rested on reducing expenses, for example by simplifying the medical selection of lives, so that the company provided insurance at cheaper premiums than the Meiji Life.

While the Meiji Life sold to the new intellectuals in urban communities, the Teikoku Life concentrated its efforts on military officers, employees in services and medical doctors. Moreover, according to its official history, the company commissioned influential local persons to be its agents. Unfortunately, we have found no detailed information on individual policyholders. The only such reference in three formal company histories of the Teikoku (Asahi) Life noted that the first policyholder was the owner of a western grocery store in Tokyo, and that the insurance amount was 300 yen.[32] Had historical documents on the Teikoku Life's early policyholders survived, we would have an idea of who bought its life assurance, but there is now almost no likelihood of finding such documents as far as I know. At best we can surmise that its important clients came from the military and medical communities, and that it gradually extended its marketing to persons of influence in the local community.

The Policyholders of the Last First-Mover: The Nippon Life

The Nippon Life was established in 1889. Its founders were bankers and businessmen located around Osaka, at that time the second largest city in Japan. The Nippon Life invested in marketing activities both in Osaka and in the surrounding area, but from the start it also expanded its business through the whole country, so that it could challenge the advantage held by the Meiji Life and the Teikoku Life in the life market. The Nippon Life commissioned influential local persons and bankers to be agents, and it soon built an agency network over the whole of Japan. The first important job for its vice-president, Naoharu Kataoka, was to travel all over the country in order both to sell the company's life assurance and to build its sales channels.[33] One consequence was that the Nippon Life's average *per caput* sum insured was lower than that of the Meiji Life.

Fortunately there is a list of all the policyholders in the early business of the Nippon Life. The list reveals that the Nippon Life adopted a different strategy from the other first-mover companies. There were many local bankers among the early policyholders and, in the list, after a banker was recorded, the names of several small policyholders generally followed him. It seems that when a local banker bought life assurance, he also used his influence to help sell the life insurance products to others. Local bankers were representative of the owner-manager and propertied class in an area, so they were the best agents for the local life market. In this way, only the Nippon Life among the first-mover companies diffused small-value life assurance into rural areas in the early Meiji period.

Partly owing to its investment in this local agency network, the average amount insured by the Nippon Life's policyholders was distinctly lower than that of the Meiji Life, as shown in Table 5.4. In addition, the expense loading of the Nippon Life was often higher than that of the Meiji Life, as shown in Table 5.5. In sum, the Nippon Life followed a low-margin, high-turnover strategy. Consequently, the company gave birth to new insurance demand in local areas. These are the reasons why this new company succeeded in building up the competitive advantages typical of a first-mover.

Policyholders in Follower Companies: An Analysis of the Application Forms for Insurance Contracts

As we have seen, a number of follower companies were no match for the first-movers. Nevertheless, some did establish themselves on firm ground. Lots of life assurance companies were established before 1897, but only seven companies, excluding the three first-movers, were still operating in 1926. Among them, the Yurin Life was a well-established company. In this section we discuss the early policyholders of the Yurin Life and identify those who bought life assurance from such follower companies. Did the follower companies sell their life assurance to a different clientele from that of the first-movers? This question will be answered by analysing the insurance application documents of the Yurin Life.

The application documents, which I happened to discover at an auction, are fragmental and limited, but no such materials currently exist in libraries and company archives, as far as I am aware. The number of application forms is 111 and they date from 30 November 1895 to 18 January 1896. They reveal detailed private information on the health, age, address, occupation, physical characteristics and so on of the Yurin Life's policyholders. For the purposes of this chapter I have extracted occupational information from this material.

Table 5.4: Average Size of Policies in the Three First-Mover Companies, 1881–1900 (in yen).[34]

Year	Meiji Amount	Meiji Policies	Meiji Average	Teikoku Amount	Teikoku Policies	Teikoku Average	Nippon Amount	Nippon Policies	Nippon Average
1881	485,300	883	550	–	–	–	–	–	–
1882	890,000	1,877	474	–	–	–	–	–	–
1883	1,074,400	2,289	469	–	–	–	–	–	–
1884	1,395,100	2,775	503	–	–	–	–	–	–
1885	1,412,200	2,794	505	–	–	–	–	–	–
1886	1,649,000	3,257	506	–	–	–	–	–	–
1887	1,985,300	4,043	491	–	–	–	–	–	–
1888	2,577,400	5,347	482	490600	1,033	475	–	–	–
1889	3,609,300	7,548	478	1,418,700	3,464	410	225,800	358	631
1890	4,670,000	10,199	458	1,986,300	5,445	365	2,001,100	5,926	338
1891	5,558,000	12,617	441	3,133,900	9,256	339	4,065,920	13,779	295
1892	6,694,400	15,614	429	5,301,700	16,925	313	5,265,800	18,953	278
1893	7,638,700	18,239	419	8,175,300	26,677	306	6,850,350	15,039	456
1894	8,958,900	22,521	398	10,375,300	34,597	300	8,732,070	31,808	275
1895	10,627,700	28,216	377	13,272,300	44,790	296	10,766,030	39,945	270
1896	11,884,300	31,994	371	16,686,300	55,296	302	13,120,000	48,435	271
1897	12,921,300	34,787	371	19,296,700	63,372	304	16,826,840	61,302	274
1898	14,049,200	37,662	373	20,992,300	69,048	304	20,861,050	73,306	285
1899	15,804,300	41,160	384	22,889,800	73,314	312	23,991,990	80,688	297
1900	18,041,200	44,951	401	26,073,200	81,072	322	27,523,110	89,679	307

Table 5.5: The Expense Ratio of the Three First-Mover Companies, 1881–1900 (in yen).[35]

Year	Meiji Expense	Meiji Premiums	Meiji Average (%)	Teikoku Expense	Teikoku Premiums	Teikoku Average (%)	Nippon Expense	Nippon Premiums	Nippon Average (%)
1881	2,936	10,212	28.75	–	–	–	–	–	–
1882	6,223	26,154	23.79	–	–	–	–	–	–
1883	7,251	31,279	23.18	–	–	–	–	–	–
1884	9,158	45,542	20.11	–	–	–	–	–	–
1885	7,445	44,054	16.90	–	–	–	–	–	–
1886	8,931	47,490	18.81	–	–	–	–	–	–
1887	11,843	66,463	17.82	–	–	–	–	–	–
1888	14,217	84,356	16.85	148	9,657	1.53	–	–	–
1889	19,371	119,897	16.16	21,069	28,891	72.93	–	6,332	–
1890	24,933	156,418	15.94	22,468	63,769	35.23	16,279	66,004	24.66
1891	30,250	191,022	15.84	32,896	94,862	34.68	34,363	128,106	26.82
1892	33,909	226,297	14.98	48,112	160,773	29.93	36,925	182,127	20.27
1893	41,312	260,848	15.84	61,683	260,300	23.70	32,076	237,272	13.52
1894	57,932	303,547	19.09	69,919	349,811	19.99	56,490	309,796	18.23
1895	71,181	368,287	19.33	78,708	442,324	17.79	70,551	386,420	18.26
1896	76,555	400,390	19.12	105,254	587,422	17.92	98,394	474,776	20.72
1897	88,810	433,931	20.47	121,797	665,604	18.30	166,769	495,014	33.69
1898	106,457	470,599	22.62	148,194	736,779	20.11	199,545	747,596	26.69
1899	125,047	519,939	24.05	172,850	799,999	21.61	212,611	983,313	21.62
1900	167,747	631,466	26.56	212,043	909,580	23.31	256,911	1,115,764	23.03

The results make it clear that there were different classes of policyholder in the early life assurance market in Japan. First, almost all the policyholders in the Yurin Life documents were small retailers, middle-class farmers, and small employees in services and transport. Table 5.6 below shows the occupational distribution of the Yurin Life policyholders. Second, as a result of this occupational structure, the average *per caput* amount insured was very low. Third, there were many cancellations. While 40 of the 105 policies covered by these documents expired, a further 58 were cancelled before expiry. Death benefits were paid out on 7 policies, and the fate of 6 policies is obscure. As far as this evidence goes, it suggests that follower companies such as the Yurin Life had a problem with the high proportion of policies that were cancelled. Lastly, the documents indicate that the Yurin Life had more female policyholders than the first-mover companies. Policies held by women were generally for small amounts. This suggests that the Yurin Life invested considerable sales effort in selling assurance to large families in rural communities. In doing so, they probably emphasized that their product was for the purpose of savings rather than for an indemnity against death.

**Table 5.6: The Occupational Distribution of the Assured of the Yurin Life,
30 November 1885–18 January 1886.**

Occupation	No.	Details
Commerce	30	Kimono fabrics, used clothes, rice & grain, metal utensils, etc.
Agriculture	20	
Manufacturing	8	Sewing, potting, printing, etc.
Construction	3	Carpenter, plasterer, etc.
Fishery	1	
Services	8	Rickshaw pullers, geishas, restaurant staff, etc.
Professionals	12	Priests, teachers, medical doctors, etc.
Civil servants	2	
Salaried man	1	
Student	1	Student of pharmacy
Miscellany	10	
No jobs	11	
No statement	3	
Obscure	1	Illegible
Total	111	

In sum, we may conclude that follower companies like the Yurin Life invested in sales forces in rural regions, and sold their small-value life policies to members of large families as a savings product. This market had not been developed by the first-movers until the follower companies entered it. The follower companies could not break the competitive advantage of the first-movers, but some managed to establish their position in this way and enjoyed a comparatively long business life. At the same time, they made a great contribution to the penetration of life assurance products among the common people.

Conclusion

The research question posed by this chapter was to clarify who bought life assurance and for what purpose in the early Japanese life market. We examined the policyholders of three first-mover companies and one follower company. As a result, we can draw the following two important conclusions. First, there was no high-value life assurance product for the richest class in Japan. It is well known that the gap between rich and poor in Japanese society was much smaller than in English society, even in the Edo period.[36] Even the Meiji Life did not expect much demand for life assurance to emanate from the rich. Thus there were no high-value life assurance contracts in early Japan. This meant that Japan did not have life assurance companies like the Old Equitable.

Second, instead of demand from the rich, life insurers anticipated a demand from the new urban intellectuals whose numbers were increasing as industrialization and Westernization progressed. The first-movers, especially the Meiji Life, were deeply involving in meeting this demand. Although the other first-movers tried to extend their sales forces into rural communities, the follower companies concentrated their efforts on supplying the demand for small policies in rural communities as thoroughly as possible. As a result, to buy life assurance became a usual practice among the common people of Japan. It is remarkable that such popularization of life assurance proceeded so rapidly.

During the process of popularization, many problems arose. For example, there were many cancellations of policies, as we saw above in the case of the Yurin Life. The more small policies they sold, the more cancellations they had. Moreover, as small-value life assurance policies increased in number, so did the number of policyholders who did not understand the product, and so did the instances of misconduct by agents. The first law for insurance supervision was enacted in Japan in 1900, partly as a measure to improve these problems. Unfortunately, however, these problems did not disappear when supervision was strengthened.

After 1900, there were some changes on the demand side. Since these are not topics that can be fully addressed in this paper, I will make only a brief reference to these changes. After 1900, some foreign life companies extended their business into Japan, by getting permits from the insurance authorities. For example, the New York Life sold its life products in Japan as early as 1903. The Canada Sun and the Equitable did the same. Their target market, however, was the richer class in Japan, to whom they sold policies of more than 5,000 yen. The wealthy in Japan at that time preferred foreign companies to domestic companies with reference to their creditworthiness.

There are two reasons why foreign life assurance companies entered Japan later than their fire and marine insurance counterparts. First, the Japanese life market was not yet well developed. As noted above, the customers in the early life market were mainly new technocrats and high-ranking businessmen living in urban areas, and the three first-mover Japanese companies already dominated this market. As a result, it was difficult for foreign life assurance companies in that they had to wait for living standards in Japan to rise. Moreover, Japanese society was much more equal in terms of its income distribution than English society. Consequently, foreign life assurance companies focused on a small market of the upper-middle class who had the requisite financial understanding of the insurance business. Second, as Morton Keller has described, American life assurance companies were busy expanding overseas after 1890s.[37] The Japanese market, therefore, was not necessarily behind the trend of US offices' overseas expansion. The latter came to have not a large, but a steady, life business in Japan for more than thirty years before the Second World War.

While life assurance penetrated into Japanese rural communities, urbanization developed further in the 1910s. The private life assurance companies did not offer their products to the poor. For this reason, the Ministry of Communications established a post office life assurance scheme, the so-called Kampo insurance, in 1915 for workers who did not buy life assurance from the private companies. The maximum insured on a Kampo policy was limited at first to 250 yen. Thus, after 1900 the demand for Japanese life assurance diversified considerably, but this is not the subject of this chapter and must await further research.

6 INDUSTRIAL LIFE INSURANCE AND THE COST OF DYING: THE ROLE OF ENDOWMENT AND WHOLE LIFE INSURANCE IN ANGLO-SAXON AND EUROPEAN COUNTRIES DURING THE LATE NINETEENTH AND EARLY TWENTIETH CENTURIES

Liselotte Eriksson

The development of life insurance is generally believed to be tightly connected to the increased income dispersion in conjunction with the rise of the wage-earning middle class in the nineteenth century. Life insurance became a necessary substitute for the safety net previously provided by the agricultural society, facilitating the existence of a middle class lacking real property. Scholars therefore view the use of life insurance as central to the improvement and diversification of the middle-class standard of living.[1]

However, at least as important as the growth of the middle class in the nineteenth century was the rise of the working class.[2] The great expansion of life insurance taking place in the late nineteenth century was thus not only accomplished through ordinary life insurance but also through industrial life insurance, which was especially designed for working-class conditions with premiums payable weekly, collected by agents at the house of the insured. The compensation of agents was done on a commission basis, sometimes both on the amount of new business written and upon the amount of premiums collected. The claim was also paid shortly after the death of the insured.[3] All this implied considerable deviations and new elements in relation to the operation of ordinary life insurance.

Industrial life insurance, with its beginnings in England in the 1850s, came to be immensely popular and expanded in many Western countries. Industrial life insurance even became the dominating line of life insurance in terms of the number of policyholders in some countries by the end of the nineteenth century. Before the introduction of public accident insurance and public pension schemes, the private insurance market addressed the needs of working-class risk management to a larger extent than governments in the nineteenth century.[4] Industrial life insurance is perhaps the line of private insurance with the most evident connection to public insurance.[5] In countries where industrial life insurance had the relatively largest market share, like the US, public insurance is still limited today. This highlights the importance of addressing the question as to why industrial life insurance grew stronger in some countries than in others.

As the industry itself claimed, industrial insurance became the most widely diffused form of savings in English-speaking countries in the early twentieth century.[6] In the UK, over 25 million industrial insurance policies were issued to a population of 43 million in 1913, which meant the number of policies exceeded the number of households. During the period 1890–1913 there was a threefold increase in industrial business in the UK.[7] According to Keneley, the expansion of the Australian life insurance market in the nineteenth century was due to the introduction of industrial life insurance companies.[8] In the US in 1905, there were 15 million industrial policies in force upon the lives of 12 million persons represented, approximately, the insurable members of 3 million families. Industrial insurance, as measured by the number of policies, increased 189 per cent over the period 1890 to 1919, while the total estimated wealth of the US increased 45 per cent, the number of savings bank depositors increased by 43 per cent and population growth was 22 per cent. The number of policyholders of industrial insurance in the US in 1907 was nearly twice the membership of fraternal societies, three times the holders of old line policies and twice the number of savings-bank depositors.[9]

Entrepreneurs in the insurance business all over Europe noticed the success of industrial life insurance in the UK and the US. Therefore a number of new industrial life insurance companies used similar organizational models as the first established industrial life insurance company, the Prudential Assurance Company of London, where industrial business was introduced in 1854. In Europe, the only country experiencing a development in industrial life insurance comparable with the Anglo-Saxon countries was Germany. The Victoria zu Berlin became the largest life insurance company in the non-Anglo-Saxon countries by the turn of the century. In other countries the industry experienced success, but a slightly less astonishing one. In Sweden and Denmark the largest industrial life insurance company sold more policies in the early twentieth century than the largest ordinary life insurance company during the late nineteenth century, but the ordinary life business was still superior in terms of total number of policies and insured amount.

Despite the success of industrial life insurance among the public, it became highly controversial among insurance specialists, representatives of old life insurance companies and among politicians.[10] Internal criticism of industrial life insurance was perhaps most extensive in the US and in the UK, where numerous articles and books were written on the subject.[11] Accusations of high expenses compared to ordinary insurance and the very high lapse rate were common complaints.[12] The offensive work of insurance agents was also criticized for making poor people engage in too expensive insurance contracts.[13] The proponents of industrial insurance, on the other hand, argued that alternatives to industrial life insurance did not exist. The price was bound to be higher per unit of insurance due to the high administration costs incurred by small policies. However, a weekly premium plan each year presented fifty-two occasions for lapsing compared to one for annual insurance. The majority of the critics of industrial life insurance acknowledged, though regretted, this fact, while they still viewed the expenses as unnecessarily high. According to some 1904 critics of industrial life insurance, a fairly representative year for US industrial insurance, 87 per cent of all policies terminating in that year ended by lapses; only 13 per cent resulted in any payment to the insured.[14] Louis Brandeis, later justice of the US Supreme Court, stated in 1906:

> For the greatest of life insurance wrongs – the so called industrial insurance – the Armstrong Committee failed to offer any remedy ... the needs and financial inexperience of the wage-earner are exploited for the benefit of stockholders or officials, the interests of the insured are ignored.[15]

Despite the European admiration of Anglo-Saxon industrial insurance, its high overhead costs were also viewed as cautionary examples.[16] Regarding British industrial insurance, the French assurance magazine *L'Argus* claimed that the policyholders in the Prudential had to pay unreasonably dearly for their policies.[17] The same magazine also regarded residents of European countries, who, in spite of the presence of sound local insurance companies, engaged with American life insurance companies, 'to be, using the most polite expression, very brave'.[18] Swedish insurance actors considered it more lucrative for the working class to buy endowment insurance instead of the kind of insurance offered by British Prudential to secure support in old age.[19] The importance of the issue is mirrored in the Swedish Insurance Association, which dedicated several meetings to discussing the high cost of industrial life insurance and its alternatives. The Nordic life insurance congress in 1901 further wished to reach an understanding and reduce the expenses in conducting life insurance business. The proposal was, however, rejected since it was believed that American companies, having the highest expenses, would never agree on a similar understanding.[20]

The critique directed against industrial life insurance was not the result of foreign competition, as long as American and English industrial life insurance companies did not take their business abroad, with the exception of Canada.[21]

Several new establishments using American industrial life insurance companies as raw models did, however, compete with existing life insurance companies.

The above discussion raises the question of whether industrial insurance deserved its bad reputation, and further, if only half the contemporary critique of industrial insurance contained some degree of truth, why was it such a success, especially in the Anglo-Saxon countries, where criticism of it was the most severe?

The Function of Industrial Life Insurance

Actors in the industrial life insurance industry aimed to be identified with perceptions of thrift and prudence, qualities which the ruling parties in many western countries wished to encourage, especially among the less well-off.[22] The function and role of industrial life insurance, however, varied in different countries, as did its achievement in improving conditions for the working class.

The remarkable diffusion of life insurance through industrial life insurance has been acknowledged for elevating the urban working class to higher income levels.[23] Murphy, for example, claims that industrial life insurance policies, except those on infants and young children, functioned the same way as ordinary insurance to the support of the family. The difference between the growth of industrial and ordinary insurance in the US is further explained by the number of persons insured in each family. In a working-class family the income of all members was crucial for the survival of the family, therefore everyone in the family got insured. Regarding the middle class, by contrast, only the breadwinner needed to be insured.[24] This assertion holds true only if industrial life insurance had the ability to reduce poverty, that is if it was comprehensive enough to support a family in the case of a loss of an income, at least for a short period of time, and economical enough to ensure the workers the most advantageous return on their premiums. This requirement of industrial insurance was not met in most countries; instead, the way of conducting industrial insurance was more expensive than ordinary life insurance and in the Anglo-Saxon countries it did not imply economic security for the remaining family.[25]

The role of industrial life insurance in America was summarized by the statistician of the first American industrial life insurance company, Frederick Hoffman: 'The chief object of industrial insurance is to provide a burial fund for every member of the wage-earner's family'.[26] This was also the case in the UK and Australia, where industrial insurance was 'little more than sufficient to pay funeral expenses'.[27] The principle of industrial life insurance was to insure for each member of the family a small sum through a whole life insurance, which in the case of the Anglo-Saxon countries only covered burial costs and perhaps the final medical bill. This implies that industrial insurance generally 'just' eased the remaining family from the immediate cost of a funeral. Industrial life insurance could keep the family from incurring debts if no reserves existed for covering costs associated with a sudden death, but it did not solve the issue of dependents or strengthen the economy of the family. Hoffman illustrated this in his *Pauper Burials and the Interment of Dead in Large Cities*. The average funeral expense of an industrial worker with a policy in the Prudential in 1918 was $121.48 and the average claim payment was $197.75. The average excess of claim payment was $76.27, a sum supposed to manage the medical costs of the last illness.[28]

Turning to the function of industrial life insurance in Europe, the picture becomes slightly more diversified. A young Swedish statistician and lieutenant, Ernst Svedelius, in 1910 received a scholarship provided by the Swedish Insurance Association to undertake an educational study of the insurance industry in Switzerland. He reported that the largest Swiss life insurance company conducting industrial insurance did not issue whole life insurance at all, instead endowment insurance was predominant.[29] Unlike whole life insurance, an endowment life insurance policy is designed primarily to provide a living benefit and only secondarily to provide life insurance protection. Therefore, endowment insurance is more of an investment than a whole life policy. Endowment life insurance pays the face value of the policy either at the insured's death or at a certain age or after a number of years of premium payment. The Swiss industrial life insurance policyholders had the option of weekly premium payments but the majority still preferred to pay the whole premium amount for a quarter in a post office account of the company. This means that a less comprehensive organization was needed to collect premium and this implies lower costs.[30] The company used the purchase and application of stamps on a specific chart to be mailed to them for premium payments.[31]

The function of Danish industrial insurance was also very different from that in the Anglo-Saxon countries, despite similarities in the organization of the business. The purpose of Danish industrial life insurance was to enable the widow of a deceased worker, for example, to start some kind of business for her continuing support; or for a maid to establish her own household. At an early date, Danish industrial insurance had a large proportion of policies issued as endowment policies. Moreover, it was called 'confirmation insurance' as parents insured their children with an endowment insurance to mature by the time of their confirmation.[32]

In Austria industrial life insurance was described as insignificant until 1914 by the eighth international congress of actuaries, when industrial insurance or so called 'war policies' became increasingly popular. These policies were generally issued on endowment plans.[33] The first Swedish industrial life insurance company, the Trygg, reported that the pattern of demand was radically different to that of the British Prudential Company. Of the total of policies issued in the Trygg, over 90 per cent consisted of endowment policies in 1908. In Trygg's weekly paper for agents, it was claimed that this illustrated the generosity of the British towards their families in contrast to Swedish policyholders who instead preferred to enrich themselves in old age by endowment policies.[34] In another Swedish industrial life insurance company, the Förenade, only 3.3 per cent of policies written in 1916 were whole life policies.[35] Germany hosted the very successful industrial life insurance company the Victoria zu Berlin, which grew to a dominant position thanks to obligatory workmen's insurance and successfully offering more advantageous conditions than state-owned institutes.[36] Fraternal associations and friendly societies are usually considered to provide a similar insurance protection at death, a sum covering funeral costs. However, Söhner, who in 1911 wrote about private industrial life insurance in Germany, stated that one difference between German burial clubs and industrial insurance was that the latter involved elements of savings and that industrial insurance was dominated by short-term contracts.[37] Another characteristic of German industrial life insurance was the dominance of insurance contracts on children, contracts that usually were extended into adulthood. In the Victoria zu Berlin half of all insurance contracts were issued on behalf of children under fifteen years of age. By contrast, in the UK and the US, insurance contracts on children constituted approximately a quarter of the business.[38] Although German industrial insurance grew stronger than in other European countries, it still remained limited in comparison to Anglo-Saxon countries. It has been argued that industrial life insurance closed a gap in social insurance, where no payment in the case of death was granted, and Söhner claims that this partly explains the lower demand for industrial insurance in Germany.[39] Furthermore, in the early twentieth century the Victoria zu Berlin offered additional accident and invalidity insurance within the bounds of industrial insurance, adapting the form of 'large life insurance', implying a function more sophisticated than burial insurance.[40]

According to Gales, industrial life insurance in the Netherlands from 1890 onwards distanced itself and its product from the business of solely covering the cost of a funeral. Industrial companies turned to intermediate insurance – insurance on the ordinary plan but on smaller amounts, an insurance placing itself between the small industrial and the larger ordinary life policy. Gales claims that wage earners were advised by the industrial insurance business itself to buy an insurance that benefited the surviving members of the family instead of one that only ensured a decent funeral. In this respect, Dutch industrial life insurance companies succeeded in creating trust among their target group, the working class, in contrast to their British counterparts.[41] Intermediate insurance was also issued in the US by companies like the Metropolitan. A major difference between the Dutch and American examples, however, was that American intermediate insurance was issued on the ordinary plan only and was not considered an industrial life insurance policy.[42]

The polarization of the forms of industrial life insurance, the dominance of the whole life burial insurance in Anglo-Saxon countries and the dominance of endowment insurance in Western Europe were fundamental international differences. In this respect it is reasonable to assume that industrial life insurance involved varying degrees of burial insurance, with Anglo-Saxon industrial life insurance implying a comparatively higher degree of burial insurance and European industrial life insurance involving a lower degree of burial insurance.

Endowment policies called for a higher premium per unit of insurance than whole life policies and were even prohibited in the state of New York, where agents were accused of selling industrial endowment insurance to people on too small amounts, insufficient for the endowment form of life insurance.[43] A similar European debate about endowment insurance has not been found. It is therefore likely that countries conducting a large part of industrial business by endowment policies sold larger policies. Some European versions of industrial insurance may therefore be considered to occupy a position right on the boundary of ordinary life insurance.[44]

The American Prudential Company started with industrial endowments in 1895, but the demand for endowments did not exceed 7 per cent during the period of study.[45] The industrial life insurance company the Metropolitan introduced endowments in 1892 and had the same experience as the Prudential.[46] In practice the early industrial insurance policies were written on the whole life plan only.[47] As stressed by the executive of the American Prudential, John F. Dryden: 'it [endowment insurance] represents an investment feature, which can hardly find a place in an industrial policy, providing first for the payment of funeral expenses and the cost of the last illness'. He also claimed that the increased cost of endowment insurance must be a serious hindrance to success, while it would be unfortunate if the primary goal of the insurance (covering cost of funeral) should be defeated by a secondary one, which would be an endowment paid during the lifetime of the insured: '[the endowment insurance] being small, would rapidly be consumed for living expenses, leaving little or nothing at death to meet the cost of burial or last illness'.[48] Supple argues that British industrial life insurance rather served to guarantee only the payment of the cost of burial and just maybe channelled tiny savings into endowment policies.[49] The above survey illustrates an obvious difference in the composition of this insurance branch between countries. Endowment insurance was predominant among Swedish, Danish, Swiss and German policyholders and gave them a pension at old age. By contrast, the Americans, the British and the Australians bought smaller policies in order to cover burial costs.

However, it was not just the function of industrial life insurance that differed internationally. An equally important aspect was the variation between countries in the cost of industrial policies. The cost of life insurance is determined by the expense incurred in running the business. As previously noted, the organization of industrial life insurance naturally involved higher expenses compared to ordinary life insurance; the salaries and commissions to the large staff consumed a great part of the annual premium income, as did the administration of the small policies and the weekly premium payments. However, these costs varied between countries. One cost that differed between countries with an extensive industrial life insurance was the cost of supervision. Keneley argues that the organization of Australian industrial life insurance involved problems associated with moral hazard and adverse selection, which incurred high agency costs. The fear of theft or fraud on the part of agents outweighed concern over the expense of maintaining a costly system of supervision of agents. The largest Australian life insurer, therefore, considered all costs in conducting industrial life insurance under 40 per cent of premium income to be economical.[50] In the US too the agent was under careful supervision and every transaction was subject to check and counter-check.[51] The same system and ignorance of the cost of supervision cannot be found in other Western countries where the organization was less extensive and the policyholders fewer.

The most common measurement used to compare the price of life insurance was the percentage of premium income used for expenses by the insurance company.[52] In comparing the price of industrial life insurance the load measure is used to avoid problems relating to deflating price series. The price, here interpreted as load, is defined as the percentage increase in an actuarially just premium that is included to pay for administration and commissions to agents. Load stands for the expense to the consumer of choosing to purchase an insurance policy instead of self-insuring.[53] This means that differences in mortality between the countries are irrelevant for the load.

The first countries to introduce industrial life insurance were the UK in 1854 and the US in 1875. Since administrative costs are a measure of the price, a lower price implies a more economical insurance for the policyholders. It might be expected that companies in, for example, the US, being in operation for more than two decades at the time of the establishment of industrial life insurance in, for example, Sweden, would have developed a more efficient way of conducting business than companies with only a few years of practice, despite catch-up effects. However, as shown in Table 6.1, during the period 1900–14, the price or load of life insurance in the US was on average 22 per cent higher than in Sweden, implying a higher administration or overhead cost share of total premium income in the US.

Table 6.1: Average Price (load) in Swedish and US Industrial Life Insurance, 1900–14.[54]

	Sweden (A)	US (B)
Sample size	40	358
Mean	1.35	1.57
T-stat of sample mean A&B	−10.1165	

There is further evidence that the British Prudential carried expensive industrial life insurance as well. The largest Swedish industrial life insurance company, the Trygg, claimed the commission for agents of collected premiums to be 18.3 per cent in the Prudential and 9.6 per cent in the Trygg, making the administration of insurance in the latter less expensive.[55] In the UK in 1919 a committee was set up which revealed that 44 per cent of the premium income on industrial policies was absorbed by expenses and commissions.[56] Industrial insurance was expensive in Sweden as well. As a comparison, the ordinary Swedish life insurance industry during the same period had an average administrative cost of 16 per cent compared to 35 per cent in industrial insurance. The generally higher cost of industrial insurance compared to ordinary insurance identifies policy size as an important aspect affecting the cost of life insurance. The price was negatively correlated with average policy size, while numerous small premiums generated higher administrative burdens than a few large premiums. A comparison between the average premium paid annually and the annual income of an average American and Swedish worker indicates that Swedish insured workers paid higher annual premiums (in current terms), which implies that the average Swedish industrial life insurance policy was larger than its counterpart in the US.[57] The size of the average industrial insurance policy in turn was partly dependent on the function of insurance.[58]

Explaining the Demand for Industrial Life Insurance

Anglo-Saxon policyholders, in particular, had to pay for demanding small industrial life insurance policies – which translated to a significantly higher price per dollar of insurance compared to European policyholders. The high Anglo-Saxon demand for small industrial life insurance is even more puzzling taking into account that an average American and UK worker earned more than his European counterparts. Despite this, although the growth of industrial insurance was impressive in many Western countries, the growth of Anglo-Saxon industrial insurance was unprecedented, for instance in 1894 industrial life insurance accounted for 40 per cent of total life insurance written in the US.[59]

A possible explanation for this could be the role of other institutions covering the cost of burials, like friendly societies, fraternal orders and burial clubs.[60] These could have crowded out industrial life insurance as burial insurance in Europe, which would explain why European industrial insurance instead became insurance for larger amounts and sometimes, as in Switzerland, for the lower middle class instead of the working class. There is little evidence, however, to support this assertion. Fraternal orders and friendly societies were very much institutions to be taken into account in the business of burial insurance, both in America and the UK.[61] More interestingly, in countries with a weak industrial life insurance business, such as Switzerland and France, burial clubs and the like languished.[62] According to Aubrun, life insurance seemed least urgent among the French population due to the relatively low economic burden for the family in the event of death, which is why burial insurance tended to be set aside in favour of two other types of insurance, sickness and accident insurance.[63] The burial clubs and other societies primarily competed with savings banks (*caisses d'épargne*).[64] This makes it hard to conclude that burial clubs had a more prominent role as a supplier of burial insurance in European countries or that an eventual crowding out effect was at hand.

The other possible explanatory aspect regarding the different functions of industrial life insurance in Anglo-Saxon versus European countries might be the entry of public insurance. At the beginning of the twentieth century, several European countries had adopted some kind of compulsory or voluntary workmen's accident insurance.[65] The insurance contributed in all cases to the burial of the insured, if death occurred at the workplace. But it did not cover unexpected deaths in the working man's family. The American insurance historian Stalson claims that the expansion of industrial life insurance essentially reflected developments in marketing.[66] It is true that the organization of agents and marketing of life insurance made it easy to purchase and maintain industrial life insurance policies. It is evident, however, that a demand for industrial life insurance was based not only on the availability to pay and purchase an industrial life insurance, but also on the function of the insurance product itself. One characteristic of industrial life insurance was that everyone in the family got insured, in contrast to ordinary life insurance. This characteristic undoubtedly sold policies. It is understandable when it was used as confirmation insurance and a mode of saving for the future of one's children, but what explains the high demand, especially in the Anglo-Saxon countries, for small industrial life policies functioning solely as burial insurance for everyone in the family? It is possible that a high demand for industrial life insurance with the function of covering burial costs mirrored a society in which funeral rituals and practices for different reasons had become very costly. According to this reasoning, the cost of dying in Anglo-Saxon countries was higher than in European countries, while industrial life insurance in Anglo-Saxon countries to a large extent performed the role of burial insurance. In Anglo-Saxon countries this kind of insurance, therefore, became a necessity for everyone in the working man's family where the unexpected death of any family member could result in economic disaster.

Burial Traditions and the Role of Culture and Commercialization

Prior to the nineteenth century, the American and British funeral was almost exclusively a family affair. But in the early years of the nineteenth century attitudes towards death and burial began to change and Britain and the US saw a development from churchyards to cemeteries. A major reason for this was urbanization, which led to overcrowded churchyards in the largest cities. Corpses were buried in shallow graves and disinterred after too brief a period to make room for others. Scientists maintained that cemeteries threatened public health because of the emanations of air released from the dead.[67] This resulted in a prohibition of intramural (inner city) cemeteries in America and all over Europe.[68] At this time churches in Britain became increasingly secularized. Besides being at risk of losing ideological and symbolic power over burial customs and death rituals, the church wanted to sustain the income from burial fees. Together with urbanization and the dilemmas of the church, this led to an increase in the establishment of cemeteries free from the control of the church and by the 1850s the monopoly of the churchyard was broken. In the US and Australia, no state church or government had been in charge of the burial of the dead. Thus, in America, Australia and the UK numerous for-profit cemeteries were founded. The world's largest cemetery in the nineteenth century was Sydney's Rockwood cemetery.[69] Recent research argues that this private control inevitably implied increasing commercialization, not the least through the emergence of the funeral industry.[70] The foundation of the emergent industry lay in the embalming and viewing of the dead, practices that gained legitimacy during the Civil War years, and which by the beginning of the twentieth century had become a regular procedure.

Europeans on the other hand turned to governments or the state church to oversee the interment of the dead.[71] According to Sloane, Europeans could be sure that governments were not burying for the purpose of profit. In France, Sweden and other countries where cemetery management was/is considered a public concern, the cultural attitude historically has been marked by less extravagant funerals. Furthermore, unlike the US and Britain, France and Sweden had laws regulating the reuse of graves after a set time period (in Sweden it is twenty-five years). In Britain it is still illegal to disturb human remains unless permission is secured from the church authorities or the Home Office, and similar conditions exist in America. In Britain it is still illegal to disturb human remains unless permission is secured from the church authorities or the home office, and similar conditions exist in America.[72]

The funeral became more expensive in all countries where intramural cemeteries were prohibited and where the deceased needed to be transported to a cemetery outside the city. A survey of the burial industry in America from 1926 illustrates that burial expenses increased in direct ratio with the size of the city, given the rising land rates, wages, rents and taxes.[73]

The privatization of burials in Anglo-Saxon countries led to costly funerals while the burial became a social marker. Thus, the major difference between the Anglo-Saxon countries and other European countries lay in the kind of funerals that were offered to the poor, as poor people were not able to cover the costs of their own funerals. If there did not exist economic means for a funeral, the alternative was to get buried at public expense – to have a pauper burial. In Anglo-Saxon countries this meant getting buried in a special graveyard for the poor, the unknown, criminals and others without their own means for a funeral. These types of graveyard, known as 'potter's fields', were established in the major towns during 1700–1800.[74] A pauper burial was free of charge, but there is a lot of anecdotal evidence of the public aversion towards them.[75] The aversion was founded partly on rumours and horror stories and partly on the true management of the burials at potter's field, for example, the possibility of becoming the subject of an anatomical examination or being poorly buried without a coffin just a couple of inches under the ground.[76] American graveyards and church-yards at this time are described by French as 'places where the mourning sank ankle deep in a repulsive mould of broken bones and pieces of coffins'.[77]

Levy and Wilson, who in 1938 investigated actual burial costs in the UK, referred to the nineteenth century where paupers were packed together as closely as possible in order to make the most of the space, and where those in charge of the common burial places did not give the bones time to decay. They stated that burial conditions abroad were in many aspects superior to those in England. In Frankfurt and Munich and in other cemeteries on the Continent, the general rule was not to allow more than one body in a grave.[78] Charles Booth claimed in 1894 that to secure a 'respectful' funeral, the English working class would well nigh starve, such was the dislike of the poor for a 'pauper' funeral.[79] The authors claimed that the cost of a funeral was seriously disrupting the economy of the absolute majority of families.[80]

The most comprehensive survey of burial costs and the funeral industry undertaken during this period is an American survey financed by one of the largest industrial life insurance companies, the Metropolitan, which employed a committee to investigate the issue of funeral costs. The director of the committee, Gebhart, wrote in a summary that funeral expenditures were relatively, but not actually, higher among the low-income groups than among the well-to-do.[81] A custom of too extravagant funerals among the less well-to-do had evolved. The *New York Sun* in 1900, for example, claimed that the poor were adopting the burial customs of the rich, with impoverishment as a result. Some objected that the money spent on funerals could be used more wisely.[82] The high cost of funerals seemed outrageous to many who claimed that vulnerable families, especially poor families, consumed by grief and guilt, had no choices and could not fully comprehend what they were purchasing when making funeral arrangements. These debates also cast a shadow over industrial life insurance. Rubinow accused industrial insurance of nursing these customs of extravagant funerals and stimulating their growth.[83] Lord Passfield acknowledged in his *Report on Industrial Insurance* in 1915 that there was an 'unmistakable interconnection between the pauper funeral and industrial insurance'. However, he still argued that industrial insurance was the means for the working classes to emancipate themselves from the once common shame of pauper funerals.[84] The statistician of the Prudential Company, Hoffman, in his *Pauper Burials and the Interment of the Dead in Large Cities*, rejected the criticism that industrial life insurance was a contributory factor in the high funeral costs of the working classes.[85]

Dying was indeed a costly business for the Anglo-Saxon working classes, and it is quite evident that industries surrounding death made large sums on the perception of a good death worked up by commercialism. Gulbin claims that in early nineteenth-century America the funeral became a way of demonstrating one's social position and one's affection for the deceased.[86] Rubinow explains the American situation:

> There is real respect of the memory of the deceased. There may be even a crude religious urge, a subconscious revival of ancestor worship; and also a very human desire to protect the social status of the living. One must keep up with the Joneses, even in dying and being buried respectably.[87]

The European way of managing burials lacked in large part the commercialism of the Anglo-Saxon funeral industry. US industrial insurance representatives were astonished to discover that 'in Germany a millionaire is carried to the cemetery in no better a hearse than a pauper! Although he could afford a more expensive coffin the preference is for the standard or normal mode of interment.'[88] Regarding Switzerland, the American burial survey of 1926, financed by the industrial insurance industry, was surprised to observe that 'On one day a poor laborer may be buried and the next day, at his side, a bank president'.[89] These expressions of astonishment reveal the impact of commercialism on cultural institutions such as funerals. A lower degree of commercialism in the European funeral industry made it culturally acceptable for a bank president to be buried next to a labourer. Funerals in Anglo-Saxon countries represented the status and social position of the deceased less than they did in Europe. The perception in Europe of a decent funeral appears, therefore, to have involved less expense. Arguably, in Sweden no such thing as a funeral industry even existed until the 1920s.[90] In France a scale of prices based upon annual income was fixed by the Municipal Burial Office: there were eight classes of funerals but even the lowest involved more than a pauper funeral, according to the American Burial Committee.[91] For adults the price for a uniform funeral in the highest income group in 1926 was $57.12, compared to the average funeral cost in the US in the same year, which reached $282.30. The immediate result of the European system was that no burial grounds similar to potter's fields existed or needed to exist in the majority of European countries. The lack of potter's fields further implied that at least well-behaved paupers were saved from sharing graves with murderers and other sinners, and that the weekly premium payment could in the best cases be used for the needs of the family or savings, and was not in the same degree as in Anglo-Saxon countries needed to secure a decent funeral.

This chapter has argued that the Anglo-Saxon countries that hosted an industrial life insurance with a primary function as burial insurance also nourished market forces, constructing perceptions and a culture surrounding funerals that implied high funeral costs. By contrast, countries hosting an industrial life insurance with a negligible function of burial insurance largely lacked the perceptions and market forces that turned funerals into very expensive affairs. The difference between the Anglo-Saxon and the European meaning of a decent funeral was also revealed in the funeral bill. The impact of funeral costs on the industrial life insurance industry is perhaps best illustrated by Switzerland. Switzerland lacked common elements of industrial life insurance and was perhaps the European country whose industrial life insurance had the most limited function as burial insurance.[92] In line with the reasoning of this chapter, the need to cover the cost of a funeral was much less important in Switzerland than in other countries, as Switzerland introduced free communal burial service in 1890. In Saxony, Germany, 51 per cent of the cities and 20 per cent of the rural communities also adopted some form of free burial.[93] Overall, funeral management was considered more as a public utility in several European communities, therefore the need for industrial life insurance to function as burial insurance became more limited in European countries than in Anglo-Saxon nations.

Concluding Remarks

Although the very idea of life insurance is to reduce the negative economic effects of death, interestingly enough, no previous research on life insurance has studied how the immediate cost of dying, the funeral, affected the development of the industry. The individual or the family in Anglo-Saxon countries was often not in a position to meet an unexpected demand for the sum of money that would cover the burial of a child or an adult. The increasing distance of cemeteries from cities meant a higher cost of funerals, but it was primarily Anglo-Saxon commercialism in the funeral industry that contributed to the construction of cultural perceptions of what a decent funeral should entail that made funerals far more costly in Anglo-Saxon countries than in Europe. Increasing commercialization was followed by increasing funeral costs. This, to a large extent, explains the different development of industrial life insurance in Anglo-Saxon and European countries. The cost of funerals and the threat of a potter's field made industrial insurance, as a consequence, almost a universal custom among the wage-earning or industrial population of the Anglo-Saxon countries. In European countries, where commercialism was limited and the costs of dying lower, industrial life insurance did not gain as much power and became more diversified. European burial traditions did not, therefore, become a cultural expression of the social status of the deceased or of the surviving relatives' care for a deceased family member.

In the early twentieth century, proponents of American public health insurance wished this also to involve a public burial insurance. Walker argues that the ambitions of the public health insurance movement were obstructed by powerful representatives of the American industrial life insurance industry.[94] Beatrix Hoffman also claims that the vice president of the American industrial life insurance company Prudential led a relentless campaign against proposals for government-run compulsory health insurance between 1915 and 1920. Although Beatrix Hoffman argues that his opposition was also an expression of his critical view of welfare states, he of course primarily acted in the interests of his insurance company employer.[95] If the arguments of the American critics of public insurance were correct, the weapons that enabled the industrial life insurance industry to launch powerful attacks on public insurance were provided by the high funeral costs and the strong preferences of the Anglo-Saxons to provide for themselves a decent funeral. In countries where industrial insurance functioned less like burial insurance, the industry might not have had the same interest in, and not have been powerful enough to counteract, the development of public insurance. The different roles of private insurance between countries therefore came to determine future attempts to improve the condition of the working classes.

7 FROM ECONOMIC TO POLITICAL REALITY: FORMING A NATIONALIZED INDIAN LIFE INSURANCE MARKET

Adrian Jitschin

Introduction

The concept of 'nationalized insurance markets' is a familiar term to all researchers of international insurance history. But how can the national character of an insurance market be defined? The dimensions of nationalization can be shaped by the economic competitive advantages of domestic insurers or by state intervention. Both circumstances have the same effect: the market becomes unattractive for international competitors.

Becoming a nationalized market turns a market almost into a black box. In the eyes of the international insurance researcher it is a kind of stigma. Understanding what makes a national insurance market specific is – generally speaking – not the subject of researchers' interest. In this chapter, with the example of India, I will pursue the specific structure of national insurance markets.

India is a very unique life insurance market. Its history is mainly distinguished by two periods: an era of juridical open-mindedness until 1956 and an era of nationalization from 1956 to 2001. In my opinion, the development of the specific Indian kind of life insurance experienced two stages: an economic shaping of the Indian insurance market during the era of *laissez-faire* juridical premises, and then, with nationalization, a political shaping of the Indian insurance market. They occurred at different times and had different effects. Both of them, however, are important for our understanding of Indian insurance and the structure of insurance markets.

The Economic Shaping of the National Indian Insurance Market

The economic shaping of the Indian insurance market happened during the inter-war period. The former dominant foreign companies left the Indian insurance market. It was not economic policy that resulted in Indian companies controlling the market, but market realities in that Indian insurance companies were beginning to overwhelm the foreign companies. During the nineteenth century, Indian insurance was practically dominated by British companies. From 1818, when the establishment of a life insurance office in Calcutta was first reported, foreign offices of British companies or start-ups founded by British citizens in India had dominated the Indian insurance market.[1] The first establishment of an insurance office founded by Indian citizens was reported for 1870 in Bombay.[2] Only a few Indian companies commenced operations before the end of the nineteenth century. Until the turn of the century, there was only one significant Indian life insurance company, which insured less than 25,000 policyholders.[3] The picture of a small life insurance market mainly dominated by British insurers did not change much before the end of the First World War.[4]

The trend changed in the years after the war. The total number of foreign life insurance companies, which had stood at 26 in 1905, fell to 24 in 1922.[5] Of these 24 companies one was American and one other was founded in Shanghai. All the others were of British origin.[6] It was not the competition of other foreign companies that broke the dominance of British companies in India. It was the strengthening of Indian insurance companies that changed the structure of supply during the decade of the 1920s. Their number increased from 42 in 1919 to 56 in 1927,[7] and they conducted much more business than before. While in the first decade of the twentieth century probably fewer than 10,000 new policies were written annually, after the First World War the number of new life insurance policies increased permanently, from 28,046 in 1920 to 36,251 in 1924 to 52,724 in 1926.[8] It may be assumed that the foreign companies received only a slight increase in business during that period. Thus, in 1928 their total new policies amounted to no more than 30,337.[9] Their business increased a little before the great depression to 39,598, but dropped again to 25,920 in 1932.[10] By comparing the total figures of policies in force for 1930 – the second year for which figures are available[11] – we see that during the 1920s Indian life insurance offices held over half a million policies – 513,955[12] – on their books, while the foreign companies only retained 202,703 policies on their books.[13] In one decade the annual new business of Indian insurance companies had quadrupled.[14] This tendency continued in the first half of the 1930s. For one year – 1931 – Indian offices were affected by the great depression. The number of their new policies dropped from 105,686 in 1930 to 96,909.[15] However, the number soon recovered. In 1935, with 204,799 new policies, there was once again a doubling of new policies in half a decade.[16] The new business of the foreign companies during that period amounted to only 33,997 policies.[17] It did not advance any further. With a stagnating number of contracts, foreign companies had become subordinate, but they still remained in the market.

It was the period between 1930 and the outbreak of the Second World War that marked the decline of foreign companies, as Indian companies had grown to dominate their own insurance market. Compared to their competitors by number of total policies, Indian companies were much bigger than the foreign companies. In terms of sums assured, however, the importance of foreign companies was not to be ignored. In 1930 their business in force still amounted to 697 million rupees.[18] The business in force of Indian companies was 849 million rupees, which was not much more.[19] Although foreign companies did not account for the majority of policies, they did transact the big policies. Their average sum assured stood at 2,975 rupees per policy in 1930, while the average sum insured by Indian companies came to 1,974 rupees that year.[20] This difference between domestic and foreign companies increased during the decade. Whilst the foreign companies' average amount insured per policy grew to 3,244 rupees, that of the Indian companies fell to 1,451 rupees.[21] What we see is a bifurcated insurance market: a high-price market served by the foreign companies, and a growing native consumer market that was served by the Indian insurance companies. The high-price market was steadily declining – in 1938 there were only 25,952 new policies issued, while the growing medium-priced market generated 298,578 new policies that year.[22] Almost no native Indians transacted life insurance with foreign companies, as a continuously growing number of Indian insurance companies were taking care of them. While at the beginning of that decade 110 Indian insurance companies were registered, their number rose to 213 in 1936.[23] Most of these companies were small establishments, only a minority of them transacted more than 1,000 policies annually (44 companies, 21 per cent). However, they operated all over the country: from north to south, from city to village, from Hindu to Muslim. In total they insured more than 2 billion rupees in 1938.[24] The market share of foreign companies was declining. For each foreign company that entered the Indian market, another one disappeared. In 1936 only 22 foreign companies were registered in India.[25] Most of them had practically suspended transacting new life insurance business. For example, the Liverpool, London and Globe, which had been working in India since 1853, was assuring during that year only 12 policies.[26] The biggest foreign companies in the Indian insurance market were at that time the Sun of Canada, the Prudential, the Allianz, the Great Eastern and the North British and Mercantile.[27] Of these five companies, three had left India by 1940.[28] Soon the small amount of business they had transacted was acquired by Indian companies.

What were the reasons behind this Indianization of life insurance? I think there are two explanations. The first was due to what may be called 'cultural' differences.[29] The Indian economy was very different from the European economy. The backbone of the end customer trade was the self-employed worker who lived from very few customers.[30] During the British Raj, so-called managing agencies organized the trade with many small sub-traders. These managing agencies had no established connections to the citizens. They needed their sub-traders as a kind of intermediary.[31] The modern kind of business company did not fit into the Indian market.[32] Beside this problem of reaching the end customers there also existed differences in everyday life. A remarkable source for this can be found in the archive of the Swiss Re. In 1934 Swiss Re sent a manager to India. His report revealed the various problems to be confronted in the market.[33] These included estimating the age of the assured, finding an appropriate doctor for the medical check, coping with the multiple languages of the country and adjusting to the funeral rites of Hinduism.[34] Transacting business in India was always a balancing challenge between modern business principles and religious unrest.[35]

The second reason that explains why Indian insurance companies were more successful than foreign companies is mundane: they transacted a low-premium business. From 1920 to 1938 the average policy sum of the Indian life insurance companies declined from 1,843 to 1,451 rupees.[36] The average amount for the business transacted by foreign companies was marked by a small but steady increase from 3,092 rupees in 1929 to 3,244 rupees in 1938.[37] In practice, foreign companies did not transact business that was below a minimum sum. By contrast, there was for each proposal an Indian insurance company that took this business. Many smaller Indian offices acted to get a foot in the door. They transacted minimum policies in the hope of getting follow-up business. Table 7.1 shows the average sum insured per policy for 53 companies transacting business in 1936. The average policy of the Norwich Union was more than eight times larger than that of the Great Social. All foreign companies are ranked in the top 15 by average sum assured. Only one Indian company is listed in the top ten. Remarkable also is the position of the biggest Indian companies[38] that are not at the bottom of the list but in the middle. They were losing market share too, though they were better able to compete.[39] The Indianization of life insurance meant lowering the premiums, a race to the bottom in which the foreigners could not compete.[40]

Table 7.1: Average Policy Amounts in 1936: Selected Companies.[41] Foreign companies are shown in italics.

Rank	Company	Average
1	*Norwich Union*	*5,456*
2	*Manufacturers*	*4,980*
3	*Crown*	*4,000*
4	*North British and Mercantile*	*3,646*
5	*Sun of Canada*	*3,503*
6	*Scottish Union and National*	*2,801*
7	*Prudential*	*2,666*
8	Provincial Union	2,230
9	*Gresham*	*2,196*
10	*Great Eastern*	*2,183*
11	National	2,177
12	New India	2,026
13	*Allianz*	*2,016*
14	Tropical	1,906
15	Sunlight	1,827
16	Industrial and Prudential	1,783
17	All India	1,772
18	Oriental	1,769
19	Lakshmi	1,736
20	Bharat	1,682
21	Bombay Life	1,660
22	Calcutta Insurance	1,606
23	Zenith	1,584
24	Empire	1,578
25	East and West	1,571
26	Hindusthan Co-Operative	1,557
27	New Asiatic	1,553
28	General	1,535
29	Asian	1,472
30	Warden	1,466
31	National Indian	1,461
32	United India Life	1,406
33	Northern India	1,397
34	Bombay Mutual	1,393
35	India Equitable	1,308
36	Metropolitan	1,277
37	Swadeshi Bima	1,233

Rank	Company	Average
38	Indian Mutual Life	1,193
39	New Insurance	1,188
40	Guardian of India	1,176
41	Western India	1,136
42	Commonwealth	1,104
43	Unique	1,078
44	Venus	1,076
45	Hukumchand Life	1,075
46	Asiatic	1,064
47	Genuine	1,050
48	South India Co-Operative	810
49	Depositors Benefit	786
50	Bhagya Lakshimi	716
51	Bombay Co-Operative	684
52	People's Insurance	680
53	Neptune	663
54	Great Social	651

The Political Shaping of the Indian Insurance Market

After gaining independence in 1947 the Indian government decided to pursue a 'socialistic pattern of society'.[42] In fact this new policy did not effect much change in everyday life during its early years.[43] The range of Indian politics was not far enough to affect most sectors of the economy. However, starting in 1951, five-year plans were implemented. This meant intervention in selected sectors. On 19 January 1956, to some surprise, Finance Minister C. D. Deshmukh announced the nationalization of life insurance.[44] The next morning state employees entered the life insurance companies' headquarters. It took nearly a year to look through all the books, to reorganize the insurance companies and to integrate them under the umbrella of the new Life Insurance Company of India (LIC). Until 2001 – that is for a period of forty-five years – the LIC held a monopoly of life insurance in India.[45]

The nationalization of life insurance had a profound impact on the amount of new business written. It can be estimated that around half of the potential life business in India has not been written due to nationalization. While during the first half of the twentieth century the insurance business of India doubled every decade, there was only a moderate increase of new business during the second half of the century.[46] New business written in 1970 was only slightly greater than the new business written in 1960.[47] As late as 1980 there was only a relatively small growth of new business.[48] The immediate impact of nationalization on the life insurance business may be compared to that of the partition of Pakistan from India.[49] The relative share of insurance as a form of saving dropped, and was replaced by other forms of saving like banking.[50] In sum, the nationalization of insurance may be judged a failure.[51]

However, apart from the question of the overall development of life insurance through nationalization, the most relevant questions are: How did the nationalization of life insurance fulfil its goals? How were its political targets achieved? First, we must find out what the reason for nationalization was. At the time, the finance minister gave an impulsive speech on nationalization. In that speech he spoke of several advances to be achieved through nationalization: he talked about lowering corruption in the sector, spreading life insurance into more rural areas, and he explained the advantages for policyholders in a government-owned insurance institution.[52] In the whole speech, however, he gave only *one reason* why the state took the step of nationalizing life insurance, namely that it was to mobilize savings, and that 'utilising them to the best advantage becomes socially purposive'.[53] He aimed to get control of the large savings of the insurance companies and to invest them for the economic development of India. In his own words:

> the nationalisation of Life Insurance is a further step in the direction of more effective mobilisation of the people's savings. It is a truism which nevertheless cannot too often be repeated, that a nation's savings are the prime mover of its economic development.[54]

The success of the nationalization of life insurance should be assessed by the success it had with the investment of its life fund.

Immediately before nationalization life insurance funds were mainly invested in government securities. Out of a total life insurance fund of 2,997 million rupees,[55] 63 per cent was invested in this way. Most of these investments, 1,373 million rupees, had gone into central government securities, while investments in state government securities, 306 million rupees, and in municipal securities, 210 million rupees, were minor.[56] If we take a look at investment policy before and after nationalization, we can see that the relative share of government securities declined after nationalization (see Figure 7.1). This is surprising. One would assume – especially given the aforementioned speech – that relatively more money would have been invested in government securities. But the opposite happened. Why? Where did these billions of rupees go?

Table 7.2 shows the yearly distribution of LIC's investments between 1957 and 1968. By the end of this period, LIC's investments were split between three main categories: government securities, loans and mortgages. The latter categories substituted a part of the traditional investment in government securities. A large proportion of loans were loans on policies. The LIC inherited the custom

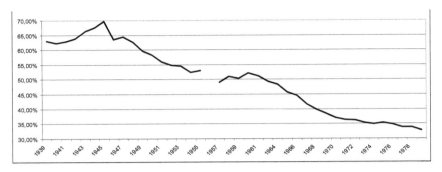

Figure 7.1: Government Securities as a Percentage Share of Life Insurance Assets, 1939–79.[57]

of insurance companies lending to their policyholders. In 1960 this amounted to 7.1 per cent of total assets, in 1970 it amounted to 7.4 per cent and in 1980 it amounted to 5.8 per cent.[58] This practice was continued with no structural change, and the loans accounted for between 5 and 10 per cent of LIC investments. This form of investment – which, arguably, is not real investment, but rather a substitute for premium income – is a basic part of Indian life insurance. However, what made the overall share of loans in the investment portfolio increase was that the LIC began to transact other types of loans. The motivation behind this change remains unclear. There is no documented strategy for this new investment policy. As economic historians, we can only diagnose that a change happened, but not pinpoint why. Also currently inexplicable is the dramatic change in the composition of the portfolio between 1956–7 and 1957–8. However, examining the long-term structural changes it is clear that after nationalization loans became an integral part of the LIC's investments, whereas before the foundation of the LIC they were negligible. Loans other than to policyholders were for the most part loans for housing schemes. For the fiscal year 1967–8 the investment in government housing schemes amounted to 945 million rupees.[59] Loans for private housing schemes amounted to 347 million rupees. These were 6.8 per cent and 2.5 per cent respectively of the LIC's total assets.[60] This was a kind of new investment in India. A big part of life insurance funds went now indirectly to building private houses.

Before nationalization the share of mortgages among the total assets never rose above 5 per cent.[61] But after nationalization it began to grow. The LIC itself explained this change with reference to a speech made by Jawaharlal Nehru in 1961. Reflecting on five years of nationalized insurance, Nehru said that an idea had struck him. 'It seemed to me that the Life Insurance Corporation could undertake large-scale building [in towns with slums] which would be an excellent investment for it and at the same time would serve an urgent social need and purpose'.[62] In this respect LIC began to extend its investment in housing.

Table 7.2: Allocations of the Annual Investments of the LIC, 1957–68 (per cent).[63]

Year	Government Securities	Corporate Securities	Loans	Mortgages	Real Estate
1957	39.1	26.0	32.6	−3.3	5.6
1958	84.7	16.9	1.2	−4.5	1.7
1959	68.4	16.3	16.8	−4.3	2.8
1960	68.0	14.3	15.4	−2.3	4.6
1961	62.7	17.9	18.0	−0.8	2.2
1962–3	48.2	21.5	29.0	0.3	1.0
1963–4	48.7	20.2	28.7	1.1	1.3
1964–5	41.0	19.1	30.0	8.4	1.5
1965–6	35.7	18.8	23.5	17.5	0.5
1966–7	38.9	7.4	29.1	23.0	1.6
1967–8	37.3	7.1	24.3	30.0	1.3

In particular, it publicized its 'Own Your Home Scheme'. This programme was designed for policyholders who wanted to live in their own property. By 1986 it had grown to over 100 million rupees.[64] Other schemes for investment were the mortgage of immovable property (M-I scheme), individual employees' housing (IEHS) and the public limited companies for the construction of houses of their employees. All these four schemes had their own terms and conditions under which credit was granted. In total, investments in the area of mortgages rose from zero in 1963 to one third of all investments by the end of that decade.[65]

Within one and a half decades the financial investment of life insurance in India was transformed. Most of the money was now directly or indirectly (via loans) invested in house building. The proportion exposed to governmental control was reduced to a third. Investments in the corporate sector were reduced. This was something of a surprise. When nationalization was announced, the target was that savings should be invested in economic development, yet private housing had been financed instead. This is somewhat surprising if we take into account the original reasons for nationalization. In my opinion, building a private house is not optimum for economic growth. While it creates employment in the short term, in the long term it does not help to develop industry, trade or education. It simply gives some employment during the period of construction and after that does not add much to the economy. In the long run investment in infrastructure, factory building, credits for micro enterprises, agrarian development, etc. would have been wiser.[66] There is no evidence, however, that the LIC ever seriously considered investing in this direction. Another remarkable feature about this is that this was never an explicit investment target for the LIC. Apart from the aforementioned speech of Nehru, there is no surviving document that suggests that LIC received instructions to invest in building. To the extent that India is a democracy, there should have been some legislative process that stipulated a new investment target for the LIC. Thus the reasoning behind the investment pattern is opaque. As it was the policyholders' money that was used, there ought to have been an explicit clarification why the LIC shifted their investments in this direction.

There is another aspect of the 'Own Your Home Scheme' worth noting. When the LIC began this house-building programme in 1964, it had already transacted housing finance for some years.[67] The 'Own Your Home Scheme' was only made available in a limited number of towns to a limited number of policyholders.[68] The majority of policyholders, those in rural areas or in smaller towns, had no opportunity to participate in the programme. The combination of financing houses and stipulating the conditions for obtaining a loan gives the scheme a rather dubious character. Those whose application was accepted received a credit for the interest of 7–8 per cent,[69] which was below the usual interest rate in India.[70] This, combined with a housing programme limited to specific groups, like LIC employees or policyholders, made it a kind of high-level bonus programme. Borrowers combined two different roles, as employees or policyholders, and as receivers of credit at a low rate. This treatment of the life insurance fund could not have been in the interest of the majority of the insured. It was in the interest of the latter to obtain a high and safe return on their investments. For these reasons it might be concluded that this part of the LIC's investment policy lacked an economic rationale.

Investment in corporate securities declined. Last but not least, therefore, the role of the LIC investment in this sector should also be discussed. When life insurance was nationalized in 1956 corporate securities accounted for 15 per cent of total assets. This amount fell to 14.4 per cent in 1968.[71] Although this was a small decline, one thing had changed: whilst these shares had previously been distributed between over 200 companies, the LIC was a single investor. It resulted in a high degree of corporate control for the LIC simply because it collected all the corporate shares previously held by various insurance companies. The impact of the LIC as an investor has been studied by M. Y. Khan and Preeti Singh. They questioned 336 companies listed on the Bombay Stock Exchange (BSE) in 1965. Of these companies, 130 (38.7 per cent) answered that the LIC was among their ten largest shareholders in that year.[72] While the LIC was limited by practice[73] not to hold more than 30 per cent of one corporation's share capital, there were plenty of companies in which it held between 5 and 25 per cent.[74] This meant that it could exercise a considerable influence over these companies without controlling them. Another aspect was that the LIC concentrated its corporate investments on stock exchange listed shares. From 1959 the LIC always invested more than half of its corporate securities in ordinary shares. Debentures and preference shares were secondary as a type of investment.[75] This meant a concentration on big companies, with smaller enterprises neglected. Because of this investment policy, the relative share of the LIC as an investor at the BSE rose. From accounting for 7.4 per cent of all equity share trades in 1965 the relative share rose to 8.1 per cent in 1974.[76] Of 408 companies listed at the BSE in 1974, 188 had the LIC as one of their ten largest investors (46.1 per cent).[77] It may also be noted that these were not small companies. In particular, the bigger and older companies were controlled by LIC.[78] In sum, Khan and Singh conclude: '[t]he LIC has been actually using its voting power in various forms against the erring management of some corporate enterprises. Such intervention in coporate [*sic*] management is an integral part of the over-all policy of the Government.'[79] Through the LIC the government had a role in the central decisions of the major companies of the country. This assured the government a control over the private sector. It was a by-product of the LIC, that voting rights for the shares that it held not only existed but were commonly used. Thus it may be concluded that this part of the LIC's investment policy not only followed the principle of maximizing returns, but also of gaining influence in private-sector companies.

Nationalization created a new investment pattern for life insurance. Less money was invested in government securities and corporate debentures. More was invested in housing and equity shares. A part of government economic policy was transacted directly by the LIC board of investors. There was an overlap between the interests of an insurance company and its interests as a state-owned investor. Instead of transacting its money in government securities and giving the government in this way control of LIC savings, the LIC tried to invest in a way that would be 'state-like'. It tried to achieve a part of national political objectives via its investments. Especially perfidious was the investment at the BSE. Acquiring equity shares as a quasi-autonomous company made it possible to intervene in the stock exchange in the government's interest. This investment formed part of the government's control over the biggest companies of the country.[80] It was a way to control the economy, not a means to promote economic development. Instead of supporting India's countless small and medium-sized companies, money was invested in the big companies. A side effect of this was, of course, the trouble that occurs when a state speculates in its own stock exchange: the LIC controlled a significant share in the equities of nearly half of the listed companies, which paralysed the trade in shares.[81] Giving credit to companies would have been in the long run a better instrument of investment. It is obvious that this kind of investment was used to acquire political control of companies.

Conclusion

Transferring life insurance to India happened in two phases: first, there was an adaptation in the economy, and then there was an adaptation in the political sphere. The adaptation to the way the Indian economy shaped insurance began under British rule and was a *de facto* transformation that occurred almost unaffected by policy. The importation of this kind of modern financial business was a Darwinian process, in which companies that adopted solutions for the specific Indian structure survived. The adaptation of life insurance in the political sphere was, by contrast, a reaction of a government that was trying to shape its country's economy. The *de facto* development of India's insurance business was not fully understood by the politicians. What they saw was the accumulated amount of money mobilized by insurance companies. What they did not realize was that the government already benefited from the investments of the insurance companies. Life insurance companies were mostly rational in the way they invested their funds. After nationalization, that investment policy changed. Insurance investment now followed political goals, rather than interest-oriented goals. Returns were not only viewed in pecuniary terms, but also in terms of social and political objectives. Money invested by the LIC in companies was used to control them. The political power of the LIC as a shareholder became an instrument of economic control. This investment pattern was not purely governed by the needs of the LIC policyholders and the economic development of the Indian nation.

The form of a 'nationalized insurance market' has multiple possibilities. In this chapter we have seen two of these possibilities operating in the case of India. Specific national conditions may mean, even within the same 'culture', very different things. Understanding an insurance market is only possible by understanding its specific dimensions of shaping and change.

8 LIFE OFFICES TO THE RESCUE! A HISTORY OF THE ROLE OF LIFE INSURANCE IN THE SOUTH AFRICAN ECONOMY DURING THE TWENTIETH CENTURY

Grietjie Verhoef

The South African economy has developed as an interlinked unitary entity only since the first decade of the twentieth century. Prior to 1910, when the Union of South Africa was constituted as a unitary state within the British Common-wealth, four separate colonies existed in the sub-region of Southern Africa. The two independent Boer Republics of the Orange Free State and the South African Republic were defeated by Britain in the South African War of 1899–1902, and incorporated as British colonies in 1902. The economies of the Boer Republics were primarily agricultural and displayed limited sophisticated commercial activity prior to the mineral discoveries of 1867 and 1886:[1] 'Even the Boer republics, in spite of the presence there of some 50,000 people of European descent, lacked the basic structure to support a viable modern economy'.[2] The Cape Colony economy was the most diversified of the four colonies by the mid-1860s. The Cape maintained a thriving agricultural manufacturing and commercial economy, soliciting the establishment of financial institutions.[3] It was into the most vibrant centre of commerce and trade in Southern Africa that insurance was first sold in the early 1800s.[4] Many insurance companies from various parts of the world commenced the sale of insurance in the South African market – using general agents. Shortly after the arrival of the 1820 British settlers in the Cape Colony, on 14 March 1831 the first South African insurance company was established. As in many parts of the world, the British insurance business heritage began its deep influence on the development of the insurance sector in South Africa.

This chapter presents an overview of the development of the long-term or life insurance industry in South Africa against the background of the development of the economy. The trend in insurance history has been to highlight the stabilizing role of long-term insurance. What role did the long-term assurance industry play in the South African economy?

Why Insurance?

The extension of human demand beyond ordinary subsistence created the opportunity for insurance. Morton Keller argued that when capital extended beyond a position of stagnation on the land and became fluid and moveable assets, the risk of some hazardous event threatening such assets emerged. Demand thus developed for some protection against sudden disaster – that is insurance.[5] 'As natural as the movement of goods by ship was the insurance of their safe arrival; when fire threatened the buildings and products of urban commerce coverage by organized underwriting developed.'[6] Life assurance was first recorded in 1583 and developed in close connection to marine insurance: men and women travelled in ships and so did cargo.[7] At the same time fire insurance schemes were being promulgated. 'Life' insurance later provided the underwriting of the risk of losing the life of a 'slave', thus actually constituting the protection of human life as 'property'.[8] Friendly societies provided for the working class, while life assurance was issued more often to the more well-to-do citizens. Friendly societies were prohibited from assuring lives for more than £100, while life assurance policies were for amounts of more than £100.[9] The first life insurance policies issued were one-year term assurances, with a rate of premium constant for all lives accepted, irrespective of age. The rate of premium was £5 or £5 5*s*.[10] Only in 1783 can records be found of a so-called 'graded' scale of premiums. These required careful consideration of mortality statistics and detailed mathematical calculations of the potential future claims on the issuer. This 'quantitative' thinking gained momentum in the mercantilist Elizabethan era.[11] One of the most satisfying general methods of creating financial security in the face of risk is that of spreading the risk among a number of persons all exposed to the same risk and prepared to make relative modest contributions towards neutralizing the detrimental effects of this risk that may materialize for any one or more of their members. This is known as 'insurance', in the economic sense of the word.[12]

Life insurance (assurance was the term generally used during the eighteenth century) became a lucrative enterprise and a tool to raise capital for a rapidly growing national economy.[13] Life assurance, as the business of risk aversion, also has a social function for those in distress. It plays an important social role in that it sells safety.[14] In seeking future security, those buying life insurance want to know that the insurer will be in a position to pay out claims should they arise. As Wright and Smith note: 'It all boils down to a problem of trust'.[15] Trust in the solvency of an insurance company is important for broader social reasons. Life insurance companies invest premiums paid by policyholders in remunerative assets, thus essentially operating as financial intermediaries between savers (or policyholders) and borrowers (entrepreneurs, households and governments). As such life insurance has

> augmented economic growth by increasing society's total savings. Those increased savings, reduce the cost of borrowing ... by increasing the supply of investment funds, thereby establishing a complex web of mutually beneficial relationships among insurers, policyholders, direct beneficiaries, and what we call 'social beneficiaries'. As increased financial intermediation has been a major cause of economic progress, life insurance companies have made significant contributions to the general weal.[16]

As life insurance depended heavily on the principle of trust and confidence some suspicion existed against such business, which explains the relatively late application of limited liability to insurance corporations.[17] The general condition was for insurance companies to be mutual in principle and thus command greater confidence. Mutuality in fire, marine and life insurance offered a mechanism of obtaining capital without exposing a small group of individuals to heavy concentrated risk. Mutualization enabled companies to begin with relatively small initial capital guarantees and had the marketing advantage of hiring commercially minded policyholders with the prospects of sharing the dividend rewards of ownership.[18] Governments often regulated the insurance industry to protect policyholders and prevent insurance companies from abusing their investment power.[19] In South Africa, however, an additional aspect of the regulation of the insurance industry was the need of government to secure access to investment funds for the domestic economy in the wake of international sanctions against the country. This development offers a unique dimension to the relationship between life insurance and the development of the South African economy.

Insurance in South Africa: Nineteenth-Century Origins

In the early years short-term insurance was conducted through agents. British companies either sent their own agents to the colonies, or colonial subjects were appointed in the colonies to represent the foreign firms. Later, branch offices of overseas operations were opened.[20] Insurance companies established themselves in the Cape Colony in the early 1830s, shortly after the arrival of the 1820 settlers.[21] The first insurance companies that advertised for business in the Cape Colony were British: the Phoenix, the United Empire and Continental Life Assurance Association and the Alliance British and Foreign Fire and Life Assurance Company. The first South African insurance company was the South African Fire & Life Assurance Company, established in 1831, followed by numerous other local fire and life assurance companies. By the 1890s various local companies were absorbed by British companies operating in the Cape Colony and the Natal Colony as well as in the two Boer Republics.[22] A high degree of concentration in the insurance industry followed that in the banking industry in the 1860s after the depression in the Cape Colony during the late 1850s and 1860s. In the banking industry, British banks, or the so-called 'Imperial Banks', came to dominate in both the British colonies as well as the Boer Republics towards the latter part of the nineteenth century.[23] The insurance sector was similarly dominated by British enterprise at this time. The only nineteenth-century life assurance company established in the Cape Colony that survived the foreign acquisition drive was the South African Mutual Life Assurance Society of the Cape of Good Hope, established in 1845.[24] The Old Mutual (as the society became known) did not grow rapidly during the first forty years in business, but after the mineral discoveries (of diamonds in 1871 and gold in 1886) foreign competition by British, Australian and American life offices encouraged increased activity by the company. The total funds administered by the Old Mutual increased from £4,214 in 1846 to £1,183,281 in 1890.[25] A total of twenty-five insurance companies were competing for business in the Cape Colony during the last two decades of the nineteenth century. Despite the fact that foreign companies appointed large numbers of agents in a widely distributed geographical network of representative offices across the British colonies, three Cape Colony based companies dominated the insurance business of the Cape by 1900.[26] These companies were the Old Mutual (established 1845), the Southern Life Association (established in 1891) and the Industrial Life Assurance Company of South Africa Limited (established in 1894). The Cape Colony taxed foreign insurance companies that earned a minimum specified premium. Foreign companies and their premium income were recorded separately.

By 1925 the insurance sector in the Union of South Africa was dominated by four companies: the African Life Assurance Society Ltd; the South African Mutual Life Assurance Society of the Cape of Good Hope (Old Mutual); the Southern Life Association and the South African National Life Assurance Company (Sanlam – Suid-Afrikaanse Nasionale Lewens Assuransie Maatskappy, established in 1918).[27] There were 34 insurance companies conducting business in South Africa, 16 of which had their head offices in South Africa, but only 9 were South African incorporated companies. The total assets of insurance companies were £822,435,000, distributed as follows: South African companies £26,698,000 and foreign companies £795,737,000. The South African companies held the bulk of their assets in the Union of South Africa. These assets in 1926 amounted to £25,833,000 compared to £9,518,000 of foreign companies.[28] By 1926, 65.3 per cent of total premium income of insurance companies accrued to South African companies. Of all new policies issued, 74 per cent were issued by South African companies and 69.4 per cent of all existing policies were held by South African companies. South African companies held 96 per cent of their assets in the Union of South Africa by 1926, and foreign companies only

1.2 per cent of their assets. South African companies were clearly dominating the local market. They obtained 91 per cent of their premium income from policies issued in the Union of South Africa compared to only 2.3 per cent by foreign companies. This balance between domestic and foreign companies' operations is to be expected, since the principal activities of insurance companies are usually in the country of domicile, rather than in foreign locations where their interests are entrusted to agents.

From the colonial period until 1943 insurance companies enjoyed a relative high level of freedom and discretion in deciding on operations and the allocation of assets. The first Union legislation regulating the insurance industry in South Africa was the Insurance Act No. 37 of 1923, tailored to the example of the British Assurance Companies' Act of 1909. The 1923 Insurance Act consolidated colonial legislation dating back to the earliest law, namely the Life Assurance Act 13 of 1891 of the Cape Colony.[29] The existing colonial legislation, based on English insurance law in the Cape and Natal Colonies, had established and maintained sufficient stability in the insurance market, which explains the thirteen years between political unification in 1910 and the passing of consolidated statutory regulation of the industry in 1923.[30] The 1923 Act required insurance companies to be registered and licensed according to the Act, deposit a maximum amount of £25,000 with the Treasury and submit an actuarial report testifying to the condition of the business. The underlying aim of the Act was recognition of the principle 'freedom with publicity', requiring full operational transparency in exchange for freedom to conduct their affairs without any prescription. Only life assurance companies were required to make compulsory investments in bonds.[31] This wide discretion was perceived to be conducive to operations delivering optimal yields on investments, which in turn would incentivize the purchase of insurance, that is, to contribute to contractual savings: 'Life assurance premiums and pension-fund contributions have become the most important channels of personal savings'.[32]

The successful mobilization of personal savings in the insurance sector was reflected in the rapid proliferation of insurance companies in South Africa. In the period between the formation of the Union in 1910 and the passing of the 1923 Insurance Act, thirty-four registered life offices conducted life assurance business in the Union. Of these, nine were domestic insurance companies and twenty-five were foreign incorporated companies (primarily British, Australian, Dutch and American concerns). In 1934 a representative organization of life offices, the Life Offices Association (LOA), was established to oversee the professional conduct of the profession. The Association's objective was 'to promote the business of life assurance by means of consultation and combined action on matters of common interest'.[33] The depression of the 1930s brought existential insecurity and a subsequent slowdown in insurance premium growth, only to resume soon towards the early 1940s. Industry consolidation followed and by 1943 there were twenty-four life assurance companies operating in the South African market.[34] Despite the presence of a large number of short-term insurance companies (more than 100) in South Africa towards the end of the Second World War, the insurance market was dominated by companies concentrating their business focus on life insurance. A comparison between the premium income of the long-term and the short-term insurers (including, marine, fire, accident) during the period after the promulgation of the 1923 Insurance Act and the adoption of the new Insurance Act 27 of 1943 displays the domination and impressive growth in the life assurance industry. Table 8.1 illustrates the domination of the life assurance industry in the insurance market up to 1943. The life assurance business constituted more than three-quarters of the insurance business in South Africa at that time.

Table 8.1: Total Premium Income, Long-Term and Short-Term Insurance, 1929–44 (£000).[35]

Year	Long-Term Insurance	Proportion of Total (%)	Short-Term Insurance	Proportion of Total (%)	Total Pre-mium Income
1929	4,960	76.2	1,541	23.6	6,507
1934	5,879	79.3	1,528	20.6	7,407
1939	8,494	77.2	2,515	22.8	11,009
1944	11,838	78.9	3,161	21.0	14,999
Annualized growth (%)	138.6		105.1		130.5
Annual compound growth (%)	6.4		5.2		6.1

In the period leading up to the Second World War, the total premium income of life assurance companies rose by 138.6 per cent (between 1929 and 1944) annualized growth. Short-term insurance (marine, fire and accident) rose by 105.1 per cent annualized and total premiums by 130.5 per cent. The annual compound growth of life premiums was 6.4 per cent, that of the short-term industry premiums 5.2 per cent and overall premiums for the entire industry 6.1 per cent. The persistent growth in the total premium income of long-term insurance over the course of fifteen years is significant when considering the economic slowdown that persisted during the depression and the aftermath of the decision by the South African government to maintain the gold standard despite the decision by Britain to abandon it in September 1931. All sectors of the South African economy suffered as a result of this choice. It was only on 28 December 1932 (15 months after the British decision to leave it) that a final decision was announced to abandon the gold standard. The South African economy showed an immediate recovery and a slowdown of capital flight.[36] Gross national income declined between 1929 and 1933, only to return to positive growth in the second half of 1934, when the improvement in the gold price restored profitable gold mining production, an overall recovery of prices and a resurgence in capital inflows and foreign trade. Real growth in the economy amounted to an annual average of 3.9 per cent between 1922 and 1933, but negative growth during the depression slowed growth to only 1.7 per cent annual growth for the whole period 1910–33. The recovery after 1933 resulted in annual growth in excess of 5 per cent between 1929 and 1939.[37] The important fact is that the annual compound growth of long-term premium income, at 6.4 per cent, exceeded the overall performance of gross national income throughout the fifteen-year period under review. In 1926 total premium income constituted 2.5 per cent of national income. This proportion increased to 3.3 per cent in 1931 and maintained that ratio until 1941, when it dropped to 3 per cent.[38]

The role of insurance as the mobilizer of domestic savings was acutely demonstrated in South Africa in the post-depression years before 1945.[39] The most important form of insurance that encouraged people to save was life assurance. Savings through general insurance (fire, marine and accident) were less significant in terms of savings mobilization for the purpose of supporting economic growth, since premiums collected within a year were largely redistributed in claims, expenses and profits.

The strong growth of the insurance industry occurred under the limited statutory regulation of insurance operations in South Africa. Based on the UK model of the Assurance Companies Act of 1909, the Insurance Act 37 of 1923 adhered to the principle of 'freedom with publicity' which allowed insurers wide discretion in the conduct of their business on condition of full disclosure.[40] The 1923 Act concerned itself primarily with the registration of insurance companies, the form and content of disclosure. Those conducting insurance business in South Africa had to have a 'Chief Office and Principal Officer in the Union' and had to be registered according to regulations in South Africa. A deposit to a maximum of £25,000 with the Treasury was required from all insurers and, in the case of life insurance, a record of bond investments and investments in industrial companies was required. Furthermore, annual official actuarial confirmation that the 'business was actuarially sound' had to be submitted to the Treasury and later the Registrar of Insurance Companies.[41] Suspicion was cast on the security of savings in life assurance companies because of the lack of regulation of investment of funds or the valuation of assets or liabilities.[42] Arndt argued that 'an insurance contract is a mere piece of paper unless not only the actuarially determined funds are being held, but also unless funds have been wisely and safely invested'. Safety of investments was seen to be enhanced by a 'desirable distribution of funds between [the] various types of assets'. Arndt wanted to see more explicit indications of various categories of debentures and qualifications in 'provisions as to first and second mortgages or even notarial bonds, but especially as regards minimum safety margins that are to be maintained in granting loans on mortgage'.[43] Compulsory deposits with the Treasury, Arndt argued furthermore, displayed no relationship to the risk to which the insurer had been exposed. Calling for improved security prerequisites of insurance risk management, the added dimension of his criticism was that the savings mobilized through life insurance had to be put to better use in the interest of the creation of capital, infrastructure and employment opportunities for the South African economy. These arguments had explicit implications for the operations of foreign insurance companies conducting business in South Africa.[44] All insurance companies would be subjected to a more prescriptive investment environment, which could dampen their enthusiasm to conduct business in South Africa.

The New Insurance Act 27 of 1943

The strong views expressed by Professor Arndt finally convinced the government to amend the Insurance Act of 1923. The new Act, the Insurance Act 27 of 1943, ushered in a period of forty five years of explicit statutory investment prescriptions for life insurance companies. The Act introduced the Roman Dutch principle of *lex mercantoria* to insurance law in South Africa.[45] The regulatory environment was formalized by the institution of a Registrar of Insurance in the Office of Financial Institutions (710) with the responsibility to exercise such powers and perform such duties assigned by the Act, such as the inspection and investigation of insurance companies and requesting regular submission of information.[46] Various amendments were promulgated to the 1943 Act in the course of the next fifty-five years. The principal position remained that life assurance companies were required, for the first time, to hold fixed proportions of their assets in prescribed securities. Section 17 and 18 of the Act required life assurers to hold 50 per cent of the value of net South African liabilities, with respect to long-term insurance business, in assets with pension and retirement annuity funds (these were the so-called Part One investments). Assets to a value of 30 per cent of net total South African liabilities (excluding the above) were required. Amongst the assets held in pension and retirement annuities, 20 per cent had to be in government bills, bonds or securities, and of the overall 30 per cent, a minimum of 15 per cent had to be in government bills, bonded securities. Apart from the prescribed investments in government paper, life insurance companies were permitted to hold the balance of their assets in policy loans, mortgage bonds, debentures, shares, property and similar investments.

The drastic interventionist nature of the prescriptions discussed above is illustrated in the distribution of investments (assets) of insurance companies between 1926 and 1935 prior to the enactment of the new requirements. South African companies had invested an average of 30 per cent of total assets in government securities, of which only 2.7 per cent was in railway securities, 15 per cent was in loans and policies, 9.7 per cent in loans to municipalities and 3.9 per cent in landed property. The largest single category of assets was invested in mortgages, namely 29.4 per cent. The total proportion of assets held in landed property and mortgages was 34.1 per cent.[47] It is clear that this historic investment distribution would have to change quite dramatically to comply with the requirements of the new Act to reach the level of 50 per cent of investments in the prescribed category.

The original purpose of the statutory asset requirements was to provide security to policyholders, since the prescribed investments were perceived to be 'safer' than investments in ordinary shares and cash in banks. In times of rising interest rates, those Part One investments were in actual fact exposed to capital losses. Furthermore, yields on government and semi-government securities were generally below free-market yields. Over the years the original purpose of these investment prescriptions disappeared and in practice they penalized widows, orphans and pensioners – the exact target market the statutory provisions had sought to protect. In fact, the statutory persistence of these requirements illustrated the need for funds by government for industrial and commercial expansion. GDP growth at market prices after the Second World War between 1945 and 1946 was 5.4 per cent, and between 1947 and 1948 it was 8.6 per cent.[48] Government needed domestic investment in key sectors of the economy: electricity consumption alone rose 71.8 per cent between 1936 and 1947 and government needed investment in the Electricity Supply Commission (ESCOM) to fund expansion. The same applied to investment in the government-owned Iron and Steel Corporation (ISCOR), since the contribution of manufacturing to GDP rose from 15 per cent in 1930 to 25 per cent in 1955, while the relative contributions of agriculture and mining were constantly declining.[49] Strong criticism of the infusion of 'grey uniformity on life offices ... seeking to control the business activities of these enterprises and eliminate divergences', was expressed, but these restrictive requirements remained binding until amended in 1998.[50] Where it is accepted that voluntary contractual savings through life insurance made an indispensable contribution to maintain national savings during times of high and rising inflation, the restrictive investment prescriptions, it could be argued, served as a disincentive to save through life insurance.[51] The yield on Part One investments of life insurers towards the late 1970s was 11 per cent for government securities and 12.5 per cent on other assets within the category of compulsory investments (such as stocks of municipal authorities and state utilities). The yield on industrial debentures was 14 per cent, thus indicating that prescribed investments reduced the return to policyholders and shareholders (where applicable). The statutory restriction on the free choice of investment instruments for long-term insurers functioned as a form of 'indirect taxation' on life insurers and their policyholders.

The 1943 Act also extended the scope of government regulation of the insurance industry. It covered four components constituting the 'vital aspects of life insurance', according to Bernstein and Benfield, namely the protection of policyholders' interests, reporting on insurance activities, the valuation of assets and liabilities, and the disclosure of financial information.[52] Apart from prescribed investments (as discussed above), the framework also regulated commission payments, controlled ownership and amalgamation of insurance interests, and authorized government to wind up a company, notwithstanding the opinion of shareholders or policyholders. This strong interventionist position of government was a function of economic policies to promote domestic industrial development. It had an impact on the overall growth of premium income of the insurance sector.

In Table 8.2 the premium income of long-term and short-term insurance companies for the between 1941 and 1951 is given. The growth performance of the two sectors shows a slight slowdown, in comparison to the growth of the same sectors of the industry prior to the 1943 Act (see Table 8.1 above). On an annualized basis long-term insurance premium income rose by 180 per cent and that of short-term insurance by 194 per cent. The short-term market also posted stronger annual compound growth at 12.7 per cent between 1941 and 1951,[53] compared to the 12.1 per cent of the long-term market for the same period. Although the overall growth in premium income of both the long-term and the short-term insurance markets is higher in the period between 1941 and 1951, compared to the period reflected in Table 8.1 (6.4 per cent and 5.2 per cent respectively), the disadvantage to long-term insurance companies of having to comply with the requirement to invest 50 per cent of their funds in Part One investments adversely affected the industry's ability to attract investment (or new policyholders). With inflation below 6 per cent throughout this period, the premium growth reflects growing confidence in insurance products or, as Wright and Smith explain, trust in the industry to take care of savings.[54] More lucrative investment opportunities were opening up at a time of rapid growth in the industrial sector (manufacturing), private enterprise and the financial sector.

Table 8.2: Total Premium Income, 1941–51 (£000).[55]

Year	Long-Term Insurance	Short-Term Insurance	Total Premium Income
1941	9,609	4,475	14,085
1946	16,067	5,971	22,038
1951	26,946	13,164	40,110
Annualized growth (%)	180	194	185
Annual compound growth (%)	12.1	12.7	12.3

Access to savings through the insurance industry provided an important source of available capital. Growing international opposition to the domestic South African political regime led to inward-looking policies to protect the South African currency, including exchange control regulations, which further restricted investment opportunities open to the insurance industry.[56] The insurance sector nevertheless remained a dominant actor in the financial services field in South Africa.

Boom and Isolation: The Growth of the Insurance Industry, 1950–2000

The period under review includes the post-war era as well as the period of international sanctions against South Africa. During this period the economy experienced unprecedented growth from the early 1950s, which persisted until the late 1970s. Then economic contraction following the oil crises set in. The period after 1970 was marked by the debt standstill and perpetual domestic political instability and violence. An analysis of the growth in premium income and assets of the life insurance industry during the last half of the twentieth century confirms the stabilizing influence of life insurance on the entire South African economy because the insurance companies had to comply with statutory domestic investment requirements.

The consistent growth in the life assurance market rendered some stability to the South African economy during turbulent times. Annual compound growth of the assets of long-term insurers rose by 16.6 per cent during the last half of the twentieth century, while the GDP of the country managed only an annual compound growth of 12.7 per cent. A strong inflow to life insurers of a substantial proportion of retirement funds (i.e. private pension policies and insured group retirement plans) occurred from the 1970s as a result of the long-term insurers' ability to demonstrate better investment returns on retirement funds under their administration. Long-term insurers increasingly acquired the administration of a growing portion of those pension funds and by the mid-1990s showed asset growth that surpassed the level of 67 per cent of GDP. These trends were responsible for the strong growth in long-term insurance companies' assets as a proportion of GDP, as reflected in Table 8.3. This proportion rose from 14.6 per cent in 1950 to 76.9 per cent in 2000.[57] The importance of this development was that those assets were retained in South Africa and satisfied the growing economy's demand for investment capital when international sanctions were increasingly hurting the economy. An international comparison of the period between 1990 and 2000 showed that in South Africa long-term insurance companies achieved remarkable success in capturing premium income representing a large share of the national GDP as indicated in Table 8.4. In 1990 long-term premium income in South Africa was 7.47 per cent of GDP, just lower than the proportion in Japan (8.33 per cent) and South Korea (8.21 per cent). By the end of the 1990s premium income of South African long-term insurers had risen to 13.1 per cent, which represented the highest proportion in the world. By 2000 this figure stood at 14.9 per cent.[58]

Table 8.3: Total Assets of Long-Term Insurance Companies and GDP in South Africa, 1950–2000 (Rm).[59]

Year	Total Assets	GDP at Current Prices	Assets as Percentage of GDP
1950	384	2,626	14.6
1955	618	3,947	15.6
1960	926	5,258	17.6
1965	1,409	7,859	17.9
1970	2,900	12,791	22.6
1975	4,796	27,323	17.5
1980	14,395	62,730	22.9
1985	42,726	127,598	33.5
1990	140,395	289,816	25.6
1995	369,754	548,100	67.5
2000	709,382	922,148	76.9
Annual compound growth (%)	16.6	12.7	

Table 8.4: Long-Term Premiums as a Percentage of GDP, 1990–2000 (%).[60]

Country	1990	1994	1998	2000
South Africa	7.47	9.42	13.14	14.86
UK	5.99	6.38	10.26	13.78
Japan	8.33	9.58	9.24	9.03
South Korea	8.21	7.96	9.55	8.77
Ireland	5.06	4.89	5.99	7.57
Switzerland	4.30	5.71	8.79	7.40
Finland	4.34	4.51	6.16	7.12
France	2.96	5.09	4.90	6.25
Netherlands	3.93	4.30	5.35	5.61
Australia	3.65	5.34	5.75	5.59
Taiwan	2.93	3.48	4.32	4.91
US	3.61	3.59	4.04	4.45
Canada	2.75	2.93	3.02	3.21
Zimbabwe	2.48	2.14	1.62	2.33

The investment of these premiums in assets in South Africa for most of the second half of the twentieth century has had a stabilizing effect on general macro-economic development, since substantial investments were made in prescribed sectors of the economy. The involvement of the long-term insurers with the financial sector also contributed to the sophistication of financial services in South Africa.[61]

The growth in the life assurance industry in South Africa since 1950 is displayed in Table 8.5. Net premium income rose by 19.3 per cent annual compound growth between 1950 and 2000. The most impressive growth occurred in the period after 1970: net premium income increased by 333 per cent between 1970 and 1980, by 926 per cent between 1980 and 1990 and by 578 per cent between 1990 and 2000. Net premium income of long-term insurers rose consistently from the 1970s, but the dramatic eruption of premium income followed the decision by government in 1985 to amend regulations preventing life insurers from accepting deposits for terms shorter than ten years and preventing them from issuing single premium bonds for shorter terms. The better investment performance of life insurance companies led to a strong demand for single premium policies. Life offices developed new products which converted lump sums into annuities, which funded annual premium endowments. Further annual premiums paid into the endowments also increased the proportion of premium income to GDP.[62] This tendency ameliorated the decline in household savings, since voluntary contractual savings thus invested offered some security to investors/policyholders under conditions of high inflation during the 1980s and 1990s. Between 1970 and 1980 the consumer price index in South Africa averaged 11 per cent; between 1980 and 1990 it was 14.6 per cent and then declined to 8.2 per cent between 1990 and 2000.[63] Between 1970 and 2000 gross saving in the South African economy declined from 24 per cent of GDP to 14.9 per cent. An increase in direct and indirect taxation also contributed to dissaving.[64]

Table 8.5: Long-Term Insurance Premium Income and Personal Savings, 1950–2000 (Rm).[65]

Year	Long-Term Net Premium Income (A)	Household Savings at Current Prices (B)	A as a Percentage of B
1950	26	153	10.7
1955	95	224	15.1
1960	135	255	52.9
1965	142	433	24.9
1970	490	573	85.5
1975	802	1,464	54.8
1980	2,124	4,066	52.2
1985	6,240	6,129	143.9
1990	21,807	4,777	456.5
1995	61,772	6,146	1005.1
2000	147,747	6,922	2120.0
Annual compound growth (%)	19.28	8.08	

Table 8.6: Premium Income and Expenditure, 1990–2000.[66]

Year	Net Premium (A) (Rbn)	% Change	Expenditure (B) (Rbn)	% Change	A – B (Rbn)	% Change
1990	21.81	–	16.63	–	5.18	–
1991	24.52	12.5	18.78	12.9	5.75	11.0
1992	31.22	27.3	26.17	39.4	5.04	−12.2
1993	38.38	22.9	32.93	25.8	5.45	8.0
1994	46.08	20.1	41.81	26.9	4.27	−21.6
1995	61.77	34.1	53.70	28.4	8.08	89.1
1996	68.40	10.7	64.10	19.4	4.31	−46.7
1997	82.47	20.6	80.74	25.9	1.74	−59.6
1998	114.52	38.8	108.43	34.3	6.09	250.5
1999	115.54	0.9	118.91	9.7	−3.37	−155.3
2000	147.75	27.9	140.68	18.3	7.07	−310.0
	–	21.6	–	24.1	–	−24.7

The 'expenditure' of long-term insurance companies between 1990 and 2000 indicates a strong outflow of funds during the decade. Despite the 21.6 per cent rise in premium income, the outflow of benefits paid, and other expenditure by the companies, was 24.1 per cent. The outflow signifies the preference for other investment products as a strategy for personal wealth accumulation. The development in the 1990s was directly linked to the mass exodus of white civil service employees due to retrenchments following the ascent of the black government. Large amounts of retrenchment packages were invested with long-term insurance companies as single premium investments from which annuity income could be earned. Contractual savings with long-term insurers have nevertheless exceeded the growth in household savings since 1950. Long-term insurers have increasingly engaged in pension fund management, since the bulk nature of the product offered more lucrative business than having to sell an equal number of life policies. The pension fund business escalated rapidly since 2000. This chapter does not extend the analysis into the first decade of the twenty-first century, but it is important to note that this trend most probably had an impact on the decision of the two largest long-term insurance companies towards the late 1990s to demutualize and embark on more comprehensive financial services business.

The total income of long-term insurers has risen as reflected in Table 8.7. Income from sources other than long-term policies began an upward trend in response to the high 'withdrawal' from long-term insurers in the form of 'benefits paid'. When more investment options opened up for investors in South Africa during the 1990s, long-term life policies were less attractive. A growing portion of long-term insurance companies' inflows were sourced less from individuals, but rather from bulk pension fund business. Long-term insurance companies were increasingly entrusted with the escalating pension fund business.

Table 8.7: Long-Term Insurance Total Operating Expenses and Total Income,
1950–2000 (Rm).[67]

Year	Long-Term Operating Expenses (A)	Long-Term Total Income (B)	A/B
1950	3	47	6.4
1955	11	62	17.4
1960	18	155	11.6
1965	51	244	20.9
1970	118	652	18.1
1975	205	1,138	18.0
1980	340	3,109	14.5
1985	1,237	9,889	12.5
1990	4,414	40,141	11.0
1995	9,085	86,970	10.4
2000	22,442	191,967	11.7
Annual compound growth (%)	20.0	18.5	

Another reason for the growing confidence in life insurance as an investment can be found in the consistent improvement in efficiency of the industry. As reflected in Table 8.7, operating expenses as a proportion of total income have been declining since the 1970s, although by 2000 there was a slight rise to 11.7 per cent. Increased operating efficiency, together with inflation-beating income and net premium growth, explain the government's reluctance to consider arguments in favour of the scrapping of statutory compulsory investments (Part One investments). Initial solvency considerations for prescribed investments by the life assurance industry were maintained primarily as a means of diverting funds to the central government and to the rest of the public sector. Table 8.8 shows the substantial proportion of life assurance investments restricted to low-return government securities. The ratio of prescribed assets to net liabilities was reduced from 40 per cent in 1959 to 30 per cent, and to 25 per cent in 1965, only to be increased to 30 per cent again in 1966 and to 50 per cent in October 1971.[68] In the UK, from where the regulatory framework for the South African life assurance industry had been inherited, there is no obligation on an insurer to maintain a proportion of its funds in fixed interest-bearing securities.

Consistent criticism against statutory prescribed investments only paid off when in 1989 prescribed asset requirements were scrapped. As reflected in Table 8.8, the ratio of life assurance companies' investments in ordinary shares and unit trusts rose dramatically from the early 1990s. It is also interesting to note that whereas mortgage investments were very important for life assurers in the earlier part of the century, their importance has declined dramatically. As a matter of fact, the four large life offices in South Africa had at some time up to the 1960s placed up to 50 per cent of their investments in mortgages. Mortgages require special knowledge and expensive administration, which gradually reduced their popularity as investments. As shown in Table 8.8, the investment in 'loans' (mortgages) declined from the 1970s to less than 14 per cent of total assets by 2000. Total investment in equities and fixed property have increased gradually over the last twenty-five years, as investors sought inflation-compensating investments. The life insurance companies were the best-performing companies in the financial sector in South Africa during the 1970s and beyond.[69] This anchor role was enhanced during the last three decades of the twentieth century.

Table 8.8: Asset Distribution of Long-Term Life Insurance Offices, 1950–2000 (%).[70]

Year	Fixed Interest Securities	Ordinary Shares and Unit Trusts	Loans	Fixed Property	Other
1950	34.2	10.2	15.2	30.0	10.1
1955	35.1	4.5	36.5	13.9	10.0
1960	28.2	9.8	44.0	7.5	10.5
1965	27.2	22.6	37.4	22.3	9.5
1970	33.7	19.6	27.5	10.2	8.9
1975	34.0	19.4	20.8	16.5	9.3
1980	38.4	22.8	10.3	15.4	13.5
1985	35.8	27.9	5.1	19.9	11.3
1990	20.1	50.4	14.1	0.6	14.7
1995	18.0	52.0	14.0	1.1	14.9
2000	13.0	61.9	11.0	1.3	12.8

Insurance to the Rescue: Life Assurance during Political Instability, 1975–2000

Life insurance companies in South Africa performed an important stabilizing function in the economy from the late 1970s. The South African government grew increasingly concerned about the security of the country, politically as well as economically. From the mid-1970s several domestic and international developments caused the government to introduce protectionist policies and especially to constrain the free movement of capital and foreign exchange. In 1976 student unrest in Soweto spread to various black townships across the country causing international uproar against the use of force to constrain school pupils protesting against the education system. The Soweto riots soon led to the declaration of a state of emergency in the country, which lasted until the mid-1980s. The state of emergency prevented the exercise of civil liberties. An increasingly restrictive foreign exchange control system was implemented.

In 1970 the Franszen Commission of Inquiry into the bank sector was appointed by the government. The report expressed *inter alia* a concern over the extent of foreign control in South African banking. By 1970 more than 73.2 per cent of total commercial bank deposits were held by foreign-controlled banks.[71] Foreign-controlled banks held 10.5 per cent of merchant bank deposits and 23.3 per cent of deposits of all the remaining bank institutions. Thus 55.8 per cent of deposits of the entire banking sector were under foreign control. Statutory restrictions were subsequently placed on foreign shareholding in South African banks. The profitability of South African banks declined and political pressure by activists was placed on foreign banks to disinvest from South Africa. The net result was that the British-controlled banks sold their controlling shareholding in South African banks to local financial institutions.[72] This large exposure of financial institutions to foreign influence was interpreted by the government as posing a serious security risk to the country. Foreign shareholding in South African banks was subsequently restricted in the Financial Institutions Amendment Act No. 101 of 1976. All banks with capital and reserves amounting to R20 million or more had to reduce foreign shareholding to not more than 50 per cent of total shares on issue.[73] New entry by foreign banks was in effect prohibited. In essence the Act sought to ensure that 'webs' of financial control were not 'quietly woven' over the South African economy, 'and in particular webs are not woven by foreigners'.[74]

Table 8.9 reflects the strong position of the long-term insurance companies in the South African economy, especially since 1980. The government's concern about the strategic importance of this industry in the hands of foreign shareholders can be understood in the context of the substantial premium income of life insurance companies as a proportion of national income. This proportion rose considerably from 1985 and trebled by 2000.

Table 8.9: Net Premium Income of Long-term Insurance Companies as a Proportion of National Income, 1950–2000 (Rm).[75]

Year	Net Premium Income (A)	National Income (B)	A/B (%)
1950	26	2 266	1.1
1955	95	7 868	1.2
1960	135	10 648	1.3
1965	142	12 816	1.1
1970	490	19 826	2.4
1975	802	26 234	3.1
1980	2,124	59 302	3.5
1985	6,240	123 126	5.1
1990	21,807	264 203	8.3
1995	61,772	537 674	11.4
2000	147,747	922 148	16.0
Annual compound growth (%)	19.3	13.0	

The insurance industry was also affected by the changes in the regulation of financial sector ownership. The Financial Institutions Amendment Act 101 of 1976 stipulated that foreign insurance institutions had to transfer their insurance business in the Republic of South Africa to domestic insurers before 1 August 1979. Mutual institutions had to obtain approval to be deemed domestic insurers in respect of their insurance business in South Africa.[76] The statutory restrictions on the operations of foreign financial institutions in terms of the Financial Institutions Amendment Act signified the perceived threat to South Africa's financial security amidst the international financial instability of the late 1970s and 1980s, as well as growing international hostility towards the Republic. Chase Manhattan Bank and other leading international banks had cancelled credit to South Africa and instituted both an investment and trade boycott against the country. The government justified the Financial Institutions Amendment Act on the basis of the considerable command of funds by insurance companies, especially long-term insurers, of total national income. Financial institutions were thus compelled to become inward-looking. Ironically, these international pressures mounted exactly when the South African monetary authorities decided to follow the international trend in liberalizing financial markets. International inflation after the oil price increases of the 1970s led to a shift in the orientation of economic policy in many countries. Emphasis shifted away from the pursuit of full employment towards price stability through the control of the money supply, realistic interest rates and the promotion of competition.[77] South Africa joined this policy direction by the appointment of the Commission of Inquiry into the Monetary System and Monetary Policy in South Africa (De Kock Commission).[78] The De Kock Commission made far-reaching proposals to the effect of fundamentally transforming monetary policy and deregulating financial institutions. To financial institutions this meant the phasing out of direct monetary controls, but the threatening international conditions prevented the full liberalization of South African financial markets in compliance with the De Kock Commission proposals.[79] The De Kock Commission advised the relaxation of exchange controls. Certain reforms were already instituted by September 1983, but a sharp depreciation of the South African currency followed, which prevented full exchange control liberalization. Between 1983 and 1990 the rand lost 50 per cent of its exchange value. In the wake of the political instability in South Africa, the Chase Manhattan Bank refused to roll over loans and demanded immediate repayment of loans made to South African private institutions in August 1985. Private sector debt had risen to R23.7 billion by 1985, but under no circumstances posed a risk of non-repayment. When Chase Manhattan called up its credit, other American banks followed suit and South Africa was forced to declare a unilateral debt standstill in August 1985.[80]

The impact of these international developments on the South African financial services industry was a comprehensively consolidating one. Foreign banks sold their shares in local banks to South African life assurance companies, since they were cash-rich and most favourably positioned to take advantage of the investment opportunity offered by these 'forced' sales. The four largest life insurance companies took control of the four large commercial banks.[81] The long-term insurance companies could effect these 'take-overs', since statutory restrictions on investments by insurance companies, especially the life offices, were finally rescinded in March 1989. Persistent criticism of the regulation of prescribed investments by institutional investors (insurance companies and pension funds) emphasized the immobilization of huge amounts of stock and inhibited trading, causing losses to investors.[82] The life assurance companies were free to invest larger proportions of their funds in shares of public listed companies offering better returns. The real growth of the life assurance companies' assets between 1970 and 1990 was 8.4 per cent compared to only 4.8 per cent of short-term insurance companies. The total income of life offices increased in real terms by 11.4 per cent between 1970 and 1990. This performance was remarkable considering that real *per capita* GDP was declining in the period 1970–90.

The performance of the life assurance companies was impressive given the restricted nature of the environment. This performance is illustrated in Table 8.10. Between 1990 and 2000, following the scrapping of prescribed compulsory investments, the long-term insurance companies' assets rose by 80.2 per cent (or by 8.02 per cent average per annum) (see Table 8.3 above). The stabilizing role of long-term life assurance companies in the financial sector in South Africa, as well as in the overall economy, is shown in the comparisons in Table 8.10.

Table 8.10: Annual Real GDP Growth, Personal Savings Growth, CPIX (Consumer Price Index excluding Mortgage Bonds) and Life Assurance Companies' Asset and Liability Growth, 1990–2000.[83]

	Real GDP	Household Savings	Long-Term Insurers' Premium Income	CPIX
Growth per annum (%)	2.6	8.1	19.3	9.8

The life assurance industry thus served as a primary source of capital to the South African economy, especially given the cautious implementation of financial deregulation (not allowing foreign investment in the long-term insurance or banking industry either inward or outward to any significant degree) and persistence with exchange control. Although international sentiment was changing favourably towards South Africa after the commencement of negotiations towards the democratic elections in 1994, monetary authorities were not prepared to deregulate the financial markets fully. Fears for capital flight similar to that of the early 1960s loomed large as much uncertainty existed about the stability of the country after the introduction of black majority rule in 1994. Foreign financial institutions were allowed back only gradually and under strict regulatory conditions. By 2000 none of the South African banks had been subjected to a foreign takeover, as had happened in New Zealand after deregulation of financial markets. The life insurance companies controlled the banking sector. There was also no international take-over bid for any of the large life offices in South Africa. In 1998 the new Long-Term Insurance Act 52 of 1998 and a new Short-Term Insurance Act 53 of 1998 were promulgated.[84] After 1990 supervision of long-term insurance companies was transferred to a newly established body, the Financial Services Board, established on the recommendation of the Melamet Commission, which had been appointed to investigate the collapse of the AA Mutual Insurance Company.[85] Composite insurers were outlawed and they jointly segregated the businesses. South Africa no longer has any direct composite insurers, although composite reinsurance companies are still allowed and exist.

The long-term insurance companies embarked on a new strategy to capitalize on their investment strength, acquired financial management capacity and the opening up of global markets to South African companies. The deregulated international financial environment, and the slowly manifesting global opportunities for South African companies, opened up various opportunities. To the life insurance companies opportunities arose to diversify their operations out of predominantly life insurance and pension funds administration into a variety of other financial services. Despite the impressive growth in assets as well as premium income, withdrawals from life assurance companies had risen by 87 per cent per annum.[86] Clients were increasingly displaying affinity for other financial instruments than life cover to provide for their future. Both the two largest life insurance companies, the Old Mutual (which controlled 33.0 per cent of the life insurance market in 1990) and Sanlam (which controlled 34.3 per cent), demutualized in 1998. These companies gradually lost market share to all the other life insurance companies conducting business in South Africa.[87] The Old Mutual listed as a primary listing on the London Stock Exchange and Sanlam on the Johannesburg Stock Exchange. The number of life insurance companies was always quite high: in 1950 there were 61 long-term insurance companies doing business in South Africa (41 local and 20 foreign). By 1980 the number was reduced to 41 in total following the statutory restrictions on foreign operating companies. By 1990 there were 39 life offices and this number rose to 43 by 2000. During the first half of the century the life insurance industry had already been dominated by only a few companies. Since the 1940s the four largest life assurance companies controlled on average 10–11 per cent of the total assets of the life insurance industry. The stronghold of the large companies increased. The market is still dominated by the Old Mutual and the Sanlam (Old Mutual controlling 19.4 per cent and the Sanlam 15.9 per cent by 2000) and the 17 largest companies controlled 92.2 per cent of the total life assurance business in 2000. The trend in business development of life assurance companies was a definite strengthening in pension fund and group life business (from 35.2 per cent of business in 1990 to 49.6 per cent in 2000), a decline in retirement annuity business (from 12.0 per cent of business in 1990 to 7.2 per cent in 2000), to a visible increase in disability and health insurance (from 0.9 per cent in 1990 to 2.1 per cent in 2000) and single premium business (from 1.2 per cent in 1990 to 7.6 per cent in 2000).

Conclusion

The life assurance industry in South Africa developed in the British tradition of life insurance and therefore developed products appealing primarily to the white population in the country. By 2000 the shift of the long-term insurance industry towards the growing black market since the 1960s gained momentum. It is not possible to state with any reliability the distribution in 2000 between white and black policyholders in South Africa. It is nevertheless assumed that life offices were primarily exposed to the white segment of the population during the establishment phase of the industry. It was assumed in 1955 that the predominant profile of holders of life insurance policies was white.[88] This distribution commenced adjustment in the early 1960s, when blacks and whites were members of corporate pension funds and pension contributions made up a growing portion of funds administered by long-term insurers. As the new government since 1994 has retrenched whites and appointed blacks to the civil service, the portion of black contributors to long-term insurers' pension funds has risen sharply. The black population was initially primarily served by so-called 'industrial' policies, which were small policies based on weekly wage subtractions. Industrial insurance was only a very small proportion of the insurance business. The large number of black employees in civil service thus increased the black client base of long-term insurance companies.

The long-term life assurance industry in South Africa performed a valuable stabilizing role in the economy, especially during the period of international sanctions and debt rescheduling. Substantial investments were kept in the country and invested in domestic industries and enterprises. The sophistication of the financial services industry, of which the long-term insurance business forms a dominant proportion, can be ascribed to the legacy of the European tradition and the lack of government intervention in the industry. Despite stringent regulatory controls over investments by institutional investors, the long-term insurance industry in South Africa was always privately owned and never nationalized. The two dominant life offices were mutual companies since their inception in 1845 and 1918 respectively. These companies demutualized in 1998 and then diversified operations to expand into a broader spectrum of sophisticated financial services aside from life cover. The slow penetration by foreign insurers into the South African market can be ascribed to the sophistication of the existing companies. This sophistication was enhanced during the period of relative isolation and was put to good use after deregulation to protect market share from foreign takeover attempts.

9 COMPETING GLOBALIZATIONS: CONTROVERSIES BETWEEN PRIVATE AND SOCIAL INSURANCE AT INTERNATIONAL ORGANIZATIONS, 1900–60

Martin Lengwiler

This chapter examines the role of international organizations in influencing and shaping the development of national welfare systems. In this process, scientific expertise played a crucial role, both on the level of international organizations and for the interactions between international and national institutions. In this sense, the chapter builds a bridge between the emerging fields of transnational history and the history of knowledge.[1] The significance of experts in international organizations is based upon an epistemic analogy, if not a relatedness, between the processes of scientification and globalization. Both are manifestations of the broad and heterogeneous tradition of a secular universalism that was particularly prominent and influential in the long nineteenth century. Universalist traditions materialized in a variety of organizations including the world exhibitions and their philanthropic sponsors, as well as the international academic congresses in the nineteenth and early twentieth centuries.[2] In the twentieth century, these organizations were amended by new international and supranational organizations, including the International Labour Office (ILO), the ILO-affiliated International Social Security Association (ISSA) and the Organisation for Economic Cooperation and Development (OECD), which also tried to shape the development of national welfare states in Europe and on a global level. Most of these organizations relied heavily on universalist expert knowledge to define the recommended social policy models; and most models were built after particular European welfare states – from the German and Scandinavian models in the first part of the century to the Anglo-Saxon and Swiss models since the 1970s.

Thus the debates within these international organizations have formed an influential transnational discourse on social policy issues, also feeding back into national social policymaking. However, it is unclear how far these transnational activities were able to shape national welfare systems in a way that would make them converge with each other, leading eventually, in the European context, to the emergence of what has been called the 'European social model'.[3] This chapter examines the interactions between the international and national levels and the role and impact of scientific expertise, while focusing on two exemplary organizations: the International Congress of Actuaries (founded in 1895) and the ILO (established in 1919).

What makes these organizations exemplary cases with which to study the role of international expert networks in the history of national welfare states? The Congress of Actuaries was one of a series of international congresses, which paralleled the rise of modern social insurance systems and which focused on the techniques and policies of insurance. Themselves a consequence of the first wave of globalization of the insurance industry, these congresses also included the International Congress of Social Insurance (Congrès internationale des accidents du travail, founded in 1886), the International Congress on Life Assurance Medicine (founded in 1899) and the International Congress for Industrial Medicine (Congrès médicale internationale pour les accidents du travail; established in 1906). As their names indicate, these insurance-related congresses were mainly frequented by expert communities (primarily mathematicians and medical and legal experts). These experts, however, had two very different organizational backgrounds: one group represented government authorities and favoured the model of social insurance, the other brought a business background and tended to support the approach of private insurance.

For two reasons, the Congress of Actuaries offers an exemplary case for this study. First, it was the main platform for debate among insurance mathematicians (actuaries) and insurance statisticians, both key disciplines for the calculation of risks and thus for the formation and organization of social insurance. Second, the actuarial congress remained the privileged platform for debates about the relation between public and private actors in social insurance systems, which is one of the dominant themes in the history of social policy and – as will be shown below – a crucial element for the institutional divergence of European welfare states. The main source for this chapter, therefore, consists of the published congress papers – a collection of papers, memoranda and minutes of the discussions at the thirteen congresses between 1895 and 1951, altogether material of nearly 20,000 pages. The argument focuses on how the international community of actuaries dealt with the conflicting interests of private and public actors and how this actuarial internationalism was able to influence national systems of social insurance. How did the rules, norms and standards agreed upon at the congresses shape social insurance systems and business practices in the insurance industry? And what were the limits of convergence – for example set by the national institutional and legal contexts?

The period examined in the first case study spans from the late nineteenth century, when the European insurance industry witnessed a considerable expansion and when at the same time the first social insurance schemes were established, through to 1950, when most of the European welfare states were reformed or rebuilt in institutional arrangements that often persist until today.[4] Over this period, when European welfare states developed their specific institutional shape, private and public organizations of insurance were integrated into mixed welfare economies, typical for most European welfare states.[5] Geographically, the first case study focuses on Britain, France, Germany and Switzerland – countries that are relevant either by the size of their insurance industry (Britain, Germany and France) or by their early and exemplary insurance legislation (Switzerland).

The second case study focuses on the social policy of the ILO and some of its affiliate organizations, from its foundation in 1919 to the early 1970s. The ILO, founded as part of the League of Nations and operating since 1946 under the umbrella of the United Nations, took a leading role in the international discourse on social policy issues, in particular in the inter-war period (during the directorship of Albert Thomas, a French socialist and syndicalist), but also from 1945 until the 1960s.[6] The organization of the ILO was based upon a tripartite model, bringing together representatives from trade unions, employers' organizations and government staff (often technical experts). In the tradition of the international trade union movement, the self-declared task of the ILO was to set international legal standards in social policy in order to prevent a destructive international competition – a 'race to the bottom' – between different national labour laws.[7]

First Case Study: The International Congress of Actuaries, 1895–1950

The first case study is organized in three steps. The first section gives an outline of the social and topical character of the Congress of Actuaries, analysing the background of the participants and the thematic focus of the thirteen meetings between 1895 and 1951. The two following sections highlight two fields of the congressional debates in which the intended transfer of ideas and convergence of practices proved to be particularly difficult: first, the debates around the statutory insurance legislation and, second, the relation between statutory or public actors and private actors in the emerging institutions of social insurance.

A Dialogue Dominated by Business Interests: Participants and Topics at the Congress of Actuaries

The International Congress of Actuaries first convened in Brussels in 1895, invited by the Belgian life insurance companies, and continued convening in a three-year cycle, only interrupted by the two world wars and the economic crisis of the 1930s.[8]

The congress originated as a reaction to the increasing internationalization of the insurance industry. The international branches of the insurance business, in particular the leading British and American insurers, were confronted with a variety of national legislations and economic policies.[9] Thus, the congress followed an already existing internationalization of business practices; the gatherings were not intended to open up new insurance markets but rather to facilitate already established market mechanisms by standardization and harmonization of business procedures. Accordingly the common aim of the congress was seen as the harmonization of the legal and technical aspects of insurance – from the collection of mortality statistics to the calculation of risk probabilities. In his opening address to the second congress in 1898, Thomas Emley Young, president of the British Institute of Actuaries – the leading scientific institution of the field – and in this role president of the congress, eloquently illustrated the need for unification by comparing insurance with the history of languages and by evoking the universal spirit of scientific endeavours:

> We confer a systematic unity upon our Professional investigations by adoption of a uniform scheme of symbolic language; we thus become the possessors and inheritors of a common and intelligible tongue, undistracted by local dialects; diversified Babel, in the ancient allegory, is re-converted into primitive speech; with this bond we more closely, though diversely scattered, re-unite into a universal Scientific citizenship; the refined and competent finish of our analytical language re-acts, as has so significantly occurred in the history of Mathematics, upon the subtle and potential possibilities of research[10]

The countries present at the congress reflected the global map of the insurance industry. The meetings were dominated by the industrialized world and by countries with a strong insurance sector, such as Britain, the US, Germany, France, Belgium, the Netherlands, Austria or Switzerland. Also among the founding members were most other Western European nations (Denmark, Spain, Portugal and Italy) as well as Russia, South Africa and Japan.[11] Over the years, all countries from Western and Eastern Europe started to send delegations, but also Canada, Australia, New Zealand, South Africa, later also India, Egypt and other African states. The first three congresses brought together between 300 and 500 participants, a number that quickly rose to 600 at the fourth congress (New York, 1903) and 1,200 at the fifth meeting (Berlin, 1906). After that, the size of the event fluctuated between 1,000 and 1,400 participants (see Table 9.2 in the annex).

The congresses were organized by the Permanent Office of the congress, located in Brussels, in collaboration with the association of actuaries of the hosting country. The Permanent Office, a characteristic element of nineteenth-century international organizations, was responsible for defining the main themes of the congress. These themes were published in advance of the meeting and had to be addressed by the papers submitted to the congress. There were two thematic categories: the more controversial themes were to be covered by papers read out and discussed at the congress, the less important themes were to be addressed by memoranda, which were neither read out nor discussed but still published in the congress papers.

The congress mainly acted as a platform for a voluntary professional dialogue (either by open discussions or by published memoirs). There were no binding decisions, not even on technical matters, although in its first meetings the congress was able to adopt formal resolutions – an opportunity abolished in 1903.[12] The analysis of the thematic fields shows the importance of technical issues, in contrast to the political, legal and professional issues. If we divide the conference themes along these lines, technical issues are by far the most frequent themes picked up by the Congress of Actuaries – about twice as frequent as political, legal and professional issues combined (see Table 9.1).

Table 9.1: Themes Covered by the Thirteen International Congresses of Actuaries, 1895–1951.[13]

General Topic	Included as Specific Topics	No. Treatments (as Title of Congress Sections)
Technical	Notation	82
	Development of interest, currency depreciation	
	Calculation of reserves, of contributions, of assets	
	Bonus distribution and participation in surplus	
	Mortality statistics, substandard risks, mathematical statistics, new types of risk (aerial risk)	
	Industrial insurance, reinsurance	
	Insurance contract; medical service	
Political	Social and economic policies; tax policies	25
	Relation to mutual insurers and social insurances (incl. topic of group insurance)	
Legal	Supervisory legislation	11
	Legislation on insurance contracts	
	Regulations on financial liquidity / reserves	
Professional	Professional or academic education and research	7
	Professional dictionary	
	History of profession	

The distribution of themes seems to reflect the comparably advanced integration of the insurance community on technical matters. In fact, the congress succeeded, voluntarily and incrementally, to establish a couple of international technical agreements and standards. In the 1890s for example, at the first two congresses, the participants agreed upon a universal mathematical notation to be used by future actuarial science.[14] Furthermore, around 1900 the congress initiated three extensive and independent mortality investigations (two in Britain after 1895, one in France in 1900), the statistics of which were later used by life insurance companies as a model for other national mortality tables.[15] Later the congress acted as the platform on which the progress of mathematical statistics in the probabilization of new risks, such as the risk of accidents, was presented and adopted by the actuarial community.[16] Occasionally, delegates also attended the congress to seek specific information, as, for example, the Hungarian James Raffmann, who was sent by his government in 1903 to look for models for a planned supervisory legislation.[17]

In all these cases the congress acted as a motor of convergence for the international insurance community. This convergence seemed to be much easier in technical matters than on the legal and political level. Moreover, if technical issues were related to political conditions, the integration was difficult even in technical matters. The establishment of international statistics on occupational accidents, for example, failed because the frequency of accidents partly depended on the legal regulations for accident prevention.[18]

The analysis of the participants – which shall be limited here to Britain, Germany, France and Switzerland – highlights the split, mentioned above, between representatives of the insurance business and government authorities. Figure 9.1 shows that private insurance representatives were by far the biggest community among the participants from Britain, Germany, France and Switzerland, with a rate of between 70 and 85 per cent of all participants. Government representatives only made up between 5 and 15 per cent, with the exception of the Berlin congress, hosted by the mother country of social insurance, where 18 per cent of the participants represented government authorities. The friendly societies (i.e. the French *mutualités* or the German *Hilfskassen*) were also regularly present at the congresses, although only in small numbers (usually around 1–2 per cent). The dominance of commercial interests at the Congress of Actuaries is also illustrated by an introductory remark of the doyen of the German actuarial community and professor of insurance economics, Alfred Manes, at the London congress in 1927. Manes welcomed the fact that the International Labour Office increasingly acted as a promoter for the international diffusion of social insurance. Expressing concern, however, he continued that it was 'a great pity that private insurance has no such International Office to promote the private insurance idea', adding that 'perhaps this Congress could take the place of that'.[19]

Interestingly, despite the leading role of commercial insurers and the marginal position of friendly societies and government authorities, no group ever lost interest in the congress. Government representatives as well as delegates from friendly societies kept frequenting the congress until the end of the time span examined here. There was no segregation between private and public sectors at the Congress of Actuaries – the meetings did not lose their relevance for business *and* statutory insurers.

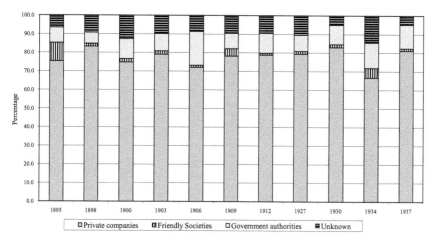

Figure 9.1: Participants at the International Congress of Actuaries, 1895–1937 (counting only Britain, Germany, France and Switzerland).[20]

The national delegations also show remarkable differences. The biggest delegation in size was usually the British camp; often more than twice as large as the French, the German and the Swiss delegations together (see Figure 9.2). Moreover, the British delegation was clearly business oriented. It regularly consisted of 80 to 90 per cent business representatives, with a percentage of government authorities of usually below 3 per cent (see Table 9.5 in the annex). The contrasting examples were the more governmental German and Swiss delegations, with a rate of government representatives of usually between 10 and 30 per cent (Germany) or even between 20 and 50 per cent (Switzerland), whereas the size of their business group more or less oscillated between 50 and 80 per cent of the national delegations (see Tables 9.3 and 9.6 in the annex).

Heated Controversies and Blocked Integration: The Debates around Statutory Insurance Legislation

How did the congress succeed in committing its participants to the intended 'common tongue' mentioned above, in particular in a field like insurance legislation where the international debate was marked by wide national disparities? Basically, the congress intended to unify the national insurance communities in all respects, even in legal and political matters where integration was most difficult. The hope for reducing the legal disparities was based on the early successes of the congress in technical matters, such as the development of a standard mathematical notation already mentioned.[21] An international standard for insurance legislation also promised to eliminate the economic obstacles posed by the myriads of national (sometimes even regional) particularities in the regulation

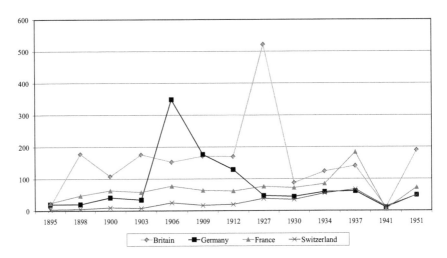

Figure 9.2: Number of Participants at the International Congress of Actuaries, 1895–1951.[22]

of insurance – an important incentive for the highly internationalized insurance business.[23] The question of integrating the different statutory insurance regulations was thus on the agenda from the first congress in 1895, and most delegates were hopeful that progress on this question was imminent.[24]

The congress was also unanimous, at least in the years before the First World War, about the direction in which a legal unification had to proceed. The debates at the early congresses show that most of the participants were critical of an interventionist economic policy with expanded supervisory legislation. The second congress in 1898 offers an illustrative anecdote. The discussion in the section on the question of legislation on life assurance was such a one-sided matter – all votes taking sides against state intervention – that the chairman had to intervene and call for somebody to make the opposite argument: 'he hoped that before the proceedings closed, some champion of restrictive legislation and Government interference in the conduct of life assurance would speak. So far there had been a rather one-sided debate.' The chair eventually invited an American delegate to offer his views on the interventionist legislation of New York and other US states.[25]

Until 1914, most speakers and discussants at the congress supported the British model of insurance supervision, based on a liberal, free-market approach and relying on the self-regulation of the insurance industry. The British legislation was based on the Insurance Act of 1870 and included a concession system, under which every commercial insurance company had to deposit a comparably modest sum of £20,000 (regardless of the size of the company), combined with a lukewarm supervisory system that only asked for the publication of the company's results every five years. The idea behind the focus on publicity was that the supervision of the insurance business should be exercised by the public, not by the government.[26] When characterizing the British model, the vice-president of the Institute of Actuaries in London, George King, in 1895 conceded that in fact there was practically no government supervision at all – at least no statutory intervention in the insurance market.[27]

The contrasting model was often represented by Switzerland, the first country with an interventionist supervisory legislation (from 1885, implemented by the Federal Insurance Office, the Eidgenössisches Versicherungsamt) and a model for other similar legislations, first by Germany (1901), then by Austria (1904), later also by other states.[28] The interventionist model provided that detailed accounts had to be published yearly, that the reserves be invested in reliable securities and that the government was allowed to stipulate specific business procedures designed to protect the rights and financial claims of the customers. The compliance with these regulations was often supervised by a centralized government office, such as the Federal Insurance Office in Switzerland or the German Supervisory Office for Commercial Insurance (Aufsichtsamt für Privatversicherung). Furthermore, the deposit, as a condition for a concession, was usually measured in a percentage of the turnover – often resulting in a much higher amount than the British lump sum.[29]

The adherents of the liberal legislation – which included the insurance industry of interventionist countries – harshly criticized the extended government supervision. The legal restrictions would unnecessarily hamper the insurance industry, and the regulation was seen as a poorly disguised protectionist policy (when, for example, it prescribed investing reserves in government assets). The forces of market competition would be a better instrument to control the insurance industry, whereas the legal regulations would always drag behind the developing business practices.[30] The critique went so far as to ridicule interventionist policies, as when a British delegate mocked the yearly publications of the Swiss Federal Insurance Office and their detailed insights into the accounts of the companies as unintelligible and counterproductive. The publication offered merely 'a multiplicity of figures ... which, to be effective, should be reduced to as small dimensions as possible'; the 'multitude of statistics and comparisons that are published ... fails in enlightening public opinion'.[31] Only a few delegates, mostly public employees of the Swiss and the German delegations, spoke in favour of an interventionist approach.[32] Even at the 1903 congress in Berlin, the capital of Bismarckian social insurance, the defenders of government interventionism were clearly on the defensive.[33]

However, the hopes for an international convergence of the legal regulations were soon disappointed. One problem was that the congressional debates did not succeed in convincing the interventionist camp of a liberal approach to government supervision. Even after years of repeated debates, the two positions remained irreconcilable. At the Berlin congress in 1906, for example, the delegates did not even agree on the title of the section on government supervision. The German version spoke of 'Vorschläge zu einer Vereinheitlichung der Rechtsvorschriften über die Staatsaufsicht', but the French and British delegations struggled to translate the concept of *Staatsaufsicht*. The French version was still close to the German original with 'Propositions pour uniformiser les dispositions légales en ce qui concerne particulièrement la surveillance exercée par l'Etat', but the English translation reduced the broad idea of government supervision to the limited task of reporting procedure. The English title spoke of 'the uniformity of legal requirements, especially as regards reports to be made to the insurance authority' – a wording that was further shortened by the American delegation to the US version of 'the uniformity of reports to insurance authorities'. The Dutch speaker, mentioning the episode, wryly added: 'It can hardly be seen as a good omen for the achievement of a uniform legislation when the attempts to clearly define what the papers of a section should deal with, turned out to be so far from being uniform'.[34]

A more important obstacle to the integrative ambition of the congress was that government legislations remained split into two camps, the liberal camp headed by the British and the interventionist camp around Germany, Switzerland and Austria. Already in 1906, the German speaker had to concede that the intended legal integration was still a distant prospect, not least for protectionist concerns of the respective governments.[35] The situation remained unchanged in the inter-war period; the integrative prospects were thus still judged pessimistically.[36]

Accommodation Instead of Confrontation: How the Insurance Business Adapted to the Social Insurance System

As mentioned above, the Congress of Actuaries brought together actuaries from three institutional backgrounds: private insurance companies, friendly societies and social insurances. These three communities often acted as competitors on the insurance market, for example in sickness insurance (i.e. health insurance) or in old age and pension insurance. Accordingly, the congressional debates about the relation of commercial, mutual and statutory insurance, which started already in the 1890s, were always potentially conflict-laden. One side of this triangle, the relation between commercial insurers and friendly societies, was comparably relaxed. The development of friendly societies was taken up as a topic by the congress a couple of times, especially at the early meetings, but it did not spark any deep controversies. Most speakers, commercial actuaries and government delegates alike, stressed the need for a further professionalization of the friendly societies, in particular on the technical level.[37]

Much more controversial were the debates about the relation between private (including commercial and mutual) and statutory actors, in particular in the expanding fields of social insurance such as the workmen's compensation and the old age insurance schemes.[38] Most actuaries from the private sector disagreed with the expansion of public insurance schemes. Systems of statutory or compulsory insurance were seen as interfering with the business of private insurers and often ridiculed as bureaucratic, paternalistic, unprofessional and technically underdeveloped.[39] A British actuary, representing the Prudential Assurance Company, one of the market leaders in life insurance, scornfully quipped: 'Companies offer the people what they want, and the Government offers the people what they think they ought to want.'[40] However, the delegates of the private sector at the same time agreed that the rise of social insurance was as inevitable as it was irreversible. The question was not whether there should be any social or statutory insurance at all, but rather what the spread of social insurance meant for commercial and mutual insurances: did it mark the beginning of the end of private insurance or did it signal the emergence of a mixed, public-private welfare system?[41]

Similar to the debates about government supervision, the discussions about the relation between commercial and social insurance were marked by two distinct positions. The contributions to the section on the 'economic relations between public and private insurance' ('Die wirtschaftlichen Beziehungen zwischen der öffentlichen und privaten Versicherung') at the 1909 congress in Vienna offer an exemplary illustration of these positions. Delegates from countries with early social insurance legislation, notably from Germany and Austria, painted a harmonic picture, based on dialogic relations between public and private actors. Although the public and private insurance sectors would profit from each other by mutual learning processes, most German and Austrian delegates agreed that at the end of the day social insurance, based on statutory insurance organizations, would prevail over private insurance.[42] One of the discussants summarized the papers by concluding that the future role of private insurance was doomed and consisted at best of a marginalized supplement to social insurance.[43]

As one might expect, the British delegates at the Vienna congress vehemently disagreed. They conceded that social insurance had grown to a relevant institution, but they were not ready to write off private insurance. Instead they argued for a mixed, public-private welfare system and for a strong role of private actors within the social insurance schemes. The congressional debates of 1909 show that this position was already clearly established before the First World War – long before the inter-war period, when it eventually became a successful strategy of the insurance industry. The British representatives, supported by their French and American colleagues, argued that the opposition of private and public insurance should not be understood as distinct and exclusionary spheres, the private belonging to commercial insurers and the public to government organizations. On the contrary, they favoured a system of social insurance in which private insurers could play at least a relevant and complementary, if not the decisive part.

This strategy was not only supported by friendly societies and similar organizations, which already played a crucial part in the public schemes for health insurance in Germany and Britain, but also by delegates from commercial insurers. Maurice Bellom, for example, a professor at the French École des Mines de Paris, argued that commercial insurers, with their technical expertise and professional experience, were in fact better prepared to carry out social insurance than government organizations. Bellom understood the notion of 'social insurance' as a non-compulsory insurance of the working class, quite similar to the industrial insurance (the small life insurance) offered by commercial insurers in Britain and the US. He thus tried to open a huge new market for commercial insurers, which hitherto – with the exception of industrial insurance – had focused on a middle-class clientele.[44]

In the years after the First World War, the relation between private and social insurance quickly developed into one of the key themes at the congresses of the 1920s and 1930s. At the opening of the first reunion after the war, in 1927 in London, the chairman of the congress noted that there was one issue in the programme that made the London congress distinct from its predecessors: 'this is the ever-increasing prominence assumed by questions of industrial and social insurance as compared with the purely professional matters which formerly had pride of place'.[45] Other speakers concurred. The British delegate James Bacon spoke of a 'tremendous extension of the system of Social Insurance' since the last pre-war congress, and Ralph Hill Stewart, of the Scottish Faculty of Actuaries in Edinburgh, stated that social insurance was 'the most interesting and at the same time complicated system of insurance with which actuaries have to grapple'.[46]

Despite the increased relevance of the topic, the strategy of commercial insurers to promote a mixed welfare economy remained the same and persisted until the 1950s, the end of the period examined. It turned out to be a largely successful strategy. This is not the place to elaborate on national welfare legislation. It should suffice to say that after the First World War the insurance industry in several European states entered the social insurance systems or strengthened its position in them. Commercial insurers were particularly active in two fields of social insurance: in health insurance, either by offering their own policies and thus competing with friendly societies, or by reinsuring the business of friendly societies; and in old age insurance, mainly by managing small employer's funds in the form of group insurances. At the same time, the debates at the congress about the relations between public and private insurance systems lost much of their previous explosiveness.[47]

The form of collaboration between commercial insurers and friendly societies (i.e. *Hilfskassen* in Germany and *mutualités* in France) within the emerging welfare systems depended on the national context. In Germany, the commercial insurers occupied the growing market for complementary private health insurance, whereas the *Hilfskassen* were integrated as managers of the social insurance system. In Britain, commercial and friendly societies both acted as approved societies under the statutory health insurance (Health Insurance Act of 1911). In France, commercial insurers started to collaborate with the *mutualités* by offering reinsurance. In Switzerland, the *Hilfskassen* occupied the private as well as most regional statutory health insurance markets. Commercial insurers were inactive in Switzerland; however, the mutual insurers witnessed a professionalization process that reduced the differences between commercial and mutual insurers.[48] In the field of old age insurance, commercial insurers often built up their own pension system, sometimes preceding statutory insurance (as in Switzerland), sometimes founding a complementary insurance system on top of the statutory provisions (as in Britain, France or Germany).[49] Therefore, in the field of old age insurance, the debates at the congress from the 1930s tended to see statutory insurance only as a basic insurance, providing a minimal level of subsistence, whereas the private or corporate pension insurance would secure the level of individual incomes.[50]

Second Case Study: The ILO, 1919–70

How effective were the activities of the ILO, the second case to be examined here? In social policy issues, the ILO did not act on its own but was supported by affiliate organizations, in particular by the ISSA, an organization founded in 1947 but with a precursor that had existed since 1927. The ISSA was a discrete but very influential association of social policy experts from academic and bureaucratic institutions. Its operations were heavily subsidized and organizationally supported by the ILO, which turned the ISSA *de facto* into a branch of the ILO.[51]

By what means did the ILO and the ISSA try to shape international social policy discourses and influence national social policy legislations? We can distinguish three mechanisms of integration, in the sense of defining a universal model for social policy decisions: a legal, a scientific-technical and a social mechanism.

The legal mechanism of integration was certainly a central part of the activities of the ILO. The organization's ordinary work consisted of agreeing upon conventions and recommendations, conventions being the more prescriptive form of decision. However, in order to come into effect in a member state, conventions had to be ratified by its authorities. Implicitly the ILO's conventions and recommendations were mostly modelled after some European form of welfare state, which the ILO sought to popularize. In the inter-war period the ILO's decisions were quite ambitious (in tune with Albert Thomas's striving directorship); the organization worked for an international harmonization of the social security legislation, modelled after the maximal standards of certain

European welfare state types. A typical example is the convention on sickness insurance of 1927. It recommended the direct adoption of the German model of statutory sickness insurance (the Gesetzliche Krankenversicherung), together with a nationalization of the existing private sickness funds. A similarly ambitious convention was the one on old age insurance, agreed upon in 1933, that was modelled after the universal insurance systems of the Scandinavian states.[52] This policy of maximal standards clearly failed. The higher the goals of a convention, the more moderate its achievements in the process of ratification. The convention on sickness insurance, for example, was to be adopted only by 10 of the 27 European member states of the ILO (until 1989) – among the prominent outliers were France, Italy, Switzerland and the Scandinavian countries (except Norway, which ratified the convention). The effect of the convention on old age insurance was even more modest. Until 1945 only France and Britain had signed the convention, followed by Italy, Bulgaria and Poland in the post-war period. All other states in Western and Eastern Europe stood apart.[53]

These sobering experiences led the ILO to change its policies and pursue a more pragmatic course in the post-war period. A case in point is the convention on minimal standards in social security of 1952, arguably the most effective convention on social insurance issues in the history of the ILO. Different from the inter-war policy, this convention did not declare one model of social insurance as authoritative, but sought to introduce an open standard. Moreover, it only set a minimal, instead of the old maximal, standard. The text of the convention listed nine branches of social insurance each with a specific minimal standard. Countries that wanted to adopt the convention only had to fulfil the standards of three of the nine insurance branches. Thus, the ILO allowed for a flexible implementation of the convention. States with completely different welfare systems were able to join the convention. Accordingly, the ratification process was comparably successful. All Western European countries – with the exception of Finland – adopted the convention within a few years.[54]

The second mechanism of the ILO for converging different national approaches to social policy relied specifically on the universalizing effects of scientific-technical expertise. After 1945, research activities became a central concern of the ILO and of the ISSA in particular. Both organizations took on important consultancy mandates, either for its member states or for other international organizations, for example for the European Council, the European Coal and Steel Community and later the European Community and the European Union.[55] In the early post-war period, research activities dealt with topics like the protection of women at work, the insurance of migrant workers or the administration and planning of social insurance systems – the central concern of these expert opinions was most often a technical benchmarking of different national systems of insurance.[56] From the recession of 1973/4, the ILO and increasingly also the OECD became a platform for the emerging international discourse on the crisis of the European welfare states. Now topics to be examined included the efficiency of social security systems, the funding of old age pension systems, or the general strategy of social security reforms in a period of economic stagnation. International organizations such as the ILO, the ISSA or the OECD did not just anticipate many of the later reform proposals of the European Commission; they also created an institutional platform for the emergence of a discourse and a perception of a European-wide crisis of the welfare state.[57]

However, the proliferation of technical expertise by international organizations did not necessarily have a universalizing effect. One of the remarkable outcomes of the scientific-technical expertise of the ILO was the recognition of the specificities of European welfare as the result of an intended but failed strategy of globalization. Since the 1930s, the ILO had actively promoted the global proliferation of the idea of social insurance, in particular outside the world of Western industrialized nations. The main instrument of this strategy was the inclusion of non-Western states as members of the ILO, supplemented by technical consultations of the political authorities of developing or emerging countries – a strategy of globalization thoroughly examined in the recent study by Daniel Maul. In the 1930s and 1940s, this strategy focused on Latin American countries, joined, from the 1950s, by Middle Eastern countries and several Asian states; from the 1960s, African countries were also included. In this process, the ILO often just followed the paths of decolonization.[58] As agents for transferring the technical know-how of social insurance, the ILO relied on the ISSA and its network of European social insurance experts.[59]

In a long-term perspective, the global triumph of the Western welfare state model did not materialize. The extra-European countries reflected upon Western approaches to social insurance – for example when dealing with the traditions of their own colonial past – but they did this from their own distinct perspectives, often taking an explicitly non-Western course of development. The effects of the ILO's strategy were ambiguous. The former French colonies in Africa introduced or maintained the French-style system of family allowances; African countries with a British colonial past continued their social services system (of a Beveridgian descent); but in Latin American countries integrated social insurance systems were formed only very slowly.[60] In the 1950s, the ILO gave up its unsuccessful strategy of globalizing the Western model and instead suggested a course of regionalization by founding several non-European regional offices, not least after being pressured by the non-Western member countries.[61] Crucially, these offices were not just agents of the ILO policy of globalizing European welfare state models. In contrast, they reflected the global discourse, initiated at the ILO headquarters in Geneva, from their regional perspective. The effect was that the debates in the regional offices did shift from a European agenda to the regionally specific problems of social and welfare policy.[62] Instead of the proliferation of the European welfare model, we can instead observe a provincialization of the eurocentric debates. The regionalization of ILO offices indeed ended in the formation of a European office in 1967, in order to deal with the European-specific dimensions of welfare policy. Significantly, the European office saw itself not as a promotion agency for the European path in welfare history any more but – a significant shift – began critically to examine the deficiencies of the European welfare model, such as the social security of migrants (conference in 1972) or the lack of integration of the agrarian population into the European social security systems (conference in 1970). Tellingly, both topics were raised by Southern European countries, whose societies were still heavily marked by an agrarian sector (mainly in the southern regions). The welfare systems of those countries typically privileged the population of the northern, more industrialized regions against the agrarian south – a typical feature of the 'southern model' of the welfare state and the reason for those governments to intervene at the ILO.[63] This example shows that the process of globalization of the European welfare model, as intended by the ILO in the early post-war period, backfired and resulted in a critique of the eurocentric approaches of the ILO as well as a self-critical view of the European model itself.[64]

The third mechanism of integration operated on a social level. International organizations such as the ILO offered their staff a stepping-stone for a further career on a national or a European level. Thus, national, international and supranational institutions were – in a collective biographical sense – closely intertwined. Adrien Tixier, for example, worked in the 1920s and 1930s on several posts for the ILO, among them as secretary of the ISSA. In 1944 he took over the position of interior minister for the provisional government of De Gaulle in London. In this function he designed, together with Pierre Laroque, the director general for social security, the introduction of the French Sécurité sociale of the fourth republic.[65] Similar figures can be found in other national contexts. The German Helmut Lehman, president of the Association of German Sickness Funds (Hauptverband deutscher Krankenkassen) in the Weimar period, was a driving figure behind the foundation of the precursor of the ISSA and held several minor posts in the ILO from the mid-1920s. After the Second World War, Lehmann pursued his career in the German Democratic Republic, ultimately becoming president of the Eastern German social insurance system in the 1950s (1950–9). A final example for the significance of these networks between national and international organizations is Richard Titmuss, one of the founding fathers of modern welfare studies and professor at the London School of Economics. Titmuss too was active in the ISSA, parallel to his academic obligations. He was a founding member of the first permanent research group of the ISSA on social security, established in 1967.[66]

Concluding Remarks

This chapter has shown that the influence of international expert networks, as institutionalized in international organizations like the Congress of Actuaries or the International Labour Office, on national social policymaking and the development of national welfare systems is multilayered and ambivalent. On the institutional and organizational level most policies of convergence, brought forward by internationalist actors, failed or were thwarted by national actors. However, international expert bodies were quite influential in shaping the state of the art of technical debates, the epistemic framework of national social policy actors as well as the *Zeitgeist* of welfare policies. On this qualitative level of technical skills, strategic policies and key interpretive concepts, international organizations formed a crucial platform for the interaction of academic experts and national policy actors.

Thus, for example, the ILO and the ISSA were not only effective in defining international technical standards for the management of national welfare systems; they also shaped the perception of welfare policies, for example by coding modern systems of social security in the 1950s and 1960s as a European phenomenon or by defining the framework for a common understanding of a crisis of the European welfare model in the 1970s. Similar conclusions can be drawn from the second case study. The themes and arguments at the Congress of Actuaries indicate that the international debates indeed played the role of a trendsetter for national policymakers as well as for business and social insurance executives. In particular, in technical fields such as the design of mortality tables or the development of mathematical statistics to calculate certain risk potentials, the Congress of Actuaries was the most important platform for the international insurance community to develop universally valid standards and agreements. However, the influence of international discourses on the national level was limited by institutional obstacles or the extraordinary course of historic events. Institutionally, the more or less interventionist traditions of welfare and insurance policies often proved stronger than the homogenizing ambitions of the congress. Thus, the legal gap between the liberal supervisory legislation in Britain and the interventionist regulation in Switzerland, Germany and other states was not reduced, despite all efforts by the participants of the congresses. Furthermore, both world wars and the increased national antagonisms around these years were able to disrupt the continuity of the international debates. The two interruptions came precisely at moments in which the national policy debates were particularly intense, and were usually followed by a fundamental change of course in the development of national welfare legislation. In these crucial moments for the shaping of national welfare systems, the international congresses were momentarily suspended and had no chance to intervene on the national level.

Annex

Tables 9.2–7: Participants at the International Congress of Actuaries, 1895–1952.[67] Note that the 1941 congress was not held because of the ongoing war. The congresses of Lucerne in 1941 and Scheveningen in 1951 only published general information about participants without any data on professional background.

Table 9.2: Total Participants at the International Congress of Actuaries, 1895–1952.

Year	Total
1895	c. 300
1898	c. 400
1900	455
1903	c. 600
1906	c. 1,180
1909	c. 1,260
1912	c. 1,340
1927	c. 1,350
1930	c. 1,080
1934	c. 1,160
1937	c. 1,260
1941	–
1951	c. 1,050

Table 9.3: German Participants at the International Congress of Actuaries, 1895–1952.

Year	Total	Private companies	Friendly Societies (Hilfskassen)	Government Authorities	Unknown
1895	20	17	2	0	1
1898	20	14	0	2	4
1900	41	34	0	4	3
1903	34	20	0	10	4
1906	349	225	4	92	28
1909	177	131	11	19	16
1912	129	93	1	17	18
1927	47	31	0	13	3
1930	44	34	0	9	1
1934	59	31	1	16	11
1937	61	43	0	14	4
1941	10	–	–	–	–
1951	49	–	–	–	–

Table 9.4: French Participants at the International Congress of Actuaries, 1895–1952.

Year	Total	Private Companies	Friendly Societies (mutualités)	Government Authorities	Unknown
1895	25	15	4	4	1
1898	47	32	1	10	4
1900	63	39	3	14	7
1903	58	41	3	11	3
1906	77	62	3	8	4
1909	64	38	2	8	16
1912	62	45	0	13	4
1927	76	67	3	4	2
1930	72	60	1	9	2
1934	85	66	9	8	2
1937	184	149	6	24	5
1941	5	–	–	–	–
1951	73	–	–	–	–

Table 9.5: British Participants at the International Congress of Actuaries, 1895–1952.

Year	Total	Private Companies	Friendly Societies	Government Authorities	Unknown
1895	13	12	0	0	1
1898	178	159	3	2	14
1900	108	88	1	1	18
1903	176	153	2	1	20
1906	153	135	0	1	17
1909	171	158	3	2	8
1912	170	151	3	4	12
1927	522	417	7	32	66
1930	88	78	2	1	7
1934	124	88	6	3	27
1937	141	127	0	3	11
1941	10	–	–	–	–
1951	190	–	–	–	–

Table 9.6: Swiss Participants at the International Congress of Actuaries, 1895–1952.

Year	Total	Private Companies	Friendly Societies	Government Authorities	Unknown
1895	4	2	0	1	1
1898	5	3	0	1	1
1900	10	5	0	5	0
1903	8	4	0	4	0
1906	25	13	0	9	3
1909	17	8	1	7	1
1912	20	11	0	7	2
1927	38	27	0	11	0
1930	35	26	1	6	2
1934	55	30	1	17	7
1937	67	48	0	17	2
1941	13	–	–	–	–
1951	49	–	–	–	–

Table 9.7: Total of German, French, British and Swiss Participants at the International Congress of Actuaries, 1895–1952.

Year	Total	Private Companies	Friendly Societies	Government Authorities	Unknown
1895	61	46	6	5	4
1898	250	208	4	15	23
1900	222	166	4	24	28
1903	276	218	5	26	27
1906	604	435	7	110	52
1909	429	335	17	36	41
1912	381	300	4	41	36
1927	683	542	10	60	71
1930	239	198	4	25	12
1934	323	215	17	44	47
1937	453	367	6	58	22
1941	38	–	–	–	–
1951	361	–	–	–	–

NOTES

Pearson, 'Introduction'

1. R. E. Wright and G. D. Smith, *Mutually Beneficial: The Guardian and Life Insurance in America* (New York: New York University Press, 2004), pp. 3–6.
2. G. Bankoff, 'Dangers to Going it Alone: Social Capital and the Origins of Community Resilience in the Philippines', *Continuity and Change*, 22 (2007), pp. 327–55.
3. An argument famously mooted by Ulrich Beck in his *Risikogesellschaft: Auf dem Weg in eine andere Moderne* (Frankfurt am Main: Suhrkamp, 1986).
4. G. Clark, *Betting on Lives: The Culture of Life Insurance in England, 1695–1775* (Manchester: Manchester University Press, 1999); V. A. Zelizer, *Morals and Markets: The Development of Life Insurance in the United States* (New York: Columbia University Press, 1979); T. Alborn, *Regulated Lives: Life Insurance and British Society, 1800–1914* (Toronto: University of Toronto Press, 2009); K. Horstman, *Public Bodies, Private Lives: The Historical Construction of Life Insurance, Health Risks and Citizenship in the Netherlands, 1880–1920* (Rotterdam: Erasmus, 2001).
5. The classic work is M. Douglas and A. Wildavsky, *Risk and Culture: An Essay on the Selection of Technological and Environmental Dangers* (Berkeley, CA: University of California Press, 1982). See also P. Slovic and E. Peters, 'The Importance of Worldviews in Risk Perception', *Risk, Decision and Policy*, 3 (1998), pp. 165–70; K. Dake, 'Myths of Nature: Culture and the Social Construction of Risk', *Journal of Social Issues*, 48 (1992), pp. 21–37.
6. Z. Kang, 'Assurances moderne en Chine: Une continuité interrompue (1801–1949)', *Risques*, 31 (1997), pp. 103–20.
7. W. Rohrbach, 'Von den Anfängen bis zum Börsenkrach des Jahres 1873', in W. Rohrbach (ed.), *Versicherungsgeschichte Österreichs*, 3 vols (Vienna: Holzhausen, 1988), vol. 1, pp. 46–432, on p. 74.
8. M. Ruffat, 'French Insurance from the *Ancien Régime* to 1946: Shifting Frontiers between State and Market', *Financial History Review*, 10 (2003), pp. 185–200, on p. 187.
9. Rohrbach, 'Von den Anfängen bis zum Börsenkrach', pp. 172–9.
10. Ibid., pp. 234–9.
11. C. Kingston, 'Marine Insurance in Britain and America, 1720–1844: A Comparative Institutional Analysis', *Journal of Economic History*, 67 (2007), pp. 379–409.
12. On the rise of the composites in the UK, see H. E. Raynes, *A History of British Insurance*, 2nd edn (London: Pitman, 1964), ch. 21.
13. R. Pearson, 'Towards an Historical Model of Financial Services Innovation: The Case of the Insurance Industry 1700–1914', *Economic History Review*, 50 (1997), pp. 235–56.

14. *Insurance Critic*, 1 (1895), p. 19; 6 (1895), p. 195.
15. R. Pearson, 'Insurance: An Historical Overview', in J. Mokyr (ed.), *The Oxford Encyclopedia of Economic History*, 5 vols (New York: Oxford University Press, 2003), vol. 3, pp. 83–7.
16. T. W. Guinnane and J. Streb, 'Moral Hazard in a Mutual-Health Insurance System: The German *Knappschaften*, 1867–1914', Economics Working Paper 70 (Yale University, 2009); Rohrbach, 'Von den Anfängen bis zum Börsenkrach', pp. 65–7.
17. Clark, *Betting on Lives*, pp. 13–16; Ruffat, 'French Insurance from the *Ancien Régime* to 1946', p. 188.
18. Clark, *Betting on Lives*, p. 77.
19. B. Supple, *The Royal Exchange Assurance: A History of British Insurance 1720–1970* (Cambridge: Cambridge University Press, 1970); B. Drew, *The London Assurance: A Second Chronicle* (London: London Assurance, 1949).
20. Clark, *Betting on Lives*, pp. 114–27.
21. Supple, *The Royal Exchange Assurance*, pp. 131, 220.
22. Alborn, *Regulated Lives*, p. 20.
23. P. Borscheid, 'Vertrauensgewinn und Vertrauensverlust: Das Auslandsgeschäft der Deutschen Versicherungswirtschaft 1870–1945', *Vierteljahrschrift für Sozial- und Wirtschaftsgeschichte*, 88 (2001), pp. 311–45, on p. 317.
24. L. Arps, *Auf Sicheren Pfeilern: Deutsche Versicherungswirtschaft vor 1914* (Göttingen: Vandenhoeck & Ruprecht, 1965), pp. 24–30.
25. Rohrbach, 'Von den Anfängen bis zum Börsenkrach', pp. 145–52, 221.
26. F. Büchner, 'Die Entstehung der Hamburger Feuerkasse und ihre Entwicklung bis zur Mitte des 19. Jahrhunderts', in Hamburger Feuerkasse, *300 Jahre Hamburger Feuerkasse* (Karlsruhe: Verlag Versicherungswirtschaft, 1976), pp. 1–50, on pp. 4–13.
27. The regulations of 1676, *Punkta der General Feur-Ordnungs Cassa*, are reproduced in Hamburger Feuerkasse, *300 Jahre Hamburger Feuerkasse*, pp. 114–24.
28. On the diffusion of German public fire associations, see P. Borscheid, *275 Jahre Feuersozietäten in Westfalen: Vorprung durch Erfahrung* (Münster: Westfälische Provinzial-Versicherungen, 1997).
29. M. Lönnborg, *Internationalisering av svenska försäkringsbolag* (Uppsala: Uppsala University, 1999), p. 56.
30. A primitive risk classification was introduced by the Hamburger Feuercasse in 1753, and later by other associations.
31. Ruffat, 'French Insurance from the *Ancien Régime* to 1946', pp. 188–91.
32. Rohrbach, 'Von den Anfängen bis zum Börsenkrach', pp. 215–16, 221–3.
33. Arps, *Auf Sicheren Pfeilern* pp. 186–8.
34. Ibid., pp. 81–98.
35. R. Pearson, *Insuring the Industrial Revolution: Fire Insurance in Great Britain, 1700–1850* (Aldershot: Ashgate, 2004), pp. 21–30.
36. US figures from D. Armstrong, 'A History of the Property Insurance Business in the United States prior to 1890' (DPhil. dissertation, New York University, 1971), tables VII, VIII, pp. 72–4. I have taken Armstrong's figures as the most comprehensive count. Figures are lower in other sources, for example, the *Statistical Abstract of the United States* (1937), table 299, p. 275, records 580 companies earning $143m net premiums from fire and marine insurance in 1890. Without reworking the original figures state by state – a major task – it is impossible to reconcile these differences at present.

37. D. Baranoff, 'Principals, Agents and Control in the American Fire Insurance Industry, 1799–1872', *Business and Economic History*, 27 (1998), pp. 91–101.

38. *Assecuranz Jahrbuch*, 16 (1895), p. 368.

39. P. G. T. Hägg, 'The Institutional Analysis of Insurance Regulation: The Case of Sweden' (PhD dissertation, University of Lund, 1998), table 14.

40. *Assecuranz Jahrbuch*, 34 (1913), p. 344.

41. *Assecuranz Jahrbuch*, 10 (1889), p. 407; 14 (1893), p. 404.

42. *Assecuranz Jahrbuch*, 1 (1880), pp. 153, 158.

43. *Assecuranz Jahrbuch*, 10 (1889), p. 278. Gesellschaft fuer Feuerversicherungsgeschichtliche Forschung e.v., *Das Deutsche Feuerversicherungswesen*, 2 vols (Hanover: Staats- und Sozialwiss. Verlag, 1913), vol. 2, table XIII, p. 590.

44. *Insurance Times*, 17 (1884), p. 106; *Post Magazine*, 35 (1874), p. 54; *12th Annual Report of the New York Insurance Superintendent for 1870*, part 1 (New York, 1871). In 1900 the surviving seven New York mutuals insured $37m against fire, compared to 55 stock companies that together insured $55bn. D. Baranoff, 'A Policy of Cooperation: The Cartelisation of American Fire Insurance, 1873–1906', *Financial History Review*, 10 (2003), pp. 119–36, on p. 133.

45. *Post Magazine*, 31 (1870), p. 235; I. MacPherson, 'The Origins of Cooperative Insurance on the Prairies', *Business and Economic History*, 26 (1977), pp. 76–87.

46. C. Trebilcock, *Phoenix Assurance and the Development of British Insurance*, 2 vols (Cambridge: Cambridge University Press, 1985–98), vol. 1, pp. 162–267.

47. Ibid., vol. 1, pp. 251–63; Pearson, *Insuring the Industrial Revolution*, pp. 157, 159, 184.

48. B. Supple, 'Insurance in British History', in O. M. Westall (ed.), *The Historian and the Business of Insurance* (Manchester: Manchester University Press, 1984), pp. 1–8, on p. 6.

49. Rohrbach, 'Von den Anfängen bis zum Börsenkrach', pp. 225–8.

50. *Assecuranz Jahrbuch*, 1 (1880), pp. 18–23.

51. R. Pearson, 'The Development of Reinsurance Markets in Europe during the Nineteenth Century', *Journal of European Economic History*, 24 (1995), pp. 557–71.

52. P. G. M. Dickson, *The Sun Insurance Office, 1760–1960* (Oxford: Oxford University Press, 1960), p. 192.

53. *Assecuranz Jahrbuch*, 19 (1898), p. 405.

54. *Assecuranz Jahrbuch*, 27 (1906), p. 328. For the critical comments, see also 23 (1902), pp. 369–70; 26 (1905), pp. 332–40.

55. R. Pearson and M. Lönnborg, 'Regulatory Regimes and Multinational Insurers before 1914', *Business History Review*, 82 (2008), pp. 59–86, in table 4.

56. *Insurance Times*, 13 (1880), p. 166.

57. Pearson and Lönnborg, 'Regulatory Regimes', tables 2 and 3.

58. Rohrbach, 'Von den Anfängen bis zum Börsenkrach', pp. 290–7.

59. *Insurance Critic*, 17 (1889), p. 124; 18 (1890), p. 217; *Insurance Times*, 23 (1890), pp. 573–4. The chronology of entry to the US is from United States Congress, Bureau of the Census, *Insurance Report* (Washington, DC, 1890), table 1.

60. Pearson, *Insuring the Industrial Revolution*, tables 1.3, 1.5.

61. 'Net' premiums are net of reinsurance. It is probable, though not entirely clear from the sources, that premiums include premiums earned abroad as well as at home for companies in these countries. Only in the case of Britain in 1900 and 1912, and Germany in 1910, is it certain that they do. All data exclude premiums earned by foreign companies in these countries. Germany's figure for 1851 includes stock companies only. German data

for other years include premium earnings by public and private mutual as well as stock companies. The French figure for 1850 includes an estimate for premiums earned by French mutuals, calculated by applying the average premium yield earned by French stock companies that year to the total sum insured by French mutuals. The result suggests that mutuals earned 36 per cent of the amount of premiums earned by stock companies that year. A similar calculation for 1889 suggests that this proportion had fallen by then to 10 per cent. These are the only two estimates we can make at present for French mutuals. The French data for 1882–1912 thus include an allowance of 10 per cent to account for earnings by mutuals. British premiums for 1850 have been aggregated from internal company accounts and include an estimate for missing data, as described in Pearson, *Insuring the Industrial Revolution*, appendix B. British and French population figures relate to 1851, 1881, 1901 and 1911; German relate to 1852, 1880, 1900 and 1910; Japanese relate to 1900 and 1910; US relate to 1850, 1880, 1900 and 1910. Currency conversion rates used: £1 = 7 Prussian taler = 20 Reichsmark = 25 francs = $4.86 = ¥10. Sources: *Assurance Magazine* (1853); *Assecuranz Jahrbuch*, 1–35 (1880–1914); *Post Magazine*, 44 (1883), 74 (1913); *Australian Insurance and Banking Review*, 24 (1900), p. 714; Armstrong, 'A History of the Property Insurance Business in the United States', table VIII; US Congress, Census, *Insurance Report*, table 7, p. 487; *Statistical Abstract of the United States* (1937), table 299, p. 275. B. R. Mitchell, *International Historical Statistics: Europe 1750–1993* (London: Macmillan, 1998), table A1; B. R. Mitchell, *International Historical Statistics: The Americas, 1750–2000* (London: Macmillan, 2003), tables A1, J1; B. R. Mitchell, *International Historical Statistics – Africa, Asia and Oceania 1750–1993*, 3rd edn (London: Macmillan, 1998), tables A1, J1; B. R. Mitchell, *Abstract of British Historical Statistics* (Cambridge: Cambridge University Press, 1962), p. 6.

62. Alborn, *Regulated Lives*, p. 30.
63. M. Wilkins, *The Emergence of Multinational Enterprise: American Business Abroad from the Colonial Era to 1914* (Cambridge, MA: Harvard University Press, 1970), pp. 64–5.
64. Supple, *The Royal Exchange Assurance*, pp. 223–4, 276. The Equitable and the New York Life, together with another US office, the Germania Life, accounted for 40 per cent of life premiums earned in Spain in 1912. This figure declined to 19 per cent by 1921, then collapsed to less than 1 per cent by the 1930s. J. Pons Pons, 'Las Empresas Extranjeras en el Seguro Español ante el Aumento del Nacionalismo Económico (1912–1940)', in J. Pons Pons and M. A. Pons Brías (eds), *Investigaciones Históricas sobre el Seguro Español* (Madrid: Fundación Mapfre, 2010), pp. 191–226, in table 7.3.
65. Calculated from *Assecuranz Jahrbuch*, 35 (1914), p. 426.
66. Borscheid, 'Vertrauensgewinn und Vertrauensverlust', figs 5, 6.
67. Original Reichsmark figures converted at £1/RM 20. Source: adapted from Arps, *Auf Sicheren Pfeilern*, p. 142.
68. Alborn, *Regulated Lives*, pp. 51–2.
69. *Sigma*, 9 (2000), table VII.
70. R. Pearson, 'Growth, Crisis and Change in the Insurance Industry: A Retrospect', *Accounting, Business and Financial History*, 12 (2002), pp. 1–18.
71. J. Cantwell, 'A Survey of Theories in International Production', in C. N. Pitelis and R. Sugden (eds), *The Nature of the Transnational Firm* (London: Routledge, 1991), pp. 16–63.
72. *Post Magazine*, 42 (1881).
73. M. K. Erramilli, 'The Experience Factor in Foreign Market Entry Behaviour of Service Firms', *Journal of International Business Studies*, 4 (1991), pp. 479–501.

74. G. Jones, 'British Multinationals and British Business since 1850', in M. W. Kirby and M. B. Rose (eds) *Business Enterprise in Modern Britain: From the Eighteenth to the Twentieth Century* (London and New York: Routledge, 1994), pp. 172–206.

75. Dickson, *The Sun Insurance Office*, pp. 226–30.

76. J. Johanson and J.-E. Vahlne, 'The Internationalization Process of the Firm. A Model of Knowledge Development and Increasing Foreign Market Commitments', *Journal of International Business Studies*, 8 (1977), pp. 23–32; K. Eriksson, J. Johanson, A. Majkgard and D. D. Sharma, 'Experiential Knowledge and Cost in the Internationalisation Process', *Journal of International Business Studies*, 28 (1997), pp. 337–60.

77. Borscheid, 'Vertrauensgewinn und Vertrauensverlust', fig. 3c.

78. P. Borscheid, 'A Globalisation Backlash in the Inter-War Period?', in P. Borscheid and R. Pearson (eds), *Internationalisation and Globalisation of the Insurance Industry in the Nineteenth and Twentieth Centuries* (Marburg: Philipps-University, 2007), pp. 129–41.

79. J. L. García-Ruiz and L. Caruana, 'The Internationalisation of the Business of Insurance in Spain, 1939–2005', in Borscheid and Pearson (eds), *Internationalisation and Globalisation of the Insurance Industry*, pp. 66–83, in table 2.

80. B. Gales, 'Odds and Ends: the Problematic First Wave of Internationalisation in Dutch Insurance during the late Nineteenth and early Twentieth Centuries', in Borscheid and Pearson (eds), *Internationalisation and Globalisation of the Insurance Industry*, pp. 84–111, on p. 87.

81. Pearson and Lönnborg, 'Regulatory Regimes'.

82. J. S. Zappino, *El Instituto Mixto Argentino de Reaseguros: La Formación de un Mercado Nacional de Seguro, 1946–1952* (Buenos Aires: Ediciones Cooperativas, 2007).

83. J. Pons Pons, 'Multinational Enterprises and Institutional Regulation in the Life Insurance Market in Spain, 1880–1935', *Business History Review*, 82 (2008), pp. 87–114.

84. Borscheid, 'Vertrauensgewinn und Vertrauensverlust', pp. 332–4.

85. *Chartered Insurance Institute Journal* (March 1998), pp. 18–20.

86. *Sigma*, 9 (2000), tables III, VIII.

87. See, for example, H. Berghoff and J. Sydow (eds), *Unternehmerische Netzwerke: Eine Historische Organisationsform mit Zukunft?* (Stuttgart: Kohlhammer, 2007); M. Maclean, C. Harvey and J. Press, *Business Elites and Corporate Governance in France and the UK* (Basingstoke: Palgrave Macmillan, 2006).

1 Llorca-Jaña, 'The Marine Insurance Market for British Textile Exports'

I am very grateful to Prof. Philip L. Cottrell, Prof. Robin Pearson, Prof. Marcello Carmagnani, Prof. Huw V. Bowen, Dr Rory Miller, Prof. Herbert Klein, Dr Bernard Attard, Dr Marc Latham and to the ESRC (PTA-030-2005-00308).

1. The term Southern Cone refers to the modern countries of Argentina, Uruguay and Chile.

2. Source: M. Llorca-Jaña, 'British Textile Exports to the Southern Cone during the first half of the Nineteenth Century: Growth, Structure and the Marketing Chain' (PhD dissertation, University of Leicester, 2008), p. 33.

3. This is also the case for other markets in the Americas. For instance, N. Buck, in his most famous work, decided 'to ignore such topics as insurance'. *The Development of the Organisation of Anglo-American Trade, 1800–1850* (New Haven, CT: Yale University

Press, 1925), p. 1. As far as I am aware, the only work dealing with the development of European marine insurance premiums to South America during the first half of the nineteenth century is that of P. Schöller, 'L'évolution séculaire des taux de fret et d'assurance maritimes 1819–1940', *Bulletin de l'Institute de recherches économiques et sociales*, 17 (1951), pp. 519–57. Another work would be J. T. Danson, *Our Next War in its Commercial Aspect, with some Account of the Premiums Paid at 'Lloyd's' from 1805 to 1816* (London: Blades, East & Blades, 1894), but it only covers a few years of our period of study.

4. Llorca-Jaña, 'British Textile Exports to the Southern Cone', p. 41.

5. F. M. Martin, *The History of Lloyd's and of Marine Insurance in Great Britain* (London: Macmillan, 1876), p. 95. See also 'Report from the Select Committee on Marine Insurance, 1810', *British Parliamentary Papers*, VII:298 (1824), pp. 1–11, on pp. 2–3.

6. H. A. L. Cockerell and E. Green, *The British Insurance Business, 1547–1970* (London: Heinemann Educational, 1976), p. 5.

7. J. R. McCulloch, *A Dictionary, Practical, Theoretical, and Historical of Commerce and Commercial Navigation* (London: Longman, Brown & Green, 1852). In 1810, it is estimated that private underwriters were responsible for 90 per cent of all marine insurance, mainly effected at Lloyd's coffee house. Martin, *The History of Lloyd's*, p. 101. See also Kingston, 'Marine Insurance in Britain and America', pp. 379, 384–5.

8. 'Report from the Select Committee on Marine Insurance', p. 6. For a new interpretation of why the two chartered corporations failed to dominate the British marine insurance market, see Kingston, 'Marine Insurance in Britain and America', pp. 385–8. According to Kingston the two chartered corporations faced a 'lemons' problem. That is, Lloyd's had superior access to risk-related information than the companies (pp. 397–9). See also A. H. John, 'The London Assurance Company and the Marine Insurance Market of the Eighteenth Century', *Economica*, n.s. 25 (1958), pp. 126–41, on p. 127.

9. Cockerell and Green, *The British Insurance Business*, p. 6. Furthermore, 'there were a number of friendly associations established among shipowners for the mutual insurance of their ships. Whether these were illegal, as the Select Committee implied, or not, they seem to have been fairly strong in the north of England.' Raynes, *A History of British Insurance*, p. 180.

10. Raynes, *A History of British Insurance*, p. 171. Indeed, Stewart & Wilson, Scottish supplier of textiles for the famous London house of Huth & Co., with branches in South America, used to effect marine insurances with Huth & Co. at London but, not unexceptionally, used the services of Black & Wingate at Glasgow. For an example, see Huth & Co., London, to Stewart & Wilson, Glasgow, 2 December 1837, Huth & Co. Papers, English Letters, University College London, Special Collections [hereafter HPEL], vol. 18. Likewise, the British mercantile house of Wylie & Hancock, with branches in Brazil and the River Plate, used underwriters in London, Liverpool and Glasgow for its textile exports to South America during the early 1810s. For an example, see Wylie, Manchester, to Dalglish, Glasgow, 14 January 1812, Wylie & Co. Papers, University of Glasgow Archives [hereafter UGD], 28/1/3.

11. Cockerell and Green, *The British Insurance Business*, p. 7.

12. Huth & Co., London, to Stansfeld, Manchester, 20 April 1829, HPEL, vol. 3.

13. For example, see Huth & Co., London, to Marine Insurance & Co., London, 26 February 1849, HPEL, vol. 59. For other merchants, it is worth mentioning that the cargoes of Hodgson & Robinson, British merchants at Buenos Aires, were insured with the London-based Indemnity Insurance Company and the Liverpool Marine Assurance

Company. Likewise, Lupton & Co., merchants of Leeds exporting to South America, used the services of Jameson & Aders, T. W. Stansfeld and E. Durant & Co. to effect insurances at Lloyd's and also insured with the Royal Exchange Assurance. For an example, see Lupton & Co., Leeds, to Luptons & Luccock, Rio de Janeiro, 4 and 6 March 1811, William Lupton & Co. Papers, Brotherton Library, University of Leeds [hereafter WLP], vol. 5; Lupton & Co., Leeds, to Luptons & Luccock, Rio de Janeiro, 3 October 1811, WLP, vol. 6. Finally, Hancock & Wylie used the services of brokers such as George Johnston & Co. and Thomas Rodie & Co. For an example, see Wylie, Manchester, to Dalglish, Glasgow, 14 January 1812, UGD/28/1/3.

14. This was also the rate charged by Gibbs & Sons, also London merchants exporting to South America. For an example, see Gibbs & Sons, London, to branches at Lima, Valparaiso, Arequipa and Tacna, 10 February 1854, Antony Gibbs & Sons Papers, Guildhall Library, MS 11471-1, Despatch N-213.

15. Sixteen volumes in total, available at the National Archives (Kew, Surrey), FO 307.

16. A typical textile cargo from Liverpool to Valparaiso had a value of between £15,000 and £60,000. See, for example, 'Abstract of shipments to Valparaiso', 1840, FO 132/18. If underwriters were taking just £100–£200 each, then the whole textile cargo was insured by dozens of individuals. Indeed, as early as 1801, the number of subscribers at Lloyd's was more than 2,000. Kingston, 'Marine Insurance in Britain and America', p. 389. Underwriters taking little risk in marine insurances is a practice that dates from medieval times. See F. Edler de Roover, 'Early Examples of Marine Insurance', *Journal of Economic History*, 5 (1945), pp. 172–200, on pp. 187–8.

17. Huth & Co., London, to Halliday, Sanquhar, 8 August 1831, HPEL, vol. 8.

18. Huth & Co., London, to Huth & Co., Liverpool, 29 November 1843, HPEL, vol. 40.

19. Huth Papers, Guildhall Library, MS 10700-5. See in particular loose papers relating to Roux.

20. Huth & Co., London, to Huth & Co., Liverpool, 17 May 1843, HPEL, vol. 38.

21. Hugh Dallas Papers, Banco de la Provincia de Buenos Aires, Argentina. For examples, see MacIntosh, Miller & Co. to H. Dallas, 15 June 1818 and 11 November 1818.

22. As did Wildes, Pickersgill & Co. upon Hodgson's request. For some examples, see Hodgson, Buenos Aires, to Fielden Brothers, Manchester, 15 May 1841, Green, Hodgson and Robinson Papers, John Rylands Library, University of Manchester [hereafter GHR], 5/1/4; and Hodgson & Robinson, Buenos Aires, to Owens & Son, Manchester, 4 August 1837, GHR/5/1/6.

23. For instance, Zimmerman at Buenos Aires requested Huth's in London to insure cargoes of hides from the River Plate to Bremen. Huth & Co., London, to Zimmerman, Frazier & Co., Buenos Aires, 21 August 1829, HPEL, vol. 4. Even smaller houses than Huth & Co., such as Fielden Brothers & Co., also effected marine insurances in London for hide cargoes sent from Buenos Aires to New York. Hodgson, Buenos Aires, to Pickersgill, New York, 6 April 1842, GHR/5/1/8.

24. Llorca-Jaña, 'British Textile Exports to the Southern Cone', pp. 234–6.

25. Ibid., pp. 79–81.

26. In 1812, during the Napoleonic Wars, premiums from British ports to Buenos Aires were quoted at 12.5–18.8 per cent. Lupton & Co., Leeds, to McNeile & Co., Buenos Aires, 7 November 1812, WLP, vol. 9.

27. D. C. M. Platt, *Latin America and British Trade* (London: A. & C. Black, 1972), p. 55; V. B. Reber, 'Speculation and Commerce in Buenos Aires: The Hugh Dallas House, 1816–1820', *Business History*, 20 (1978), pp. 18–37, on p. 29.

28. In the words of a London merchant to his Liverpool branch: 'we have effected the insurances you order ... but cannot fix the premium until you state how the goods are packed'. Huth & Co., London, to Huth & Co., Liverpool, 27 August 1842, HPEL, vol. 35.

29. Huth & Co. wrote: 'our underwriters generally ask for a higher premium when the name of the ship is not given'. Huth & Co., London, to Rawson & Saltmarshe, Halifax, 20 September 1833, HPEL, vol. 12. In another case, Wylie wrote to his partner on the spot in these terms: 'your brother and I came down here last night ... [to] effect some insurances per Grace, which we find some difficulty in doing, the ship not being known here, nor in Lloyds book'. Wylie, Liverpool, to Hancock, Bahia, 14 February 1812, UGD/28/1/3.

30. Though probably exaggerating, Huth & Co. were of the opinion that when fixing the premium, underwriters paid more attention to the nature of the voyage than to the vessel's name. Huth & Co., London, to Huth & Co., Liverpool, 11 and 22 July 1843, HPEL, vol. 39.

31. In the 'Report from the Select Committee on Marine Insurance' it was reported that during the winter months 'a great number of underwriters withdraw from Lloyd's Coffee-House. The merchants ascribe this to a dislike to winter risks' (p. 7).

32. For instance, premiums at Lloyd's for shipments from Liverpool to Valparaiso in 1837 were 50 shillings per £100. Once the news of the war between Chile and Peru reached Britain, the premium went up to 90 shillings per £100. Llorca-Jaña, 'British Textile Exports to the Southern Cone', p. 215. Likewise, during the Napoleonic Wars, marine insurance premiums for cargoes from Britain to Buenos Aires were as high as 9.6 per cent (e.g. in 1813). In contrast, in 1816 the premium had been reduced to 2.28 per cent. Danson, *Our Next War*, pp. 90–1.

33. M. Hopkins, *A Manual of Marine Insurance* (London: Murray, 1867), pp. 202, 205, 208. See also Schöller, 'L'évolution séculaire des taux de fret', pp. 528–30.

34. Martin, *The History of Lloyd's*, p. 137; Llorca-Jaña, 'British Textile Exports to the Southern Cone', pp. 214–25.

35. Fielden Brothers reached the extreme of insuring some bales within a cargo, while other bales going in the same vessel were not insured at all. Fielden Brothers, Manchester, to Hodgson & Robinson, Buenos Aires, 20 January 1835, GHR/5/2/7. The business correspondence of these merchants does not allow us to extract further details about the nature of these bales. It could be the case, for example, that those goods uninsured were probably 'unsaleable' goods, or textiles that had remained in hand for a long period of time. They could also have been goods badly suited to the taste of the inhabitants of the River Plate, and upon which there was little hope of making a profit.

36. Source: Llorca-Jaña, 'British Textile Exports to the Southern Cone', p. 103.

37. See Hodgson & Robinson, Buenos Aires, to Owens & Son, Manchester, 10 June 1835, GHR/5/1/5; Crossley & Sons, Manchester, to Hodgson & Robinson, Buenos Aires, 3 June 1831, GHR/5/2/3; Crossley & Sons, Manchester, to Hodgson & Robinson, Buenos Aires, 18 January 1833, GHR/5/2/5.

38. Huth & Co., London, to Rawson, Halifax, 31 October 1832, HPEL, vol. 10.

39. Walker, Manchester, to Hodgson & Robinson, Buenos Aires, 9 July 1833, GHR/5/2/5; Broadbent, Manchester, to Hodgson & Robinson, Buenos Aires, 18 August 1836, GHR/5/2/8.

40. *British Packet*, 17 September 1842. As stated by Huth & Co.: 'no separation of packages being permitted in our Custom House ... our home market is mostly supplied from the auctions with goods but partially damaged'. Huth & Co., London, to Stansfeld, Leeds, 10 December 1835, HPEL, vol. 14.

41. Huth & Co., London, to Stansfeld, Leeds, 10 December 1835, HPEL, vol. 14. From 1817, Lloyd's decided to separate sound from damaged goods, as observed by Wright: 'in many ports it had hitherto been the custom to sell the entire contents of a package for the underwriters' account, although only a small part of it might have sustained damage; and the result of a forced sale in a bad market [at public auctions] was often a heavy loss to the underwriters'. C. Wright, *A History of Lloyd's* (London: Lloyd's, 1928), p. 284. This policy, however, was first implemented in the US and continental Europe, rather than in Latin American markets that had to wait longer.

42. The 'value is not mentioned ... value must be proved'. Martin, *The History of Lloyd's*, pp. 122–3.

43. The 'goods or property insured are valued at prime cost at the time of effecting the policy ... [the value] is agreed'. Ibid.

44. Campbell, Liverpool, to Hodgson & Robinson, Buenos Aires, 1 April 1834, GHR/5/2/6.

45. Huth & Co., George Faulkner, Thomas Broadbent and Owen Owens & Son, as a rule, insured for values between 10 per cent and 40 per cent over the invoice cost. For examples, see Faulkner, Manchester, to Hodgson & Robinson, Buenos Aires, 15 March 1834, GHR/5/2/6; Broadbent, Manchester, to Hodgson & Robinson, Buenos Aires, 15 March 1836, GHR/5/2/8; Broadbent, Manchester, to Hodgson & Robinson, Buenos Aires, 6 October 1832, GHR/5/2/4.

46. For some examples, see Huth & Co., London, to Webster & Sons, Morley-Leeds, 20 April 1829, HPEL, vol. 3; Huth & Co., London, to John Halliday, Sanquhar, 11 January 1831, HPEL, vol. 7.

47. McCulloch, *A Dictionary*, p. 715.

48. That is, 'that at the time of so sailing the said vessel was staunch and strong and had her hatches well and sufficiently caulked and covered and was well and properly manned, fitted and equipped for the performance of said voyage'. Chilean National Archives, Valparaiso Judicial Papers [hereafter ANCH-AJV], vol. 469-1: Valparaiso, 1834. See also vol. 73-19: Valparaiso, October 1833; vol. 77-10: Valparaiso, 1837; and vol. 91-22: Valparaiso, 1854.

49. To establish general averages, a commission was always appointed to undertake a survey. It usually comprised ships' captains, ship-builders and insurance companies or underwriters' agents. See ANCH-AJV, vol. 321-14: Valparaiso, April 1823. In this case the commission consisted of port surveyors of Lloyd's and the Marine Insurance Company of Hamburg, and a shipwright. See also vol. 73-19: Valparaiso, 1833, when the survey was conducted by four British masters. In another case, the survey was commissioned to a Lloyd's agent, a port surveyor, a master mariner and a master shipwright, all of whom were British (vol. 293-2: Valparaiso, November 1843).

50. For examples, see ANCH-AJV, vol. 73-19: Valparaiso, October 1833; vol. 75-1: Valparaiso, September 1835; vol. 91-21: Valparaiso, September 1854.

51. There were many issues in the legal processes required to declare general averages. To start with, the judge had to establish the real amount of money borrowed, the costs of repairs, the value of the ship, the value of the cargo, the income for freights, the monies given for passengers to pay for repairs, legal costs, consular stamps, expenses to feed crew as well as salaries while the ship was being repaired, and the value of the part of the cargo that had to be thrown away to save the ship (or jettison). Another, and more difficult, issue was establishing the market value of vessels after repairs and to compare this with its market value before the accident.

52. See, for instance, what happened to Huth, Gruning & Co. as consignees of a particular cargo. ANCH-AJV, vol. 77-10: Valparaiso, July 1837. See also vol. 77-12, and the case of the *Iceni*, in 'Bond of indemnity of British brig Iceni', 20 August 1834, National Archives, FO 446/4.

53. Figure 1.3 shows that, from the early 1850s, the index of Southern Cone's total imports (in volume) grew faster than Southern Cone's per capita consumption of British textiles. Before the early 1850s, British export prices of cottons, the main staple exported from Britain to the Southern Cone, declined continuously and markedly, but after the early 1850s export prices for cottons remained at a similar level. Llorca-Jaña, 'British Textile Exports to the Southern Cone', p. 211. Absolute growth of textile volumes exported by Britain from the 1850s to the 1870s was mainly due to an increase in population. In 1850, the population of the Southern Cone was some 2.7 million people, while in 1879 it was some 5.1 million people. Ibid., p. 65.

54. Before the 1820s, for textiles shipped from Liverpool to Rio de Janeiro (which had lower premiums than to Valparaiso), premiums quoted in WLP (vols 3–9) were 5.25 per cent in 1808, 4.5 per cent in 1809, 6–7 per cent in 1810–11, 5.25 per cent in early 1812 and 19 per cent in November 1812. During the years 1822–4 comparable rates for exports to continental Europe were 1.25–1.5 per cent.

55. Other variables also affected marine insurance premiums, in particular developments in shipping (which are treated below). It is believed, for instance, that in long hauls (e.g. Europe–South America), a material cause for the fall in premiums was the introduction of bigger and more secure vessels. Schöller, 'L'évolution séculaire des taux de fret', p. 530.

56. This integrated index of United Kingdom textile exports in volume was constructed with weighted averages of three individual indexes of quantum for cottons, wool manufactures and linens. The weights given each year to each textile branch were the associated shares cottons, wool manufactures and linens had in the value of United Kingdom exports to the Southern Cone for these three categories added together. Source: Llorca-Jaña, 'British Textile Exports to the Southern Cone', p. 299.

57. Source: ibid., p. 215.

58. Source: ibid., p. 216.

59. Another factor that may have contributed to a fall in marine insurance premiums was an increase in competition among marine insurers after new marine insurance companies entered into the market from 1824. Had this been the case, we would expect to see a general fall in marine insurance premiums for British textile exports to all markets. Premium data for cargoes from Britain to continental Europe, however, show that premium rates remained at a similar level before and after 1824 (between 1 and 1.25 per cent the invoice value of cargoes). Nevertheless, it is likely that there was not one marine insurance market for British textile exports, but many: a market for cargoes to nearby locations (e.g. continental Europe) and other markets for distant outlets, such as the Southern Cone. Consequently, it could still be the case that competition after 1824 pressed down on premium rates to distant markets (e.g. Chile), but I can find no evidence to confirm this.

2 Stadlin, 'Actuarial Practice, Probabilistic Thinking and Actuarial Science'

My special thanks go to Katja Trodella of the communications department at Zurich Financial Services for reviewing this paper. I thank also Thomas Antunes, head of the historical archive of Winterthur AXA, for his pieces of advice and for granting me access to relevant historical documents.

1. H. Bühlmann, 'The Actuary, the Role and Limitations of the Profession since the mid-Nineteenth Century', *Astin Bulletin*, 27 (1997), pp. 165–71, on p. 166.
2. Ibid., p. 168.
3. Most accounts of the history of non-life actuarial science start with the work of the Swedish mathematician Filip Lundberg on collective risk theory and stochastic processes published in the first decade of the twentieth century. Cf. H. Ammeter, 'Grundlagen und Hauptprobleme der Sachversicherungsmathematik', *Mitteilungen der Vereinigung schweizerischer Versicherungsmathematiker* 65 (1965), pp. 147–61; H. Ammeter, 'Die Entwicklung der Versicherungsmathematik im 20. Jahrhundert', *Mitteilungen der Vereinigung schweizerischer Versicherungsmathematiker* 70 (1970), pp. 317–32; S. Haberman, *Landmarks in the History of Actuarial Science (up to 1919)*, Actuarial Research Paper 84 (London: Department of Actuarial Science and Statistics, City University London, 1996).
4. An exception is English fire insurance where Pearson's *Insuring the Industrial Revolution* provides many insights at least for the period up to the mid-nineteenth century.
5. M. Gürtler, *Die Kalkulation der Versicherungsbetriebe* (Berlin: Mittler, 1936), p. xxxiv.
6. Ibid., pp. vi, xxxiv, 268, 288.
7. P. Bernstein, *Against the Gods: The Remarkable Story of Risk* (New York: Wiley, 1996), p. 225.
8. H. Fehlmann, 'Die Entwicklung der Unfallversicherung', in *Das Versicherungswesen in der Schweiz*, Sonderabdruck aus dem 'Bund' (Bern: Pochon-Jent, 1927), pp. 34–40, on p. 36.
9. The other core task is reserving. H. Bühlmann, 'The Actuary', *Insurance: Mathematics and Economics* (1992), pp. 223–8, on p. 226.
10. In this paper the term 'risk' has three different meanings: 1. the risk an insurance company underwrites, e.g. the risk to pay a certain sum in case the person x dies in a fatal accident. In this sense, 'risk' is also used as a substitute for the insured, as the insured is the reason why it exists; 2. the concrete risks for which an accident insurance company provides coverage in the form of pecuniary compensation, i.e. accidental death, permanent and temporary disability caused by an accident; 3. risk in the vague colloquial sense, such as the risk to travel by trains or a risk society. The term 'casualty insurance' is used synonymously with 'accident insurance'. The other branch of casualty insurance, which is liability, lies outside the scope of this paper.
11. The following is based on W. A. Dinsdale, *History of Accident Insurance in Great Britain* (London: Stone & Cox, 1954).
12. £1 = 20*s.* (shillings) = 240*d.* (pence).
13. Cited in D. Defert, '"Popular Life" and Insurance Technology', in G. Burchell, C. Gordon and P. Miller (eds), *The Foucault Effect: Studies in Governmentality* (Chicago, IL: University of Chicago Press, 1991), pp. 211–34, on p. 220.
14. E. Engel, 'Materialien zur Unfallversicherung', *Zeitschrift des Königlich Preussischen Statistischen Bureaus*, 7 (1867), pp. 171–85, on p. 183.

15. To apply the term of law to observable regularities of social events such as accidents can also be seen as an indication that the founders of Sécurité Générale were familiar with the discourse in contemporary statistical and social sciences. For these areas the Belgian statistician Quetelet had introduced the concept of social physics and laws. This meant, for example, discerning regularities in suicides and crimes by quantitative statistical investigation with the aim to discover the natural laws of social life. Cf. L. Krüger, L. Daston and M. Heidelberger (eds), *The Probabilistic Revolution*, 2 vols (Cambridge, MA: MIT Press, 1987), vol. 1; M. Lengwiler, *Risikopolitik im Sozialstaat: Die schweizerische Unfallversicherung 1870–1970* (Köln: Böhlau, 2006), pp. 87–91.

16. E. Engel, 'Die Unfallversicherung', *Zeitschrift des Königlich Preussischen Statistischen Bureaus*, 6 (1866), pp. 294–7, on p. 295.

17. Ibid.

18. Alte Berichte, Report 1883, Unternehmensarchiv Winterthur-AXA, Winterthur [hereafter Winterthur Archive], 691.102.299.304, p. 3.

19. The following is based on Engel, 'Die Unfallversicherung', p. 294.

20. The following is based on Engel, 'Materialien zur Unfallversicherung', pp. 171–3.

21. G. Zeuner, *Abhandlungen aus der Mathematischen Statistik* (Leipzig: A. Felix, 1869), pp. 138–9.

22. *Mathematical Investigations Regarding the Creation and Derivation of the Formulas to Calculate Net Premiums and Reserves for all Insurances Branches of the Swiss Rentenanstalt* (Zurich, 1861); *Mathematical Investigations Regarding the Creation and Derivation of the Formulas to Calculate the Profit Reserves and Profit Commissions for the Respective Insurance Branches of the Swiss Rentenanstalt* (Zurich, 1864); Schweizerische Lebensversicherungs- und Rentenanstalt Zürich, *Fünfundsiebzig Jahre Schweizerische Lebensversicherungs- und Rentenanstalt Zürich 1857–1932* (Zurich 1932), p. 16.

23. Schweizerische Lebensversicherungs- und Rentenanstalt Zürich, *Fünfundsiebzig Jahre*, p. 17.

24. Analytically, births are a continuous function of time, the number of births taking place at exactly the same point in time is indefinitely small. This in turn prohibits the mathematically exact definition of a large enough group of people required to research mortality laws in a definitive way. Zeuner, *Abhandlungen*, p. 3.

25. Ibid., pp. 95–6.

26. Ibid., pp. 178–9.

27. Ibid., p. 196.

28. Ibid., pp. 198–9.

29. Ibid., p. 204.

30. Ibid., pp. 205–6.

31. Arps, *Auf Sicheren Pfeilern*, p. 66.

32. Ibid., p. 69.

33. This account is based on the tariff booklets in the company's collection of printed materials in ZAZ 1738 Drucksachenbelege 1873–2008, Corporate Archives, Zurich Financial Services, Zurich [hereafter Zurich Archive].

34. In the annual report for 1879 and agent instructions of 1880 there are remarks invoking statistics as basis for rate-making, but they remain completely erratic. Ibid.

35. ZAZ 1601 Einzel-Berufs-Statistik 1889–1902, Zurich Archive.

36. ZAZ 672 Korrespondenz ausländischer Filialen mit dem Hauptsitz 1882–91, Zurich Archive.

37. ZAZ 704 Korrespondenz der Agentur Bellinzona mit dem Hauptsitz 1889–93, Zurich Archive.
38. ZAZ 588 Erinnerungen von A. L. Tobler 1941, Zurich Archive.
39. Zubler gave his account of this in a general introduction to the Zurich's French business that he wrote in 1924, as well as in his documentation on the French workmen's compensation business. Both reports are in ZAZ 997 Aufzeichnungen Zubler über Filiale in Paris mit Ergänzungen 1878–1955, Zurich Archive.
40. Ibid., Einführung ins französische Geschäft, p. 11.
41. Ibid., Frankreich Arbeiter – Versicherung, pp. 23–4.
42. Ibid.
43. A. von Sprecher, *75 Jahre 'Zürich': Band II – Aus der Werkstatt der 'Zürich', 1872–1947* (Zurich: Orell Füssli, 1948), p. 37.
44. J. Jung, *Die Winterthur: Eine Versicherungsgeschichte* (Zurich: NNZ-Verlag, 2000), pp. 159, 423.
45. Tarife ab 1876, Winterthur Archive, 691.101.205.301.
46. Jung, *Die Winterthur*, p. 322.
47. Ibid., n. 62.
48. H. Braun, *Geschichte der Lebensversicherung und der Lebensversicherungstechnik*, Veröffentlichungen des Deutschen Vereins für Versicherungswissenschaft 70, 2nd edn (Berlin: Duncker & Humblot, 1963), p. 404.
49. Cited in Jung, *Die Winterthur*, p. 326.
50. Tariff for whole life accident insurance of 1881, in Tarife ab 1876, Winterthur Archive, 691.101.205.301.
51. Alte Berichte, report of 1886, Winterthur Archive, 691.102.299.304, p. 3.
52. The following is based on Widmer's report, cited in Jung, *Die Winterthur*, pp. 63–5.
53. Ibid., p. 67.
54. Alte Berichte, report of 1883, Winterthur Archive, 691.102.299.304.
55. Ibid., p. 13.
56. Report of 1886, ibid., p. 1.
57. The following is based on the detailed description provided in the introduction of the report of 1891, ibid., pp. 4–6.
58. The following is entirely based on the reports of 1886, 1889 and 1891, ibid.
59. Report of 1889, ibid.
60. Report of 1901, ibid.
61. Defert, '"Popular Life" and Insurance Technology', p. 216.
62. Cf. note 15 above.
63. H. von Sprecher, *'Zürich': Die Gesellschaft in den Ersten Fünfzig Jahren ihres Bestehens 1872–1922* (Zurich: Buchdr. Berichthaus, 1923), p. 43.
64. Cf. Gürtler, *Die Kalkulation*, pp. 20–6.
65. A recent example is the application of extreme value theory and copula methodology to the valuation of derivative products. Cf. P. Embrechts, P., *Revisiting the Edge, Ten Years On*, Research Paper (Zurich: ETH Zurich, 2008); F. Salmon, 'Recipe for Disaster: The Formula that Killed Wall Street', *Wired Magazine* (2 February 2009).

3 Pons Pons, 'The Difficulties of Spanish Insurance Companies to Modernize'

1. A summary of the economic principles of the autarkic regime can be found in C. Barciela, 'Guerra Civil y Primer Franquismo (1936–1959)', in F. Comín, M. Hernández and E. Llopis (eds), *Historia Económica de España, Siglos X–XX* (Barcelona: Crítica, 2002), pp. 331–68, on p. 339. The majority of authors consider the autarkic period to last until approval of the stabilization plan in 1959. Autarky led to a significant balance of payment deficit. The stabilization plan was intended to correct this situation. Reforms were carried out which in the long term resulted in the internal and external deregulation and liberalization of the economy. The concept of 'Primer franquismo' is also used for this period, translated here as 'the first stage of the Francoist regime'.

2. A. Carreras and J. Tafunell, *Historia Económica de la España Contemporánea* (Madrid: Crítica, 2003), p. 278; Barciela, 'Guerra Civil', p. 339.

3. Foreign investments were regulated by the Ley de Ordenación y Defensa de la Industria Nacional of 24 November 1939. This law limited the participation of foreign capital in a company to a maximum of 25 per cent of the share capital. It also limited the method of capital participation and obliged representation of foreign capital on the boards of directors to be through Spanish nationals. This regulation, based on autarky, hardly changed until 1959. E. Martínez Ruiz, *El Sector Exterior durante la Autarquía: Una Reconstrucción de las Balanzas de Pagos de España (1940–1958)*, Estudios de Historia Económica 43 (Madrid: Banco de España, Servicio de Estudios, 2003), p. 99.

4. Its creation in August 1939 was a further step in a whole series of rules regulating international payments, including the Law of Monetary Crimes of June 1938. These laws made the repatriation of profits derived from productive activity more difficult, as these could only be exported with specific authorization.

5. For an account of the repercussions of the war on the insurance sector, as regards life insurance policyholders, claims, accident rates, etc., see M. Maestro, *Formación del Mercado Español de Seguros* (Madrid: INESE, 1993), pp. 63–8; and J. Garriguez and E. Maynes, *Dos Dictámenes sobre Liquidación de Pérdidas Sufridas por las Inversiones Afectas a las Reservas Matemáticas de los Seguros de Vida a Consecuencia de la Revolución Comunista Española* (Barcelona, 1940).

6. J. Pons Pons, 'Diversificación y Cartelización en el Seguro Español (1914–1935)', *Revista de Historia Económica*, 3 (2003), pp. 567–92; J. Pons Pons, 'Mutua General de Seguros (1907–2007): Cien Años de Historia del Seguro Español' (unpublished manuscript, 2007).

7. In this state-dependent trade unionism, of a vertical nature, employers and workers were incorporated in an apparent relation of equality, although this was belied in reality. Barciela affirms that while workers lost their class-based unions and were defenceless in industrial tribunals, employers maintained a certain autonomy within the system, which gradually increased with time. C. Barciela, 'Autarquía e Intervencionismo, 1939–1950', in C. Barciela, M. I. López, J. Melgarejo and J. M. Miranda, *La España de Franco (1939–1975): Economía* (Madrid: Síntesis, 2001), pp. 23–154, on p. 45.

8. The Syndicate was created on 12 July 1940 as a compulsory trade union organization. E. Valenzuela de Quinta, *Protagonistas del Mutualismo de Accidentes de Trabajo: 100 Años de Historia (1900–2000)* (Madrid: Asociación de Mutuas de Accidentes de Trabajo y Enfermedades Profesionales de la Seguridad Social, 2000). For the model of labour relations based on the National Syndicate, see Á. Soto Carmona, 'Rupturas y Continuidades

en las Relaciones Laborales del Primer Franquismo, 1938–1958', in C. Barciela (ed.), *Autarquía y Mercado Negro: El Fracaso Económico del Primer Franquismo, 1939–1958* (Barcelona: Crítica, 2003), pp. 217–45, on pp. 232–3.

9. *Boletín Oficial del Estado or Official State Gazette* [hereafter *BOE*], 16 December 1941.

10. The first to be created, in an exceptional manner, was the Confederación de Montepíos, Mutualidades y Entidades Gestoras y Colaboradoras de Previsión. This confederation had its origin in article 37 of the Regulation of 1943 and was constituted on 25 October 1947 by virtue of the Order of the Ministry of Labour of 8 July 1947. Valenzuela de Quinta, *Protagonistas del Mutualismo*, pp. 176–7.

11. For the internationalization of the insurance business in Spain at this stage, see García-Ruiz and Caruana, 'The Internationalisation of the Business of Insurance in Spain'; and for its legislative evolution and the historical problems of the sector, see J.-M. Guillem Mesado and J. Pons Pons, 'La Legislación en el Sector Asegurador (1935–1955): La Prolongación y Crecimiento de los Problemas Históricos del Sector', *Revista Española de Seguros*, 135 (2008), pp. 263–91.

12. Carreras and Tafunell, *Historia Económica*, p. 318.

13. La Estrella, *Medio Siglo del Seguro Privado Español* (Madrid, 1959).

14. This was the main argument used in the study of the insurance sector published by the company La Estrella in 1959, ibid.

15. *BOE*, 23 March 1944.

16. Guillem Mesado and Pons Pons, 'La Legislación', p. 288. On 18 February 1927 the initial capital established by the law of 14 May 1908 and the posterior regulation of 1912 was modified. In this case the share capital required of insurance companies was two million pesetas, with 25 per cent paid up, and for the commercial companies that operated in the branches of insurance of land and maritime transport, fire, accidents, hail and theft it was fixed at 2 million pesetas with a minimum paid-up capital of 750,000 pesetas. For the branches of sickness and plate glass only 50,000 pesetas of capital was required with a minimum 15,000 pesetas paid up. J. Pons Pons, 'Las Entidades Aseguradoras y la Canalización del Ahorro en España', *Revista Española de Seguros*, 115 (2003), pp. 337–58, on p. 339.

17. There were branches, such as industrial accident insurance, where for historical reasons the state had fostered the development of mutual institutions, J. Pons Pons, 'El Seguro de Accidentes de Trabajo en España: De la Obligación al Negocio (1900–1940)', *Investigaciones de Historia Económicas*, 4 (2006), pp. 77–100.

18. This period of heavy investment occurred in all economic sectors in general from 1939 to 1942 and was followed by a new boom from 1945 to 1947. E. Torres Villanueva, 'La Empresa en la Autarquía, 1939–1959. Iniciativa Pública versus Iniciativa Privada', in Barciela (ed.), *Autarquía y Mercado Negro*, pp. 169–216, on pp. 172–3.

19. Sources: Memoria Estadística del seguro privado del ejercicio (1951, 1960), Dirección General de Banca, Bolsa e inversions; Memoria Estadística del seguro privado del ejercicio (1970), Subdirección General de Seguros.

20. Factors established by Jiménez Arana and compiled in ibid., pp. 175–6.

21. For legislation on insurance between 1935 and 1955 and its influence on the prolongation and growth of historical problems in the sector, see Guillem Mesado and Pons Pons, 'La Legislación'.

22. J. Pons Pons, *El sector seguros en Baleares: Empresas y empresarios en los siglo XIX y XX* (Palma de Mallorca: El Tall, 1998).

23. Source: Memoria Estadística de Seguro (1951); *Revista del Sindicato Vertical del Seguro*, extraordinary edition (1961, 1971).

24. An example of this strategy can be seen in the Mutua General de Seguros, which in the 1940s and 1950s tried to create an insurance group, including a reinsurance company. The mutual's control of two companies, the Cresa and La Constancia, was exercised in this way, distributing the shares among the principal members of the mutual's board of directors. Pons Pons, 'Mutua General de Seguros'.

25. Preamble to the decree of 29 September 1944, in *BOE*, 19 October 1944.

26. La Garantía was founded in Bilbao on 7 December 1918 in the presence of the notary Celestino María del Arenal.

27. The Cresa company, for example, had share capital of a mere 2 million pesetas. The limited average financial scale of these companies was a characteristic of new companies created in the first stage of the Franco regime. The average scale of the joint-stock companies created in 1959 was only a third of those created in 1939 and less than a quarter of those created in 1934. Torres Villanueva, 'La Empresa en la Autarquía', p. 186.

28. Some exceptions were established in the case of mergers, some foreign companies with special authorization, or those that it was decided to authorize for reasons of 'national convenience', which gave the government the last word. *BOE*, 18 July 1949, p. 3195.

29. Decree of 11 July 1952, in *BOE*, 26 July 1952.

30. Sources: Memoria Estadística del seguro privado del ejercicio (1951, 1960), Dirección General de Banca, Bolsa e inversions; Memoria Estadística del seguro privado del ejercicio (1970), Subdirección General de Seguros.

31. Source: *Revista del Sindicato Vertical del Seguro*, 3:34 (October 1946).

32. R. Huerta Huerta, *Inversiones Extranjeras en España: Estudio Multidisciplinar* (Madrid: for the author, 1992); M. Muñoz Guarasa, *La Inversión Directa Extranjera en España: Factores Determinantes* (Madrid: Civitas, 1999), pp. 94–5.

33. The Spanish government, under pressure from the Allies, joined in the freezing of German companies' assets after the Second World War. The result of this entire process can be summarized briefly with regard to the insurance sector: the Allies got a very small part of these assets through expropriation, Spanish capitalists did some lucrative business (such as in the case of La Constancia) and the German companies recovered most of their property except in the case of small companies which, due to the difficulties created by the special circumstances at this time, were liquidated. E. Frax, and M. J. Matilla, 'Los Seguros Negocios del Franquismo: El Proceso de Bloqueo, Expropiación y Liquidación de las Compañías de Seguros con Capital Alemán', ponencia de la sesión B17 ('El mercado de seguros en la España contemporánea', organized by M. A. Pons Brías and J. Pons Pons), VIII Congreso de la Asociación Española de Historia Económica, Santiago de Compostela, 13–16 September 2005.

34. This restriction was initiated during the Civil War with the decree of 5 July 1937, which froze balances in pesetas when they were the property of non-residents. This regulation did not disappear with the Ley de Desbloqueo of 7 December 1939, as the obligation to request prior authorization from the Spanish Institute for Exchange Control to take capital out of the country was maintained. Torres Villanueva, 'La Empresa en la Autarquía', p. 207.

35. García-Ruiz and Caruana, 'The Internationalisation of the Business of Insurance in Spain'.

36. Source: *Revista del Sindicato Vertical del Seguro*, extraordinary edition (1951, 1961, 1971).

37. According to Carreras and Tafunell, in the last century and a half the Spanish have not had to endure such prolonged and dramatic impoverishment as that experienced between 1936 and 1950. The Civil War reduced Spain to a per capita level of GDP less than half that of EU countries. Carreras and Tafunell, *Historia Económica*, p. 280.

38. Source: *Revista del Sindicato Vertical del Seguro*, extraordinary edition (1951, 1961, 1971).

39. The law of compulsory automobile insurance (law 122/1962) was passed on 24 December 1962. However, a posterior decree postponed its application until 1 June 1965. Pons Pons, 'El Seguro de Accidentes de Trabajo', p. 97.

40. The compulsory nature of this insurance was in contention for a long time. During this time a number of meetings were organized by the Sección Española de la Asociación Internacional de Derechos de Seguros (SEAIDA) and the Dirección General de Seguros. For its origins, see Maestro, *Formación del Mercado Español*, p. 124.

41. In some cases, the loss of the branch of industrial accidents was a serious blow. For example, in 1966, the last year of private management of this insurance, this branch comprised 66 per cent of the entire business of Mutua General de Seguros. Pons Pons, 'Mutua General de Seguros'.

42. M. Vilar Rodríguez, 'El Sistema de Cobertura Social en la Inmediata Posguerra Civil (1939–1958): Una Pieza más de la Estrategia Represiva Franquista', in *VI Encuentro de Investigadores sobre el Franquismo* (Zaragoza: Fundación Sindicalismo y Cultura. CCOO, 2006), pp. 619–36.

43. To understand the adoption of technology in an information-intensive industry such as insurance, especially life insurance, from the use of the predecessor of the computer, the tabulators, up to the adoption of computers, see J. Yates, *Structuring the Information Age: Life Insurance and Technology in the Twentieth Century* (Baltimore, MD: Johns Hopkins University Press, 2005); M. Campbell-Kelly, 'Large-Scale Data Processing in the Prudential, 1850–1930', *Accounting Business and Financial History*, 2 (1992), pp. 117–39.

44. In 1951 there was a change of government which introduced a change of tendency. Politicians who favoured the old policy of autarky stepped down (e.g. Suanzes) while others came in who were in favour of a reform which some groups of employers and financiers were requesting, without questioning the regime itself. The proposed reform was basically a relaxation of interventionism. Barciela, 'Guerra Civil', p. 359.

45. The National Commission of Industrial Productivity was created by the decree of 1 May 1952. The Commission included industrial engineers and the government conceded extraordinary credits to meet its needs (law of 22 December 1953). A decree of 22 April 1955 extended its functioning for three years and on 12 July 1955 the Commission was entrusted with setting up and running a school of industrial organization. The objectives of the Commission were to increase productivity levels, improve technical knowledge and strengthen the economic connections between human capital, autochthonous natural resources and industrial equipment. M. Vilar Rodríguez, 'Mercado de Trabajo y Crecimiento Económico en España (1908–1963): Una Nueva Interpretación del Primer Franquismo' (PhD dissertation, University of Barcelona, 2004). For productivity in the industrial sector, see Martínez Ruiz, *El Sector Exterior*; J. A. Miranda, 'El Fracaso de la Industrialización Autárquica', in Barciela (ed.), *Autarquía y Mercado Negro*, pp. 95–122; J. A. Miranda, 'La Comisión Nacional de Productividad Industrial y la "Americanización" de la Industria del Calzado en España', *Revista de Historia Económica*, 22 (2004), pp. 637–68; M. T. Sanchís Llopis, 'Relaciones de Intercambio Sectoriales y Desarrollo Industrial. España, 1954–1972', *Revista de Historia Industrial*, 11 (1997), pp. 149–74.

46. Soto Carmona, 'Rupturas y Continuidades', p. 223.
47. Martínez Ruíz, *El Sector Exterior*, p. 10.
48. La Estrella, *Medio Siglo*, pp. 109–10.
49. Jesús Serra participated in its creation as the representative of La Catalana. J. Pons Pons, 'Jesús Serra Santamans', in E. Torres Villanueva (ed.), *Los 100 Empresarios Españoles del Siglo XX* (Madrid: Editorial Lid Empresarial, 2000), pp. 451–5, on p. 454. The Mutua General de Seguros was a member of the Productivity Committee in 1955.
50. J. J. Garrido Comas, *Notas de Andar y Ver: Memorias de J. J. Garrido y Comas* (Madrid: Fundación MAPFRE estudios, 1997), p. 184.
51. In 1940 there was an invitation to submit tenders for the supply of four electric calculators to the Dirección General de Estadística. *BOE*, 14 November 1940. In 1943, exemption from custom duties was granted for five calculators destined for the Instituto Geográfico y Catastaral. They were Triumphator calculators from the German company Triumphator Werk Heer & Co. based in Leipzig-Mölkau. *BOE*, 15 January 1943.
52. Sources: Memoria Estadística del seguro privado del ejercicio (1951, 1960), Dirección General de Banca, Bolsa e inversions; Memoria Estadística del seguro privado del ejercicio (1970), Subdirección General de Seguros.
53. Extract from the oral report given by Mr Gaminde to Mutua General de Seguros' Advisory Committee in its session of 20 March, relating to the interest in, and possibilities of, the mechanisation of the administrative services of the said company, Mutua General de Seguros Archive (unclassified).
54. M. Vilar Rodríguez, 'El Mercado de Trabajo como Estrategia Política del Régimen Franquista (1936–1975)', in J. De la Torre Campo and G. Sanz Lafuente (eds), *Migraciones y Coyuntura Económica del Franquismo a la Democracia* (Zaragoza: Prensas Universitarias de Zaragoza, 2008), pp. 153–77.
55. Ibid.
56. La Estrella, *Medio Siglo*, p. 110.
57. At the height of autarky, Maquinas Comerciales Watson was on the point of closing down on various occasions. In 1949 the name was changed to IBM-SAE. The company had 35 workers. E. De Diego, *Historia de la Industria en España: La Electrónica y la Informática* (Madrid: Editorial Actas, 1995), pp. 57–8.
58. An IBM 650 was installed in RENFE in 1958 and a UNIVAC (UCT model) in the Junta de Energía Nuclear in 1959. Other smaller IBM 1620s were installed in Engineering Schools. Ibid., pp. 58–9.
59. S. López, 'Los Precedentes de la Informática y la Automática en España (1925–1971)', in R. Enrich, G. Lusa, M. Mañosa, X Moreno and A. Roca (curators), *Tècnica i societat en el món contemporani: I Jornades, Maig 1992* (Sabadell: Museu d'Historia de Sabadell, 1994), pp. 211–28, on pp. 213–14.
60. Yates, *Structuring the Information Age*, p. 108.
61. 'De la Pluma de Ave a la Automatización', a talk given in Madrid on 21 October 1958. Tattevín belonged to a French insurance group. At that time, this group possessed Europe's first high-powered electronic computer in the insurance sector.
62. In the case of the US it spread through associations such as the Society of Actuaries, the Life Office Management Association (LOMA) and the Insurance Accounting and Statistical Association (IASA). J. Yates, 'The Structuring of Early Computer Use in Life Insurance', *Journal of Design History*, 12 (1999), pp. 5–24, on p. 8.

63. 'El Empleo de Máquinas de Fichas Perforadas en una Entidad de Seguros: La Utilización de Fichas Perforadas para las Operaciones de Emisión de recibos', report 3 (Madrid: ICEA, April 1963).
64. The rounding of céntimos in all operations, which simplified the task of mechanization, was introduced in the Mutua General de Seguros in 1959. Pons Pons, 'Mutua General de Seguros'.
65. Source: abstract of the meeting held in Madrid on 25 November 1958, in the head office of the Compañía General Española de Seguros. Mutua General de Seguros archive.
66. 'The employment of punched-card equipment in an insurance institution', CAPA, translated by ICEA in its report 3.
67. Tabulator technology applied to insurance was developed after the Second World War. Starting in 1947, IBM presented the 600 line tabulating equipment which involved numerous innovations. The 604 electronic calculator was introduced in 1948. American insurance companies were among the most sophisticated users of punched-card machines in the late 1940s and during the 1950s. Yates, *Structuring the Information Age*, pp. 104–9.
68. These limitations affected all sectors of the economy. Barciela highlights the difficulties of importing machinery and spare parts as one of the factors which explain the low productivity at this time. Barciela, 'Guerra Civil', p. 349.
69. Source: information taken to Board meeting, 9 May 1963, Mutua General de Seguros archive.
70. According to Soto Carmona, the adjustment between supply and demand in terms of qualifications did not take place in the market but rather within companies, which meant an extra expense for them. Soto Carmona, 'Rupturas y Continuidades', pp. 224–5.
71. According to Guillen, there were about 800 people in programming companies (software) in Spain in 1969. However, as the need for specialists increased by about 40 per cent a year there were about 6,000 skilled computer workers by the end of 1976, of which about 70 per cent were systems analysts and technicians and the rest programmers. A. Guillen, *ITT e IBM en España: El 'Holding' de la ITT y el Monopolio de IBM en España* (Bilbao: Zero, 1977), p. 46.
72. As Keneley has shown, insurance companies resorted to the internal labour market to cover jobs associated 'with the processing of large amounts of information and the interpretation of highly specialized and technical concepts'. M. J. Keneley, 'In the Service of the Society: The Labour Management Practices of an Australian Life Insurer to 1940', *Business History*, 48 (2006), pp. 529–50, on p. 546.
73. See, for example, the analyses carried out in G. de Usera, 'El Seguro Privado y el Desarrollo Económico', *Anales del Instituto de Actuarios Españoles*, 4 (1964), pp. 1–15; or the analysis of the insurance panorama in the 1960s made in F. V. Planes, 'Panorámica Actual del Seguro Español', *Riesgo y Seguro* (1963), pp. 324–8.
74. *BOE*, 25 July 1962.
75. *BOE*, 7 January 1964.
76. *BOE*, 5 October 1966.
77. *BOE*, 11 January 1967.
78. *BOE*, 24 December 1963.
79. *BOE*, 24 May 1967.
80. Valenzuela de Quinta, *Protagonistas del Mutualismo*, p. 280.
81. For the complete list of companies and their representatives, see I. Hernando de Larramendi, *Así se hizo Mapfre: Mi Tiempo* (Madrid: Actas Editorial, 2000), p. 296.

82. For the role of Jesús Serra Santamans in promoting this association, see Pons Pons, 'Jesús Serra Santamans'. Victor Gaminde Cortejarena, Director General of the Mutua General de Seguros, also belonged to its executive council.

83. Planes, 'Panorámica Actual', p. 326.

84. De Diego, *Historia de la Industria en España*, p. 81.

85. Ibid.

86. By comparison, the value of computers installed in France in 1965 represented 0.68 per cent of GDP and 1.31 per cent in 1969. Ibid.

87. The first applications of computers in the American insurance industry were introduced from 1954 onwards. Yates, 'The Structuring of Early Computer Use', p. 9.

88. In 1970, banking was the industry that had the greatest number of computers, with 88. Insurance companies had 20, lagging behind another five sectors. Guillen, *ITT e IBM en España*, p. 47.

89. De Diego, *Historia de la Industria en España*, p. 81.

90. This was the year in which the first models of the IBM 1401 series arrived, the first of which were installed in Sevillana de Electricidad and in Galerías Preciados. This computer came onto the market in 1960, and was the successor of the 650 model. The 1401 was a small-scale, low-cost computer system with transistors and core memory. Yates, *Structuring the Information Age*, p. 195.

91. For the characteristics of this model and its diffusion in the 1960s, see ibid., p. 202.

92. Source: 1969 data, 'Survey on Mechanisation in Insurance Institutions', report 94 (Madrid: ICEA, June 1971), (A-22).

93. Yates, 'The Structuring of Early Computer Use'.

94. Source: 1969 data, 'Survey on Mechanisation in Insurance Institutions', report 94 (Madrid: ICEA, June 1971), (A-22).

95. The Fremap, along with the Mutualidad General Agropecuaria and the Mesai, had created Sdomsa (Servicio de Organización y Mecanización). Hernando de Larramendi, *Así se hizo Mapfre*, p. 361. The Mutua General de Seguros and the Mutua General, Mutua Patronal nº 10 created SECYPROSA in 1978. Pons Pons, 'Mutua General de Seguros'.

4 Werner, 'Multilateral Insurance Liberalization'

1. For studies on trade barriers in the insurance sector, see D. L. Bickelhaupt and R. Bar-Niv, *International Insurance: Managing Risk in the World* (New York: Insurance Information Institute, 1983); R. Carter and G. M. Dickinson, *Obstacles to the Liberalization of Trade in Insurance*, Thames Essay 58 (London: Trade Policy Research Centre, 1992).

2. The terminology used in this chapter regarding forms of and barriers to international trade in insurance is derived from the General Agreement on Trade in Services (GATS), the most broad-based and systematic approach to insurance liberalization to date. International activities, including trade (or 'cross-border supply of services') and the operations of foreign insurers (or 'commercial presence'), are restricted by barriers to market access and national treatment. Besides these two economically significant modes of trans-border supply of services, the GATS framework agreement makes reference to two more modes, which involve the cross-border movement of individuals (or 'natural persons'): consumption abroad and presence of individuals.

3. The main hypothesis of this chapter was first developed in W. Werner, 'Öffnung der Versicherungsmärkte bei OECD, EU und WTO: Mühsamer Abschied vom

Finanzmarktprotektionismus der Bretton Woods Periode', *Zeitschrift für die gesamte Versicherungswissenschaft*, 94 (2005), pp. 841–64.

4. In 1948, sixteen states belonged to the OEEC: Austria, Belgium, Denmark, France, Greece, Great Britain, Iceland, Italy, Ireland, Luxembourg, the Netherlands, Norway, Switzerland and Turkey. The Federal Republic of Germany and Spain became full members of the organization in 1949 and 1959 respectively. Canada and the US were associated members as of 1950. The six founding members of the EEC are Belgium, the Federal Republic of Germany, France, Italy, Luxembourg and the Netherlands.

5. The OEEC's early liberalization initiatives on insurance trade were discussed almost exclusively in the legal literature. See, for example, Lorenz-Liburnau, who reported regularly on changes in the insurance provisions of the Code of Liberalisation of Trade and Invisible Transactions. H. Lorenz-Liburnau, 'Integration der Europäischen Versicherungswirtschaft in Vergangenheit, Gegenwart und Zukunft', *Die Versicherungsrundschau*, 17 (1962), pp. 70–85. An exception is Dürr, who offers an analysis from an economic point of view. E. Dürr, *Die Liberalisierung des Internationalen Versicherungsverkehrs* (Berlin: Duncker & Humblot, 1956).

6. While concepts used in the EU for the liberalization of the services trade are not identical to those used under the GATS framework agreement, the following terms are roughly equivalent: 1. cross-border supply of services: free movement of services; 2. commercial presence: freedom of establishment; 3. service consumption abroad by a natural person; and 4. service provision abroad by a natural person: free movement of persons.

7. For a discussion of the early development of European reinsurance markets, see Pearson, 'The Development of Reinsurance Markets in Europe'.

8. The firm commitment of reinsurance companies to furthering the liberalization of international reinsurance trade is exemplified by the writings of Marcel Grossmann. Already at the end of the 1940s he described the problems that reinsurance companies face if they are restricted to national markets. For an example of his early proposals on the liberalization of international reinsurance trade, see M. Grossmann, 'Rückversicherungszahlungen in Drittlandwährungen', *Schweizerische Versicherungs-Zeitschrift*, 17 (1949/50), pp. 331–7.

9. The protectionist effects of prudential regulation are analysed by H. D. Skipper, 'Protectionism in the Provision of International Insurance Services', *Journal of Risk and Insurance*, 54 (1987), pp. 55–85.

10. For examinations of the role of prudential regulation in the multilateral liberalization of insurance trade, see R. K. Shelp, *Beyond Industrialization* (New York: Praeger, 1981), p. 131; Carter and Dickinson, *Obstacles to the Liberalization of Trade*, p. 40; H. D. Skipper, 'International Trade in Insurance', in C. E. Barfield (ed.), *International Financial Markets: Harmonization versus Competition* (Washington, DC: AEI Press, 1996), pp. 151–224, on p. 209.

11. See W. Werner, *Handelspolitik für Finanzdienste*, Schriften zur Monetären Ökonomie (Baden-Baden: Nomos, 2004).

12. See OECD, *Supervision of Private Insurance in Europe* (Paris: OECD, 1963).

13. Another trade policy initiative of the OECD which focused on FDI was the Multilateral Agreement on Investment (MAI). This agreement was to become a broad-based legally binding instrument covering a large number of industries. Negotiations, however, were cancelled in 1998. For more details on the MAI and the National Treatment Instrument, see Werner, *Handelspolitik*, p. 118.

14. See Carter and Dickinson, *Obstacles to the Liberalization of Trade*, p. 126; W. Witherell, 'The Liberalization of International Service Transactions: The Experience of Developed Countries', in United Nations Centre on Transnational Corporations, *Services and Development: The Role of Foreign Direct Investment in Trade*, ST/CTC/95 (New York: United Nations, 1989), pp. 143–50, on p. 147.

15. Consequently, quite a few authors count as principles of the Single Market programme not only mutual recognition and minimum harmonization but also home country control.

16. Commission of the European Communities, *Insurance*, The Single Market Review, Subseries II (Impact on Services), 1 (Luxembourg: OOPEC, 1998).

17. See R. Beckmann, C. Eppendorfer and M. Neimke, *Financial Integration within the European Union: Towards a Single Market for Insurance*. Institut für Europäische Wirtschaft, Diskussionsbeiträge 40 (Bochum: Ruhr University, 2002); R. Beckmann, C. Eppendorfer and M. Neimke, 'Financial Integration within the European Union: Towards a Single Market for Insurance', in P. Cecchini, F. Heinemann and M. Jopp (eds), *The Incomplete European Market for Financial Services*, ZEW Economic Studies 19 (Heidelberg: Physica-Verlag, 2003), pp. 1–29.

18. W. Werner, *Das WTO-Finanzdienstleistungsabkommen* (Munich: Oldenbourg, 1999).

19. For an overview of developing countries' protectionist views on international trade in insurances, see early studies by the United Nations presented in UNCTAD, *Insurance in the Context of Services and the Development Process*, TD/B/1014 (Geneva: UNCTAD, 1984). For a more liberal view, see UNCTAD, *Services and the Development Process*, TD/B/1008 (New York: UNCTAD, 1985); UNCTAD, *The Outcome of the Uruguay Round: An Initial Assessment. Supporting Papers to the Trade and Development Report 1994*, TDR/14 (New York: UNCTAD, 1994), pp. 145–84.

20. M. Kono et al., *Opening Markets in Financial Services and the Role of the GATS* (Geneva: World Trade Organization, 1997); S. Claessens and T. Glaessner, *Internationalization of Financial Services in Asia*, Policy Research Paper 1911 (Washington, DC: World Bank, 1997).

21. See, for example, J. J. Schott, *The Uruguay Round: An Assessment* (Washington, DC: Institute for International Economics, 1994).

5 Yoneyama, 'Policyholders in the Early Business of Japanese Life Assurance'

1. For the Old Equitable, see M. E. Ogborn, *Equitable Assurances: The Story of Life Assurance in the Experience of the Equitable Life Assurance Society 1762–1962* (London: George Allen & Unwin, 1962); and C. Walford, 'Equitable', in his *Insurance Cyclopaedia*, 5 vols (London: Layton, 1871–8), vol. 2, pp. 570–640.

2. For the Prudential, see H. Plaisted, *Prudential Past and Present* (Cardiff: Rees' Electric Press, 1916), and R. W. Barnard, *A Century of Service, the Story of the Prudential 1848–1948* (London: Times Publishing, 1948).

3. Although in the context of labour history, Paul Johnson has discussed clearly the demand side of a worker's family. For his excellent study, see *Saving and Spending: The Working-Class Economy in Britain, 1870–1939* (Oxford: Clarendon Press, 1985). Viviana A. Zelizer asked why Americans began to buy life insurance after 1850s. Her answer was

that it was because they changed their view of insurance through the impact of the sales efforts of the new mutual companies. See her *Morals and Markets*.

4. Cf. the essays in C. E. Núñez (ed.), *Insurance in Industrial Societies: Economic Role, Agents and Markets from the Eighteenth Century to Today* (Seville: University of Seville, 1998).

5. The Meiji Life, the first Japanese life assurance company, sold five types of life products, namely whole life insurance, whole life with a limited term of premium payment, endowment insurance, term insurance and savings insurance for children. At first, the Meiji and other life companies expected that whole life insurance would be most purchased, but consumers in the early Japanese market supported endowment insurance. They seldom bought insurance for another's account, so that most policyholders were the same persons who were insured.

6. The first-mover is a concept originated by Chandler, who describes a first-mover as an industrial company that undertook a three-pronged investment in new products, and that built its advantage against challengers. For details, see A. D. Chandler, *Scale and Scope: The Dynamics of Industrial Capitalism* (Cambridge, MA: Harvard University Press, 1990), pp. 34–6. A reconstruction of the concept of first-movers for financial companies needs to be undertaken; however there is no space to do so in this chapter.

7. The Iwakura Mission was the first formal inspection group to the West in Japan. The chief delegate was Tomomi Iwakura, who was a key government official. The Mission consisted of 107 members, including students studying western technology, politics and cultures. The Mission left Yokohama on 12 November 1871, and returned to Japan on 13 September 1873. They visited America, the UK, France, Belgium, the Netherlands, Germany, Russia, Denmark, Sweden, Italy, Austria and Switzerland. Immediately after the Meiji Restoration it was widely regarded as important for Japan to learn from the West.

8. High-ranking government officials in the Meiji administration mainly came from the Han (feudal domain) of those who had been associated with the winning party in the Revolution of 1867–8. Yasuda had fewer connections to this group than other businessmen.

9. Sources: Asahi Life Insurance Company, *The 80 Year History of Asahi Life Insurance Company* (Tokyo: Asahi Life Insurance Company, 1968); *The Centenary History of Yasuda Life* (Tokyo: Asahi Life Insurance Company, 1975); *The 123 Year History of Yasuda Life* (Tokyo: Asahi Life Insurance Company, 2003).

10. Kikugoro Onoe I (1817–83) became a member when he was 63 years old, and his family was paid benefits within two years.

11. Sensai Nagayo (1838–1902) became a member when he was 42 years old, and he was not paid benefits before the association's reorganization in 1894.

12. That is to say 'examining physicians'. In contemporary Japan no one other than a medical 'doctor' was permitted to undertake the medical examination of a prospective client.

13. Now called the Meiji Yasuda Life Insurance Company. For details, see http://www.meijiyasuda.co.jp/regular/english/ [accessed 29 July 2009].

14. The former is now called the Asahi Mutual Life Insurance Company. For the Nippon Life Insurance today, see http://www.nissay.co.jp/okofficial/english/ [accessed 29 July 2009].

15. A review of life assurance companies was published by a contemporary journalist in 1926, listing these seven companies. Cf. T. Inami, *Hoken ha dokohe* [*Where is the Insurance Company Going?*] (Bunga-Do, 1926).

16. The Nagoya Life was renamed the Taiyo Life in 1908. The Taiyo Life has enjoyed a long history and is now the main affiliate under T&D Holdings, Inc. For current information, see http://www.td-holdings.co.jp/e/group/ [accessed 29 July 2009].

17. Its original name was the Kokumin Life. It was a small local company and was wound up in 1930s.

18. The Kyosai Life was created by the Kyosai 500 in 1894. It was the main forerunner of the Yasuda Life. The Yasuda merged with the Meiji to form the Meiji Yasuda in 2004.

19. The Yurin Life finally transferred its business to the Meiji Life in 1943, when the company was 49 years old.

20. The Sogo Life was renamed the Nihon Kyoritsu in 1907, and finally merged with the Teikoku Life in 1942.

21. In 1940 the Jinjyu Life merged with the Nomura Life, whose former name was the Shinshu-shinto Life. The Nomura Life was renamed the Tokyo Life in 1947. The Nomura is now the largest securities company in Japan.

22. The Shinshu-shinto Life was renamed the Kyoho Life in 1914. Shinshu-shinto means believers of the True Pure Land sect of Buddhism. It became the main forerunner of the Tokyo Life. The Tokyo Life fell into insolvency in 2001 and is now reorganized as an affiliate under T&D Holdings, Inc.

23. Source: Hoken Ginko Jiho, *Honpo Seimei Hoken Gyoshi* [*History of Life Insurance Business*] (Tokyo: Hoken Ginko Jiho / Insurance and Banking News Report, 1933), part 10, p. 29.

24. Fukuzawa published *Seiyo Tabi Annai* [*A Travel Guide of Western Culture*] in 1867. He introduced life assurance, fire insurance and marine insurance in the supplement of this book.

25. Hoken Ginko Jiho, 25 October 1908, in T. Yui and M. Tatsuki (eds), *Historical Documents of Japanese Life Assurance in the Early Period* (Tokyo: Meiji Life, 1981), pp. 346–7.

26. Utinomiya-shi Keirekidan, 1932, in Yui and Tatsuki (eds), *Historical Documents*, p. 351. Yataro Iwasaki was an influential businessman at that time. His business later became the financial combine Mitsubishi Zaibatsu.

27. Kojyunsha was the first social club for businessmen in Japan, established in 1880. It is said that Fukuzawa founded the Kojyunsha business club.

28. They are listed in Meiji Life, *Meiji Seimei 50nenshi* [*50 Years History of Meiji Life*] (Tokyo: Meiji Seimei Hoken, 1933), p. 102.

29. After graduating and taking a job teaching English, Koizumi went to London and Berlin for study in 1876–8. He studied under Leone Levi at London, and attended lectures at Berlin universities, including those of Professor Adolf Wagner. After returning to Japan, he joined the promoters of the Yokohama Specie Bank, and became a vice-president of the bank in 1879.

30. Source: T. Yui and M. Tatsuki, *Meiji Seimei 100-nenshi* [*Documents of Meiji 100 Year History*] (Tokyo: Meiji Seimei Hoken Sogogaisha, 1982), pp. 693–8.

31. After graduating from the Keio Gijyuku, Asabuki entered the Mitsubishi Company in 1878. Later, he was involved in the Mitsui business and became one of the most influential business leaders in Mitsui Zaibatu.

32. Asahi Life Insurance Company, *The 80 Year History*, p. 14.

33. Taizo Abe, the first president of the Meiji Life, also travelled across the country. Naoharu Kataoka's travels, however, were longer and more thoroughgoing. After Kataoka resigned his presidency, he became a statesman. During the financial panic of 1927, he was Min-

ister of Finance. Famously, he lost his cabinet post over an inappropriate remark that was a direct trigger of the panic.

34. Source: Hoken Ginko Jiho, *Honpo Seimei Hoken Gyoshi*, part 10, p. 21.
35. Source: ibid.
36. O. Saito, *Hikaku Keizai Hattenron* [*Comparative Study of Economic Development: A Historical Approach*] (Tokyo: Iwanami, 2008).
37. M. Keller, *The Life Insurance Enterprise, 1885–1910: A Study in the Limits of Corporate Power* (Cambridge, MA: Harvard University Press, 1963).

6 Eriksson, 'Industrial Life Insurance and the Cost of Dying'

1. Supple, *The Royal Exchange Assurance*, pp. 113–14; S. Murphy, 'Security in an Uncertain World: Life Insurance and the Emergence of Modern America' (PhD dissertation, University of Virginia, 2005), pp. 263–4.
2. Supple, *The Royal Exchange Assurance*, p. 218.
3. Small policies were available in, for example, Sweden, France and the US before the introduction of industrial life insurance.
4. Savings banks, for example, were established in Sweden in 1884 to stimulate the saving among the broad public, especially among the mobile workforce. The availability was, however, counteracted by the low savings rate and the initiative remained a small part of total savings. In Germany, health insurance clubs were given public support, but the private insurance company the Nordstern experienced still greater success. In England, the liberal politician William E. Gladstone introduced a public insurance scheme as early as 1865 but this was abandoned as a failure in 1928. Instead, the private insurance company the Prudential grew strong. The British public insurance institutions, despite their efforts, did not issue more than 9,000 policies in comparison with the Prudential, which issued 11,000,000 policies at the beginning of the 1890s, 'Barn- och arbetareförsäkringen i England', *Försäkringsföreningens Tidskrift* [*The Swedish Insurance Association Periodical*, hereafter *FFT*] (1895), p. 243; *FFT* (1884), pp. 72–7.
5. 'Den sjätte internationella aktuariekongressen i Wien den 6–13 Juni', *FFT* (1909), p. 91.
6. F. L. Hoffman, 'Industrial Insurance', *Annals of the American Academy of Political and Social Science*, 26 (1905), pp. 103–19.
7. Supple, *The Royal Exchange Assurance*, pp. 219–23.
8. M. J. Keneley, 'The Evolution of the Australian Life Insurance Industry', *Accounting, Business and Financial History*, 11 (2002), pp. 145–170, on pp. 157–8.
9. H. J. Davenport, 'Can Industrial Insurance Be Cheapened?', *Journal of Political Economy*, 15 (1907), pp. 542–5, on p. 543.
10. For a critique of non-Anglo-Saxon industrial insurance, see P. A. Söhner, *Die Private Volksversicherung, ihr Wesen und ihr Wert und die Wichtigeren Reformbestrebungen* (Tübingen: J.C.B. Mohr, 1911), p. 45.
11. Davenport, 'Can Industrial Insurance Be Cheapened?', p. 543; C. R. Henderson, *Industrial Insurance in the United States* (Chicago, IL: University of Chicago Press, 1909), p. 150; M. Taylor, *The Social Cost of Industrial Insurance* (New York: A. A. Knopf, 1933).
12. See Barnard, *A Century of Service*, p. 75.
13. Such criticism of high expenses was established even before the introduction of industrial life insurance, as illustrated by W. Karup, *Handbuch der Lebensversicherung* (Leipzig: A. Fritsch, 1885), pp. 30–1.

14. Davenport, 'Can Industrial Insurance Be Cheapened?', p. 543; According to Epstein, in 1906 American industrial life insurance companies were criticized for allowing their executives some of the highest salaries in the country; A. Epstein, *Insecurity: A Challenge to America* (New York: H. Smith & R. Haas, 1933), pp. 118–19; D. Morrah, *A History of Industrial Life Assurance* (London: Allen & Unwin, 1955), p. 243; Ben Gales claims that the Dutch industrial life insurance had a reputation for being second rate, Gales, 'Odds and Ends', p. 90.

15. *Independent*, 61 (1906), p. 1475.

16. The Swedish Insurance Association pointed to the high expenses of the British Prudential, *FFT* (1917), pp. 3–5.

17. 'Ur litteraturen och pressen', *FFT* (1890), pp. 30–2.

18. 'Två Amerikanska bolags manifest', *FFT* (1892), pp. 18–32.

19. *FFT* (1881), pp. 29–30.

20. 'Kan reglering af anskaffningskostnader vid lifförsäkring företagas?', *Gjallarhornet* (1901), p. 215.

21. L. I. Dublin, *A Family of Thirty Million: The Story of Metropolitan Life Insurance Company* (New York: Metropolitan Life Insurance Co., 1943), p. 208. No attempt was made by the British Prudential to carry industrial business beyond the UK; Barnard, *A Century of Service*, p. 102.

22. Supple, *The Royal Exchange Assurance*, pp. 116–17.

23. M. E. Davis, *Industrial Life Insurance in the United States* (New York and London: McGraw-Hill Book Co., 1944), pp. 22–4.

24. Murphy, 'Security in an Uncertain World, p. 432.

25. Epstein, *Insecurity*, pp. 118–19.

26. Hoffman, 'Industrial Insurance', pp. 103–19. For more evidence on US industrial insurance as a service primarily for covering burial expenses, see F. L. Hoffman, *History of the Prudential Insurance Company of America (Industrial Insurance) 1875–1900* (Newark, NJ: Prudential Press, 1900), p. 1.; Henderson, *Industrial Insurance*, p. 149; R. Whaples and D. Buffum, 'Fraternalism, Paternalism, the Family, and the Market: Insurance a Century Ago', *Social Science History*, 15 (1991), 97–122, on p. 119; R. Lubove 'Economic Security and Social Conflict in America: The Early Twentieth Century', *Journal of Social History*, 1 (1967), pp. 61–87, on p. 86. Rubinow too claimed that 'Industrial insurance is funeral insurance; this purpose was clearly admitted by the fathers of the business in its early days'. I. M. Rubinow, *The Quest for Security* (New York: Henry Holt & Co., 1934), p. 465.

27. Supple, *The Royal Exchange Assurance*, pp. 219–20.

28. F. L. Hoffman, *Pauper Burials and the Interment of Dead in Large Cities* (Newark, NJ: Prudential Press, 1919), pp. 24–5. The purpose of the study was to argue that industrial insurance did not fuel the purchase of extravagant funerals.

29. 'Lifförsäkringsverksamheten i Schweiz', *FFT* (1911), p. 10.

30. International Congress of Actuaries, *Transactions of the International Congress of Actuaries* [hereafter *Transactions*] (1927), vol. 1: English Papers and Abstracts, pp. 60–1.

31. 'Lifförsäkringsverksamheten i Schweiz', *FFT* (1911), p. 10.

32. *Transactions* (1927), vol. 1, pp. 9–15; A. Løkke, 'Tryghed og Risiko – Forsikring i Danmark 1850–1950', in O. Feldbæk, A. Løkke and S. J. Jeppesen (eds), *Drømmen om Tryghed: Tusind års Dansk Forsikring* (Gylling: Gad, 2007), pp. 262–78, on pp. 262–5.

33. *Transactions* (1927), vol. 1, pp. 3–5.

34. 'Några siffror från ett jättebolags verksamhet', *Tryggs veckoblad*, 18 (1909), p. 4.

35. De Förenade, *Lifförsäkrings-Aktiebolaget De Förenade* (Stockholm: De Förenade, 1934), p. 15.
36. Ehler claims that German industrial insurance was influenced by Bismarck's invalidity and pension insurance. H. J. Ehler, *Die Verbandszusammenschlüsse in der Privaten Lebensversicherung* (Karlsruhe: Verlag Versicherungswirtschaft, 2003), p. 29.
37. Söhner, *Die Private Volksversicherung*, pp. 7, 14; *Transactions* (1927), vol. 1, pp. 16–17.
38. Söhner, *Die Private Volksversicherung*, pp. 14–15.
39. A. Surminski, *Im Zug der Zeiten: 150 Jahre Victoria* (Düsseldorf: Victoria Versicherungs-Gesellschaften, 2003), p. 42; Söhner, *Die Private Volksversicherung*, p. 11.
40. K. Hamann, *Hundert Jahre Victoria Versicherung* (Berlin: Victoria Versicherung, 1953), pp. 83–4.
41. B. P. A. Gales, 'A Fonds Perdu? The Business of Funeral Assurance in the Netherlands', in Núñez (ed.), *Insurance in Industrial Societies*, pp. 127–42, on p. 137.
42. Dublin, *A Family of Thirty Million*, p. 98.
43. Ibid., p. 135.
44. De Förenade, *Lifförsäkrings-aktiebolaget*, p. 11.
45. *Spectator Insurance Yearbook* (1904), pp. 374–5.
46. M. James, *The Metropolitan Life: A Study in Business Growth* (New York: Viking, 1947), p. 120.
47. Dublin, *A Family of Thirty Million*, p. 153.
48. Quoted in Hoffman, *History of the Prudential*, pp. 189–90.
49. Supple, *The Royal Exchange Assurance*, pp. 219–20.
50. M. J. Keneley, 'Monitoring and Motivating Outworkers: The Case of the AMP and the Sale of Industrial Life Insurance 1905–1940', *Labor History*, 49 (2008), pp. 319–40, on pp. 333–4.
51. Hoffman, 'Industrial Insurance', p. 107.
52. 'Om beräkning af lifförsäkringsbolags förvaltningskostnadsprocentsats enligt Dr Amthors metod', *FFT* (1909), pp. 123–33.
53. Load has been used, for example, by M. A. Thomasson, 'From Sickness to Health: The Twentieth-Century Development of U.S. Health Insurance', *Explorations in Economic History*, 39 (2002), pp. 233–53, on p. 242.
54. Sources: Swedish official statistics of the insurance industry (1899–1915); *Spectator Insurance Yearbook* (1901–15).
55. 'Några siffror från ett jättebolags verksamhet', *Tryggs veckoblad*, 18 (1909), 1 maj.
56. P. Cohen, *The British System of Social Insurance* (London: P. Allen, 1932), pp. 246–9. This was in spite of the fact that in 1909 an act had been passed to improve the administration of life insurance companies in the UK, which included provisions dealing with industrial insurance. Supple, *The Royal Exchange Assurance*, pp. 221–3.
57. Around 1900, the American workers paid an annual insurance premium of 1.19 per cent of their annual wage. Calculated from K. G. Jungenfelt, *Löneandelen och den ekonomiska utvecklingen: en empirisk-teoretisk studie* (Stockholm: Almqvist & Wiksell, 1966); Historical Statistics of the United States, Table Ba4335-4360. Annual earnings of full-time employees, by industry: 1900–1928; Swedish Official Statistics, *Private Insurance* (Stockholm, 1900–28); *Spectator Insurance Yearbook* (1900–28).
58. Henderson, *Industrial Insurance*, p. 149.
59. J. O. Stalson, *Marketing Life Insurance: Its History in America* (Cambridge, MA: Harvard University Press, 1942), pp. 813–14; *Spectator Insurance Yearbook* (1915), pp. 128–32; (1904), pp. 134–6.

60. These were often assessment organizations where the insurance organization could charge policyholders additional sums if the loss experience became worse than had been estimated for in the premium.

61. The great expansion of life insurance in the US that took place after 1860 was attended by a corresponding development of fraternal societies, which aimed to provide, as in the case of industrial insurance, a cheaper form of insurance than was furnished by the ordinary life insurance companies. Both the American fraternal orders and British friendly societies were in competition with the industrial life insurance companies. W. S. Nichols, 'Fraternal Insurance in the United States: Its Origin, Development, Character and Existing Status', *Annals of the American Academy of Political and Social Science*, 70 (1917), 'Modern Insurance Problems', pp. 109–22; A. Landis, *Friendly Societies and Fraternal Orders* (Winchester, TN: for the author, 1900), pp. 4–5.

62. According to a Swedish statistician, Swiss assessment organizations and burial clubs covered only a small part of the market, *FFT* (1911), pp. 57–60.

63. R.-G. Aubrun, *Mutual Aid Societies in France* (San Francisco, CA: Exposition Universelle De San Francisco, 1915), p. 28.

64. Both Mitchell and Aubrun claim that French mutual aid societies remained deaf to the actuarial science available. The greater part of the 25,000 societies up to 1915 had therefore made sick benefits their essential function, since many societies did not cover accidents and few allowed pensions. A. Mitchell, *The Divided Path: The German Influence on Social Reform in France after 1870* (Chapel Hill, NC: University of North Carolina Press, 1991), p. 227; Aubrun, *Mutual Aid Societies in France*, pp. 14–15.

65. For example, Denmark in 1898; England, 1906; France, 1898; Germany, 1884; and Sweden, 1901. The insurance was only obligatory in Germany.

66. Stalson, *Marketing Life Insurance*.

67. See K. V. Iserson, *Death to Dust: What Happens to Dead Bodies?* (Tucson, AZ: Galen Press, 1994).

68. S. French, 'The Cemetery as Cultural Institution: The Establishment of Mount Auburn and the "Rural Cemetery Movement"', in D. E. Stannard (ed.), *Death in America* (Philadelphia, PA: University of Pennsylvania Press, 1975), pp. 70–92, on pp. 73–4.

69. R. Nicol, *Final Pageant: The Past, Present and Future of Death* (Sydney: Uniting Church Historical Society, 1998); R. Nicol, *At the End of the Road* (Sydney: Allen & Unwin, 1994).

70. D. C. Sloane, *The Last Great Necessity: Cemeteries in American History* (Baltimore, MD, and London: Johns Hopkins University Press, 1991), pp. 3–14.

71. There were some private initiatives in, for example, Paris. In France the grave was rented for 6–20 years and thereafter the remains were moved and the grave reused. The French lot-holders could never be sure that overcrowding and economic pressure would not result in the dead being removed.

72. J. Mitford, *The American Way of Death Revisited* (New York: Alfred A. Knopf, 1998), pp. 202–14.

73. J. C. Gebhart, *The Reasons for Present-Day Funeral Costs: A Summary of Facts Developed by the Advisory Committee on Burial Survey in the Course of an Impartial Study of the Burial Industry* (New York: Metropolitan Life Insurance Co., 1927), p. 19.

74. R. W. Habenstein and M. Lamers, *The History of American Funeral Directing* (Milwaukee, WI: National Funeral Directors Association, 1981), pp. 157–62.

75. Henderson, *Industrial Insurance*, p. 150.

76. Hoffman, *Pauper Burials*, p. 13.

77. French, 'The Cemetery as Cultural Institution', p. 76.
78. A. Wilson and H. Levy, *Burial Reform and Funeral Costs* (London and New York: Oxford University Press, 1938), pp. 26–7.
79. C. Booth, *The Aged Poor in England and Wales* (London: Macmillan, 1894), p. 314.
80. Wilson and Levy, *Burial Reform*, pp. 58–9.
81. Gebhart, *The Reasons for Present-Day Funeral Costs*, p. 38.
82. Hoffman, *Pauper Burials*, p. 5. See also Habenstein and Lamers, *The History of American Funeral Directing*, p. 215.
83. Rubinow, *The Quest for Security*, p. 467.
84. 'Special Supplement on Industrial Assurance', *New Statesman* (13 March 1915), pp. 1, 36.
85. Hoffman, *Pauper Burials*, p. 27.
86. A. M. Gulbin, 'From the Graveyard to the Cemetery: Evolving Attitudes that have affected American Funeral Rites and Customs from the Seventeenth through the Nineteenth Century' (MA dissertation, Keene State College, NH, 1986), pp. 34–8.
87. Rubinow, *The Quest for Security*, p. 467.
88. Hoffman, *Pauper Burials*, pp. 84–5.
89. Gebhart, *The Reasons for Present-Day Funeral Costs*, p. 23.
90. A. Bremborg Davidsson, *Yrke: Begravningsentreprenör* (Lund: Lund University, 2002), p. 30.
91. Gebhart, *The Reasons for Present-Day Funeral Costs*, p. 23.
92. As previously mentioned, Swiss industrial life insurance issued mainly endowment policies on a monthly not a weekly basis.
93. Gebhart, *The Reasons for Present-Day Funeral Costs*, p. 38.
94. F. A. Walker, 'Compulsory Health Insurance: "The Next Great Step in Social Legislation"', *Journal of American History*, 56 (1969), pp. 290–304.
95. B. Hoffman, 'Scientific Racism, Insurance, and Opposition to the Welfare State: Frederick L. Hoffman's Transatlantic Journey', *Journal of the Gilded Age and Progressive Era*, 2 (2003), pp. 150–90, on pp. 150–1.

7 Jitschin, 'From Economic to Political Reality'

1. R. M. Ray, *Life Insurance in India. Its History, Law, Practice, and Problems* (Bombay: Allied Publishers, 1941), p. 7.
2. S. R. Bhave (ed.), *Saga of Security: Story of Indian Life Insurance 1870–1970* (Bombay: Life Insurance Corporation of India, 1970), p. 38.
3. D. McLauchlan Slater, *Rise and Progress of Native Life Assurance in India* (Bombay, 1897), p. 30; Oriental Governmental Security Life Assurance Company Limited (ed.), *A Short History of the Oriental Governmental Security Life Assurance Company Ltd*, Silver Jubilee Souvenir (Bombay, 1924), pp. 43ff., 79.
4. A. N. Agarwala, *Insurance in India: A Study of Insurance Aspect of Social Security in India* (Allahabad: Allahabad Law Journal Press, 1960), p. 47.
5. United States Congress, Bureau of Manufactures, *Insurance in Foreign Countries*, Special Consular Reports 38, House of Representatives Document 165 (Washington, DC: Government Printing Office, 1905), p. 121; Agarwala, *Insurance in India*, p. 59.
6. Agarwala, *Insurance in India*, p. 59.
7. Ibid., p. 58.

8. Oriental Governmental Security, *A Short History*, p. 45; Ray, *Life Insurance in India*, pp. 20ff.; Agarwala, *Insurance in India*, p. 60.

9. G. R. Desai, *Life Insurance in India: Its History and Dimensions of Growth* (Madras: Macmillan India, 1973), p. 34.

10. Ibid.

11. This depended on changes in insurance legislation, which also captured the number of policies and detailed information for foreign companies.

12. Agarwala, *Insurance in India*, p. 72.

13. Desai, *Life Insurance in India*, p. 34.

14. See Agarwala *Insurance in India*, pp. 60, 72.

15. Desai, *Life Insurance in India*, p. 32.

16. Ibid.

17. Ibid., p. 34.

18. Ibid.

19. Agarwala, *Insurance in India*, p. 72.

20. Ibid., p. 74.

21. Ibid.

22. Desai, *Life Insurance in India*, p. 34.

23. Agarwala, *Insurance in India*, p. 71; Indian Government, Controller of Insurance, *Indian Insurance Year Book 1937* (New Delhi, 1938), p. 3.

24. Desai, *Life Insurance in India*, p. 32.

25. *Indian Insurance Year Book 1937*, p. 58.

26. Desai, *Life Insurance in India*, p. 5; *Indian Insurance Year Book 1937*, p. 58.

27. *Indian Insurance Year Book 1937, passim*.

28. *Indian Insurance Year Book 1940*, pp. 39ff.

29. The term 'cultural' can be misunderstood in the context of insurance companies. It is a substitute for different kinds of business behaviour. Differences named 'culture' are often of diverse nature. They range from behaviour of individuals over specific business transaction procedures at specific places, to deep rooted differences in understanding the world because of ideologies or religions. I prefer to draw conclusions from the different behaviour of Indian and British insurance companies, than to speak of different 'cultures'.

30. As Nissel found out in his PhD dissertation in 1977 the trader–customer ratio in Bombay on average is only 20:1, which in practice means one trader for only three families. These traders were a type of Indian grocer: they transacted every kind of business that can be imagined in a small packed shop of less than 15 square metres. H. Nissel, *Bombay: Untersuchungen zur Struktur und Dynamik einer indischen Metropole* (Berlin: Institut für Geographie der Technischen Universität Berlin, 1977), p. 38.

31. D. Rothermund, *An Economic History of India: From Pre-Colonial Times to 1991* (London: Routledge, 1993), pp. 62–4.

32. With regard to the general insurance market, we find that British insurance companies were much more successful there than in the life insurance market. In this market their customers were in business; including both traders and big corporations. It was no problem to transact this business, after the hurdle of getting in contact with customers was overcome.

33. SwissRe Archive, Zurich, FA 5.2–11 Reiseberichte (Indien I).

34. In general the body of the deceased is burned within four to six hours after death. This makes it often impossible to find out if it is actually the policyholder who has died or someone else. On all aspects of this, see ibid.

35. It may be added that no company tried to enforce its business principles against resistance. All foreign insurance companies in India were wise enough to avoid zones of risk. But Indian companies in general faced up to this challenge better, being more accustomed to the market.

36. Agarwala, *Insurance in India*, pp. 62, 74.

37. Ibid., p. 74.

38. The Oriental, the Hindusthan Co-Operative and the Bombay Mutual.

39. For example the Oriental, which had a market share of 42.2 per cent in 1924 (total sum assured, Indian offices only), fell to 40.0 per cent in 1932 and 20.8 per cent in 1947. Oriental Governmental Security, *A Short History*, p. 79; Desai, *Life Insurance in India*, p. 32; *Indian Insurance Year Book 1933*, p. 40, *Indian Insurance Year Book 1947*, pp. 44, 48.

40. As a consequence, this race meant also lowering the standards of life insurance in India. It is reported that many of the smaller companies did not really know what they were doing: they copied the forms of their competitors and simply lowered their figures. The Oriental Life was the only Indian company that regularly employed actuaries and calculated its premiums on mortality and business transacted. All the other companies were more or less gambling.

41. Minimum criterion: 1,000 new policies that year. Data from *Indian Insurance Year Book, 1937*, pp. 40–6, 58. The average sum has been calculated by the author.

42. The political manifesto of this policy is the chapter 'Objectives of Planned Development' in Indian Government, Planning Commission, *Third Five-Year Plan* (New Delhi, 1960), pp. 1–9. On the political context of the nationalization of insurance, see M. C. Rau, *Jawaharlal Nehru* (New Delhi: Ministry of Information and Broadcasting, 1973), p. 230.

43. A concise introduction to this phase of the Indian economy was written by A. Panagariya, *India. The Emerging Giant* (New York: Oxford University Press, 2008), pp. 22–46, especially footnote 4 on page 24 is remarkable in this context.

44. The *Review* wrote in its headline in its next edition after nationalization: 'Somewhat like a bolt from the blue – except that the insurance sky in India has hardly been speckles blue – but suddenly and unexpectedlyt [*sic*], he [*sic*] Indian Government has issued an ordinance nationalising all life insurance ...', *Review*, 27 January 1956, p. 47. Deshmukh's speech is printed in H. D. Malaviya, *Insurance Business in India* (New Delhi: All India Congress Committee, 1956), appendix III, pp. 71–7. Malaviya was engaged in the political process that led to nationalization. As a functionary in the Congress party, he demanded the nationalization of insurance. Just a month after nationalization he published this book, though it is no understatement to call it a pamphlet whose scientific value is limited. It simply justifies political action *ex post*.

45. The liberalization of life insurance was a long process, which began in 1993 with a commission, followed by a parliamentary decision in 1998, and the opening of the market in 2001, though still in a limited way. Currently only 26 per cent of insurance companies can be owned by foreign companies and there are still many other regulations in force that restrict the insurance market.

46. Calculation by the author from data in Desai, *Life Insurance in India*, pp. 32–4. For the calculation after nationalization see below.

47. Life Insurance Company of India, *Annual Reports* (1960, 1970). New business grew from 1,249,821 policies to 1,396,540, while total business rose from 7,456,000 policies in force to 13,939,000 policies in force.

48. Life Insurance Company of India, *Annual Reports* (1970, 1980). New business grew from 1,396,540 policies to 2,095,839, while the total business rose from 13,939,000 policies in force to 22,039,000 policies in force. Looking at total figures the growth seems to be satisfactory, but it is not if one takes into account that during that period the population doubled and the GDP at current prices rose tenfold. Cf. S. Sivasubramonian, *The National Income of India in the Twentieth Century* (Oxford: Oxford University Press, 2000), pp. 492–6. The growth rate was not only lower than before 1956, but also the growth was much lower than the growth of the total service sector.

49. On the consequences of partition, see C. N. Vakil, *Economic Consequences of Divided India: A Study of the Economy of India and Pakistan* (Bombay: Vora, 1950), pp. 522–6. From 1946 (before partition) to 1948 (after partition) new business fell from 596,000 policies to 467,000 policies (down 22 per cent). From 1955 (before nationalization) to 1956 (after nationalization) new business felt from 796,030 policies to 549,401 policies (down 31 per cent). It is hard to estimate how much of the decline during those years was due to the specific political events. At most, both events were short-term setbacks for insurance development, not general changes in the trend.

50. V. K. R. V. Rao, *India's National Income, 1950–1980: An Analysis of Economic Growth and Change* (New Delhi and Beverly Hills, CA: Sage Publications, 1983), p. 66. Rao estimates for the sector of financial services in the GDP the relation of insurance to banking at 40.13:59.87 before nationalization, and 29.91:70.09 in the quinquennia between 1965 and 1980. Unfortunately Rao does not clarify what the basis for these figures was. It may be assumed that this is a ratio of life sums insured to banking deposits in million rupees. This meant – compared to banking – a relative decline of 36.3 per cent (calculation by the author). The problems that banking faced with government economic policy were substantial, too, but they must be examined elsewhere.

51. For example, Dilip Thakore comes to a harsh judgement. D. Thakore, 'The Case for Deregulating the Insurance Sector', at http://www.rediff.com/business/1998/aug/08dilip.htm [accessed 26 April 2010].

52. Malaviya, *Insurance Business in India*, pp. 74–5, 76–7.

53. Ibid., p. 72.

54. Ibid.

55. M. Mohsin, *Investment of Life Insurance Corporation's Fund* (Aligarh: Aligarh Muslim University, 1966), p. 105.

56. Ibid., p. 107.

57. Central government securities and state securities combined. Data from *Indian Insurance Year Book*, 1940–56; Life Insurance Company of India, *Annual Reports* (1957–79).

58. Calculated by the author from data in Life Insurance Company of India, *Annual Reports*.

59. The fiscal year of the LIC was transformed in 1962 from the calendar year to an April to March settlement. This was an adaptation of the governmental budget year.

60. Life Insurance Company of India, *Annual Report* (1968). For an image of typical housing financed by the LIC, see D. Kumar (ed.), *Tryst with Trust* (New Delhi: Life Insurance Corporation of India, 1991), between pp. 224 and 225.

61. O. P. Bajpai, *Life Insurance Finance in India* (Varanasi: Vishwavidyalaya Prakashan, 1975), p. 120.

62. Quoted in Bhave, *Saga of Security*, p. 302.

63. Source: Bajpai, *Life Insurance Finance in India*, p. 165.

64. Life Insurance Company of India, *Annual Report* (1986).

65. Bajpai, *Life Insurance Finance*, p. 165.

66. For example, Muhammad Yunus started his project of Grameen banking micro credits in India's neighbour Bangladesh – see M. Yunus, *Grameen Bank, as I See It* (Dhaka: Grameen Bank, 1994) – and yet during the Green Revolution the assets of the LIC were not channelled into agricultural investment. An innovative contemporary Indian economist would have had better ideas for investment than a current economic researcher could ever think about. The problem was that the LIC was unwise not to install a research department or suchlike. Investing in new channels and small enterprises failed from a lack of information. On this, compare the short, but sage, note of Bajpai, *Life Insurance Finance*, p. 9.

67. *Hindu Business Weekly* (28 September 1964), p. 4.

68. According to the *Hindu Business Weekly* in the first eight months out of 768 applications for a loan under the 'Own Your Home Scheme' only 130 were granted (16.9 per cent). Later figures for the relation between applications and given credits are not given. *Hindu Business Weekly* (28 September 1964), p. 4.

69. *Hindu Business Weekly* (6 January 1964), p. 7.

70. For an overview of interest rates compare Reserve Bank of India, *Handbook of Statistics on the Indian Economy 2002–03* (New Delhi: Reserve Bank, 2003), p. 99. Usual interest rates were between 8.5 per cent (advance rate of Reserve Bank) and 15 per cent (key lending rates for commercial banks).

71. Bajpai, *Life Insurance Finance*, p. 146.

72. M. Y. Khan and P. Singh, 'Life Insurance Corporation and Corporate Control in India', *Indian Economic Journal*, 29 (1981), pp. 51–64, on p. 52.

73. A sample from 1972 showed that of 135 companies the LIC had invested in, it held more than 30 per cent in only one company. Moreover, investment between 20 and 30 per cent was unusual. Only eight of the companies were in this category. At the other end of the spectrum there were only three companies in which LIC shares were below 1 per cent. The usual corporate share of the LIC lay between 2 and 15 per cent, which made it a significant but not dominant shareholder. L. C. Gupta, *Corporate Management and Accountability: Towards a Joint Sector* (Madras: Macmillan India, 1974), p. 67.

74. Khan and Singh, 'Life Insurance Corporation', p. 56.

75. Compare on this Bajpai, *Life Insurance Finance*, p. 162.

76. Khan and Singh, 'Life Insurance Corporation', p. 54.

77. Ibid., p. 52.

78. Ibid., p. 60.

79. Ibid., p. 64.

80. LIC policy made no secret of this fact. For example, on 7 April 1974 the LIC paid for an advertisement in the *Hindu* (p. 4) in which it advised the shareholders of the Punjab National Bank not to accept a cash option recommended by the company's management. The political power of the LIC was a truism in the economic sector – but never formulated explicitly – a kind of Damoclean sword hanging over the stock listed companies.

81. Compare on this Bajpai, *Life Insurance Finance*, p. 147.

8 Verhoef, 'Life Offices to the Rescue!'

I wish to thank the following colleagues for their valuable comments on the earlier draft of this chapter: Giepie Els, Pieter von Wielligh, Robert Vivian, Robert Wright and Robin Pearson. The responsibility for errors and omissions in the final version remains mine.

1. Diamonds were discovered in 1867 and gold deposits in 1886, which brought major international interest in the exploration of the newly discovered wealth. See C. W. de Kiewiet, *A History of South Africa: Social and Economic* (London: Oxford University Press, 1941); A. Müller, *Ekonomiese Geskiedenis van Suid-Afrika* (Pretoria: Academica, 1982); D. H. Houghton, 'Economic Development, 1865–1965', in M. Wilson and L. M. Thompson (eds), *Oxford History of South Africa*, 2 vols (London: Oxford University Press, 1969–71), vol. 2, pp. 1–48, on pp. 1–4.

2. Houghton, 'Economic Development', p. 4.

3. D. H. Houghton, *The South African Economy* (London: Oxford University Press, 1976), pp. 191–2; De Kiewiet, *A History of South Africa*, pp. 6–8; C. G. W. Schumann, *Structural Changes and Business Cycles in South Africa, 1800–1936* (London: Staples Press, 1938), pp. 43–5.

4. R. W. Vivian, 'Anniversaries', *Cover*, 19 (2006), 44; R. W. Vivian, 'A Royal Farewell', *FA News* (April 2004), pp. 12–13.

5. Keller, *The Life Insurance Enterprise*, p. 3; Wright and Smith, *Mutually Beneficial*, p. 1.

6. Keller, *Life Insurance Enterprise*, p. 3. For the similar development trend in Japan, see Nippon Life Company, *The 100 Year History of Nippon Life: Its Growth and Socio-economic Setting 1889–1989* (Osaka: Nippon Life Company, 1989), pp. 2–4.

7. Raynes, *A History of British Insurance*, pp. 117–19.

8. L. Dennett, *A Sense of Security: 150 Years of Prudential* (Cambridge: Granta Editions, 1998), pp. 7–8; Wright and Smith, *Mutually Beneficial*, pp. 5–7.

9. Dennett, *A Sense of Security*, pp. 7–9; Keller, *The Life Insurance Enterprise*, p. 5.

10. Raynes, *A History of British Insurance*, pp. 123–4.

11. Ibid., p. 125.

12. M. F. Reinecke, S. van der Merwe, J. P. van Niekerk and P. Havenga, *General Principles of Insurance Law* (Durban: Lexis Nexis Butterworths, 2002), p. 2.

13. Keller, *The Life Insurance Enterprise*, p. 3.

14. D. M. Davis, *The South African Law of Insurance* (Cape Town: Juta, 1993), p. 19; Reinecke et al., *General Principles of Insurance Law*, p. 3.

15. Wright and Smith, *Mutually Beneficial*, p. 4.

16. Ibid., p. 5.

17. Keller, *The Life Insurance Enterprise*, pp. 5–7; Wright and Smith, *Mutually Beneficial*, pp. 5–7.

18. Keller, *The Life Insurance Enterprise*, p. 7; O. M. Westall, *The Provincial Insurance Company, 1903–1938* (Manchester: Manchester University Press, 1992), pp. 197, 229; Wright and Smith, *Mutually Beneficial*, pp. 10–12.

19. Wright and Smith, *Mutually Beneficial*, p. 7.

20. South African Government, *Summaries of Returns Deposited with the Treasury by Insurance Companies during the Year Ended 31 December 1927* (Pretoria: Government Printer, 1928), pp. 8–9; O. Knaggs, *Norwich Life 1706–1990* (Cape Town: Oliver Knaggs and Associates, 1990), pp. 4–5; Ogborn, *Equitable Assurances*, pp. 10–11; R. W. Vivian,

'South African Insurance Markets', in J. D. Cummins and B. Venard (eds), *Handbook of International Insurance* (New York: Springer, 2007), pp. 677–738, on p. 698.

21. R. W. Vivian, 'A History of the South African Fire and Life Assurance Company', *South African Journal of Economic History*, 11 (1996), pp. 145–57, on pp. 146–8; H. Spyrou, 'The Development of Insurance Business in the Union of South Africa', *South African Journal of Economics*, 23 (1955), pp. 325–40, on p. 325; R. Van Selm, *History of the South African Mutual Life Assurance Society, 1845–1945* (Cape Town: Mutual Life Assurance Society, 1945), p. 2.

22. R. W. Vivian, 'A History of the London and Lancashire Fire Insurance Company in South Africa', *South African Journal of Economic History*, 17 (2002), pp. 138–61, on pp. 142–3; Spyrou, 'The Development of Insurance Business', pp. 325–6; R. W. Vivian, *The Story of Mutual and Federal 1831–1995* (Johannesburg: Mutual and Federal Insurance Company, 1995), p. 22.

23. S. Jones, *The Great Imperial Banks in South Africa: A Study of the Business of Standard Bank and Barclays Bank, 1861–1961* (Pretoria: Unisa Press, 1996); E. H. D. Arndt, *Banking and Currency Development in South Africa* (Cape Town: Juta, 1928).

24. Van Selm, *History of the South African Mutual*; Spyrou, 'The Development of Insurance Business', p. 325.

25. Van Selm, *History of the South African Mutual*, p. 88.

26. J. M. Morgan, *The Development of the Insurance Institute Movement in South Africa: A History* (Johannesburg: Cuppleditch Communication, 1992), p. 11; Vivian, 'A History of the London and Lancashire', pp. 147–8.

27. E. H. D. Arndt, *An Analysis of the Investment Policies of Life Insurance Companies in the Union of South Africa: The Need for More Constructive Legislation*, 4th edn, Publications of the University of Pretoria series 3: Arts and Social Sciences 1 (Pretoria: University of Pretoria, 1938), p. 18; General Managers Reports 3/1/116: 20 May 1937, Standard Bank Archives, Simmonds Street, Johannesburg. See also T. V. Bulpin, *Die Southern 75 Jaar van Diens* (Cape Town: Southern Life Association, 1966), p. 24; Sanlam, *Die weerste Vyftig Jaar* (Belvieel: Sanlam, 1968), pp. 30–3.

28. E. H. D. Arndt, *Insuring our Insurance: A Survey of Insurance Legislation with Recommendations for the Union* (Pretoria: Union Booksellers, 1941), pp. 6, 10–11.

29. Davis, *The South African Law of Insurance*, pp. 13–15; B. C. Benfield, 'South African Life Assurance Legislation; A Survey', *South African Journal of Economics*, 65 (1997), pp. 568–94, on pp. 570–3; M. Bernstein, 'The South African Insurance Market', paper presented to South African Actuarial Society, 13 December 1977, p. 6; Spyrou, 'The Development of Insurance Business', pp. 330–1; Arndt, *An Analysis of the Investment Policies*, p. 31.

30. Reinecke et al., *General Principles of Insurance Law*, pp. 10–14.

31. B. C. Benfield, 'South African Life Assurance: Circumstance, Significance and Technique' (PhD dissertation, University of the Witwatersrand, 1987), pp. 149–50; B. Goodall, 'Short and Long Term Insurers and Private Pension and Provident Funds', in A. Hamersma and N. H. H. Czypionka (eds), *Essays on the South African Financial Structure* (Johannesburg: SBSA, 1975), pp. 125–34, on pp. 130–1.

32. Goodall, 'Short and Long Term Insurers', p. 129.

33. Spyrou, 'The Development of Insurance Business', p. 326.

34. South African Government, *Summaries of Returns Deposited with the Treasury by Insurance Companies during the Year Ended 31 December 1943* (Pretoria: Government Printer, 1944); R. W. Vivian, *Morgan's History of the Insurance Institute Movement of*

South Africa, 1898–1999 (Cape Town: IISA, 2001), pp. 22–3; Morgan, *The Development of the Insurance Institute Movement*, pp. 12–15.

35. Sources: South African Government, *Summaries of Returns Deposited with the Treasury by Insurance Companies* (1925, 1940). South African Government, *Annual Report of the Registrar of Insurance Companies* (1944, 1945).

36. S. Jones and A. Müller, *The South African Economy 1910–1990* (London: Macmillan, 1992), p. 109; C. H. Feinstein, *An Economic History of South Africa: Conquest, Discrimination and Development* (Cambridge: Cambridge University Press, 2005), pp. 95, 122, 166.

37. Jones and Müller, *The South African Economy*, pp. 21–3, 48–9; Houghton, *The South African Economy*, pp. 40–1.

38. Spyrou, 'The Development of Insurance Business', p. 333.

39. P. Scott, 'Towards the "Cult of the Equity"? Insurance Companies and the Interwar Capital Market', *Economic History Review*, 55 (2002), pp. 78–104; Arndt, *An Analysis of the Investment Policies*; Wright and Smith, *Mutually Beneficial*, p. 5.

40. Benfield, 'South African Life Assurance Legislation', p. 574.

41. Bernstein, 'The South African Insurance Market', p. 6; Benfield, 'South African Life Assurance Legislation', p. 574; Benfield, 'South African Life Assurance', pp. 144–5, 149–50.

42. E. H. D. Arndt, 'Safety for Savings', *South African Journal of Economics*, 2:3 (1934), pp. 273–87.

43. Arndt, *An Analysis of the Investment Policies*, p. 48.

44. Arndt, *Insuring our Insurance*, pp. 15–16; Bernstein, 'The South African Insurance Market', p. 6; Benfield, 'South African Life Assurance', pp. 150–6; Benfield, 'South African Life Assurance Legislation', pp. 575–7.

45. Reinecke et al., *General Principles of Insurance Law*, p. 14.

46. Benfield, 'South African Life Assurance Legislation', p. 578; Bernstein, 'The South African Insurance Market', p. 6.

47. Arndt, *An Analysis of the Investment Policies*, pp. 13–17.

48. South African Reserve Bank, *A Statistical Presentation of South Africa's National Accounts for the period 1946 to 1970* (Pretoria: Government Printer, 1975), p. 12.

49. South African Government, Bureau for Census and Statistics, *Union Statistics for Fifty Years, Jubilee Edition, 1910–1960* (Pretoria: Government Printer, 1960), 1965, p. S-3.

50. S. H. Frankel, 'Review of E. H. D. Arndt', *South African Journal of Economics*, 9:4 (1941), pp. 313–14; G. H. Beak, 'South African Insurance Legislation and the Security of Policyholders', *Transactions of the Actuarial Society of South Africa*, 11 (1973), pp. 60–72; D. W. Goedhuys, 'South African Monetary Policy in the 1980s: Years of Reform and Foreign Financial Aggression', *South African Journal of Economic History*, 9 (1994), pp. 144–63, on p. 154.

51. Spyrou, 'The Development of Insurance Business', p. 335; South African Government, Department of Finance, *Report of the Commission of Inquiry into the Long Term Insurance Industry* (Pretoria: Government Printer, 1976); Goodall, 'Short and Long Term Insurers', pp. 125–7; Bernstein, 'The South African Insurance Market', p. 10.

52. Bernstein, 'The South African Insurance Market', p. 18; Benfield, 'South African Life Assurance', p. 160.

53. A. Laing, 'Change and Development in Short Term Insurance in South Africa, 1950–1985', *South African Journal of Economic History*, 3 (1988), pp. 33–44, on pp. 33–8.

54. Jones and Müller, *The South African Economy*, pp. 91–3; Wright and Smith, *Mutually Beneficial*, pp. 4–5.

55. Sources: South African Government, *Summaries of Returns deposited with the Treasury by Insurance Companies* (1940). South African Government, *Annual Report of the Registrar of Insurance Companies* (1944, 1951).

56. Goedhuys, 'South African Monetary Policy', pp. 156–7.

57. A. R. Munro and A. M. Snyman, 'The Life Insurance Industry in South Africa', *Geneva Papers on Risk and Insurance*, 20 (1995), pp. 127–40, on p. 130.

58. Sigma Economic Studies Database, 1990–2000, Swiss Re Archive, Zurich.

59. In 1960 South Africa changed the use of the British pound sterling currency to the use of the South African rand. The exchange rate was £1 = R2 in 1960. This exchange rate remained roughly unchanged until the later 1970s. Sources: South African Government, *Annual Report of the Registrar of Insurance Companies* (1945–2000); South African Reserve Bank, *Quarterly Statistical Bulletin* (1950–2002), p. S-104.

60. Source: World Insurance, Sigma Economic Studies Database, 1990–2002, Swiss Re Archive, Zurich.

61. Munro and Snyman, 'The Life Insurance Industry', pp. 127–30.

62. Ibid., p. 132.

63. G. Maasdorp, 'Economic Survey, 1970–2000', in S. Jones (ed.), *The Decline of the South African Economy* (Cheltenham: Edward Elgar, 2002), pp. 7–30, on p. 27; P. Mohr, 'An Overview of the South African Economy in the 1990s', *South African Journal of Economic History*, 18 (2003), pp. 16–30, on p. 18.

64. Maasdorp, 'Economic Survey', p. 26; Benfield, 'South African Life Assurance', pp. 190–3.

65. Source: SARB, Quarterly Statistical Bulletin, 1950–2001; South African Government, *Annual Report of the Registrar of Insurance Companies* (1950–2001). Total premium income includes total recurrent premiums and single premiums.

66. Source: Financial Services Board, Long Term Insurance Reports, 1990–2001. 'Expenditure' refers to benefits paid, management expenses, commission and other expenditures. The bulk of expenditure was benefits paid.

67. Source: South African Government, *Annual Report of the Registrar of Insurance Companies* (1950–90); Financial Services Board, Long Term Insurance Reports, 1990–2001. Total income includes premium income, investment income and other income.

68. Goodall, 'Short and Long Term Insurers', p. 127.

69. Munro and Snyman, 'The Life Insurance Industry', pp. 138–9.

70. Source: South African Government, *Annual Report of the Registrar of Insurance Companies* (1950–2001).

71. South African Government, *Third Report of the Commission of Enquiry into Fiscal and Monetary Policy in South Africa (Franszen Commission)*, RP87/1970 (Pretoria: Government Printer, 1970), pp. 213, 218.

72. G. Verhoef, 'The Dynamics of Banking in South Africa, 1980–1993', *South African Journal of Economic History*, special issue (1994), pp. 84–109, on pp. 84–6.

73. *South African Banker*, 71 (1974), p. 23; 74 (1977), p. 12.

74. D. T. Nicholson, 'Look at the Recent Changes in Banking Legislation in South Africa', *South African Banker*, 73 (1976), pp. 149–53, on p. 149.

75. Source: SARB Quarterly Bulletin, 1950–2001; South African Government, *Annual Report of the Registrar of Insurance Companies* (1950–2001).

76. South African Government, *Annual Report of the Registrar of Insurance Companies* (1977), p. 3.

77. M. L. Rosa, *Central Banking and Banking Regulation* (London: LSE Financial Markets Group, 1996); A. Fazio, 'Financial Stability and Growth', in L. De Rosa (ed.), *International Banking and Financial Systems: Evolution and Stability* (Aldershot: Ashgate, 2003), pp. 225–32; R. W. Ferguson, 'Consolidation in the Financial Sector', in De Rosa (ed.), *International Banking and Financial System*, pp. 233–8.

78. South African Government, *Final Report of the Commission of Inquiry into the Monetary System and Monetary Policy in South Africa (De Kock Commission)*, RP70/1984 (Pretoria: Government Printer, 1984).

79. Verhoef, 'The Dynamics of Banking', pp. 85–93.

80. The debt standstill was negotiated in four stages and by June 2001 the total debt was repaid. See Goedhuys, 'South African Monetary Policy', pp. 159–63.

81. Standard Bank was controlled by the Liberty Life; Nedbank was controlled by the Old Mutual Life Assurance Company; Volkskas Bank, Trust Bank and the former United Building Society – the largest and oldest building society – by the SANLAM; and the Rembrandt Group controlled by the Rupert Family; Barclays Bank DC&O was taken over by the Southern Life Company. These takeovers were completed by 1990.

82. See Beak, 'South African Insurance Legislation'.

83. Source: South African Reserve Bank, *Quarterly Statistical Bulletin* (1990–2001). South Africa experienced a net capital outflow between 1985 and 1991 as a result of the debt standstill agreement. This development explains the dramatic growth in domestic investment since the growth capacity of the South African economy had been proven.

84. Benfield, 'South African Life Assurance Legislation', pp. 588–91; B. C. Benfield and R. W. Vivian, 'Insurance in the 1990s', *South African Journal of Economic History*, 18 (2003), pp. 275–88; Vivian, 'South African Insurance Markets', pp. 697–9.

85. South African Government, *Annual Report of the Registrar of Insurance Companies* (1977), p. 3.

86. See Vivian, 'South African Insurance Markets', p. 699.

87. Financial Services Board, Long Term Insurance Annual Report, 1999; 'Finance and Economics: All Change in South Africa', *Economist*, 346:8056 (1998), p. 75; Benfield and Vivian, 'Insurance in the 1990s', pp. 285–7.

88. Spyrou, 'The Development of Insurance Business', p. 334.

9 Lengwiler, 'Competing Globalizations'

1. For transnational history, see P. Clavin, 'Defining Transnationalism', *Contemporary European History*, 14 (2005), pp. 421–40; for the history of knowledge, see J. Vogel, 'Von der Wissenschafts- zur Wissensgeschichte: Für eine Historisierung der "Wissensgesellschaft"', *Geschichte und Gesellschaft*, 30 (2004), pp. 639–60; for the transnational aspects of social policy, see C. Conrad, 'Vorbemerkung zum Themenheft "Sozialpolitik Transnational"', *Geschichte und Gesellschaft*, 32 (2006), pp. 437–44.

2. For the world exhibitions, see H. Meller, 'Philanthropy and Public Enterprise: International Exhibitions and the Modern Town Planning Movement, 1889–1913', *Planning Perspectives*, 3 (1995), pp. 295–310; for the early international organizations, see M. Herren, 'Sozialpolitik und die Historisierung des Transnationalen', *Geschichte und Gesellschaft*, 32 (2006), pp. 542–59; for the significance of universalist traditions in the history of the nation states and for processes of globalization, see the sociological 'world

polity approach' of John W. Meyer and its Stanford school. A series of crucial articles has recently been collected: J. W. Meyer, *World Society: The Writings of John W. Meyer* (Oxford: Oxford University Press, 2009), pp. 36–65.

3. L. Raphael, 'Europäische Sozialstaaten in der Boomphase (1948–1973): Versuch einer Historischen Distanzierung einer "Klassischen Phase" des Europäischen Sozialmodells', in H. Kaelble and G. Schmid (eds), *Das Europäische Sozialmodell: Auf dem Weg zum Transnationalen Sozialstaat* (Berlin: Edition Sigma, 2004), pp. 51–74; H. Kaelble, 'Das europäische Sozialmodell – eine historische Perspektive', in Kaelble and Schmid (eds), *Das Europäische Sozialmodell*, pp. 31–50.

4. Arps, *Auf Sicheren Pfeilern*, pp. 308ff.; see also P. Baldwin, *The Politics of Social Solidarity: Class Bases of the European Welfare States 1875–1975* (Berkeley, CA: University of California Press, 1991).

5. See, for example, U. Ascoli and C. Ranci (eds), *Dilemmas of the Welfare Mix: The New Structure of Welfare in an Era of Privatization* (Berlin: Kluwer Academic, 2002).

6. C. Guinand, *ILO und die Soziale Sicherheit in Europa, 1942–1967* (Bern: Peter Lang, 2002); see also D. Maul, *Menschenrechte, Sozialpolitik und Dekolonisation, die IAO 1940–1970* (Essen: Klartext, 2007).

7. D. Maul, 'Der Transnationale Blick: Die Internationale Arbeitsorganisation und die Sozialpolitischen Krisen Europas im 20. Jahrhundert', *Archiv für Sozialversicherungen*, 47 (2007), pp. 349–70, on pp. 351–6.

8. Congresses convened in Brussels (1895), London (1898), Paris (1900), New York (1903), Berlin (1906), Vienna (1909), Amsterdam (1912), London (1927), Stockholm (1930), Rome (1934), Paris (1937), Lucerne (1941), Scheveningen (1951). The interruption between 1912 and 1927 was due to the First World War and the succeeding inflation crisis. International Congress of Actuaries, *Transactions International Congress of Actuaries* [hereafter *Transactions*] (1927), vol. 5, pp. 110–11. The four-year gap between 1930 and 1934 was explained by the economic crisis, whereas the Second World War severely hampered the organization of the twelfth congress in Lucerne. The congress was originally planned for 1940 and the papers were sent in during the summer of 1939 before the outbreak of the war, but in the end no convention was held. As a statement on their belief in the values of international cooperation despite the wartime situation, the organizing committee decided to publish the papers in 1941, see *Transactions* (1941), vol. 1, pp. 13–14.

9. Opening address of A. Bégault (Brussels) in *Transactions* (1906), vol. 3, pp. 3–4; see also P. Borscheid, 'Systemwettbewerb, Institutionenexport und Homogenisierung: Der Internationalisierungsprozess der Versicherungswirtschaft im 19. Jahrhundert', *Zeitschrift für Unternehmensgeschichte*, 51 (2006), pp. 26–53.

10. *Transactions* (1898), p. 23; see also (1895), 2nd edn, pp. 8–10.

11. *Transactions* (1895), pp. 15–30.

12. *Transactions* (1903), vol. 2, pp. 45–6.

13. Source: *Transactions* (1895–1951).

14. *Transactions* (1895), pp. 31–72; (1898), pp. 582–640.

15. *Transactions* (1903), vol. 2, pp. 85–9.

16. See the contributions of Hans Ammeter in *Transactions* (1951), vol. 1, pp. 631ff., vol. 3, pp. 297, 305, 315.

17. *Transactions* (1903), vol. 3, pp. 229ff.

18. See the contribution of Walter Thalmann in *Transactions* (1937), vol. 2, pp. 89ff.

19. *Transactions* (1927), vol. 5, pp. 221–2.

20. Source: *Transactions* (1895–1937); for the absolute numbers, see the annex to this chapter, Table 9.7. Note: data for 1941 and 1951 not available.
21. *Transactions* (1937), vol. 3, pp. 93–104.
22. Source: *Transactions* (1895–1937); for the absolute numbers, see the annex to this chapter, Tables 9.3–6. Note: the high numbers of German participants in 1906 and British ones in 1927 were due to the venues of the congress (1906 in Berlin and 1927 in London) and the hosting status of the respective national delegation.
23. *Transactions* (1903), vol. 1, pp. 1104–12.
24. See for example the prognosis of Léon Marie, a French delegate, that the development of insurance legislation follows a common trend (to less government intervention), *Transactions* (1898), pp. 338–40.
25. *Transactions* (1898), p. 345.
26. Companies had to publish the accounts every five years and submit summary financial results yearly to the supervisory authority. There was one exception to this liberal supervision: the control of companies offering industrial insurance – a low-cost and extremely popular form of life insurance – were under the close scrutiny of the state, a supervision implemented by the Industrial Assurance Commissioner; *Transactions* (1895), p. 475 (quoting King); (1898), pp. 344–5; (1903), vol. 1, pp. 1009–20; (1895), pp. 212, 258–60; (1937), vol. 3, pp. 93–104.
27. *Transactions* (1895), pp. 475–6.
28. *Transactions* (1906), vol. 2, pp. 447–58, 467–77, 521–6. The German Reichsgesetz über die privaten Versicherungsunternehmer (the law regulating government supervision) dated from 1901, and the Austrian law from 1904. The French legislation after 1900 was also partly inspired by the Swiss model. Ibid., vol. 2, pp. 467–77.
29. *Transactions* (1895), pp. 466–9; (1903), vol. 2, pp. 1032–3.
30. *Transactions* (1895), pp. 258ff., 466–9; (1898), pp. 300–7, 335, 340–2, 343–4; (1903), vol. 1, pp. 963–70, 1007–52.
31. *Transactions* (1903), vol. 1, p. 1030.
32. Examples are Alfred Manes, a key figure in the German Association of Actuaries and professor of insurance economics in Berlin; Fritz Rosselet, a Swiss government actuary at the Federal Insurance Office; and Christian Moser, another Swiss government actuary and professor of mathematical statistics at the University of Berne; *Transactions* (1903), vol. 1, pp. 971–91, 1057–75; (1912), vol. 1, pp. 317–23.
33. See the discussions and the various criticisms of the Swiss and German legislation; *Transactions* (1903), vol. 2, pp. 229–50.
34. The original remark in German is: 'Es kann schwerlich als ein günstiges Omen für die Erreichung einer uniformen Gesetzgebung angesehen werden, dass die Versuche, genau anzugeben, worüber man eigentlich eine Abhandlung verlangt, so wenig uniform ausgefallen sind'. *Transactions* (1906), vol. 2, p. 609.
35. *Transactions* (1906), vol. 2, pp. 581–99, esp. p. 582; (1937), vol. 3, pp. 105–10.
36. *Transactions* (1937), vol. 3, pp. 93–104, 105–10.
37. For the case of Britain, see *Transactions* (1898), pp. 527–33, 534–42, 572–3; for a similar argument for the French *mutualités*, see ibid., pp. 380–91.
38. For an early treatment, see *Transactions* (1898), pp. vii–ix, and the respective sections at the congress.
39. *Transactions* (1898), pp. 572–3.
40. *Transactions* (1909), vol. 3, p. 257.

41. Only occasionally did some marginal actuaries sketch the outlines of a future without social insurance, for example James Klang, director (*Generaldirektor*) at the Austrian branch of the Phenix, who envisioned a future where social insurance proved to be a transitory phenomenon that convinced the working class of the idea of insurance – to the extent that workers were ultimately ready to switch to the more professional commercial insurance products. See *Transactions* (1909), vol. 3, pp. 219–20.

42. With detailed historical information on the learning processes between social and private insurance, see the paper of A. Emminghaus, the director of the Gotha life insurance company, the market leader in Germany, in *Transactions* (1909), vols 1–2, pp. 995–1005, 1007–21; vol. 3, pp. 220–5; see also (1937), vol. 5, pp. 231–2.

43. *Transactions* (1909), vol. 3, p. 204; vols 1–2, p. 1021; see already in (1903), vol. 1, pp. 625–55; vol. 2, pp. 178–83.

44. *Transactions* (1909), vols 1–2, pp. 1033–50, esp. pp. 1034, 1042ff.; see also discussions of this section in vol. 3, pp. 132–46, 202–66; for the perspective of friendly societies, see *Transactions* (1909), vols 1–2, pp. 1055–67; see also (1903), vol. 1, pp. 656–70.

45. Opening address of Am. Bégault, chairman of the congress, in *Transactions* (1927), vol. 5, p. 111.

46. *Transactions* (1927), vol. 5, pp. 207, 227–8.

47. Since the late 1930s such themes were treated at the congress in the form of memoranda, implying that they were not discussed at the meetings any more. The topics of the papers suggest that after the end of the 1930s the time for heated political debates at the congress was over. The arguments in the papers and the discussions seem to shift from a political to a technical level.

48. For Britain, see *Transactions* (1927), vol. 1, pp. 221–36, 237–60; (1937), vol. 2, pp. 151–70; for France, see (1909), vols 1–2, pp. 1033–50; for Switzerland and Germany, see (1930), vol. 3, pp. 3ff., 26ff., 223–44; vol. 4, pp. 398–425; see also M. Lengwiler, 'Competing Appeals: The Rise of Mixed Welfare Economies in Europe, 1850–1945', in G. Clark (ed.), *The Appeal of Insurance* (Toronto: University of Toronto Press, forthcoming).

49. See *Transactions* (1934), vol. 4, pp. 92–105, 109–27; (1937), vol. 2, pp. 151–70 (on Britain), 171–87 (on Germany), 189–206, 379–85 (on Switzerland); vol. 5, pp. 230–6; for Germany, see also C. Conrad, *Vom Greis zum Rentner, Strukturwandel des Alters in Deutschland, 1830–1930* (Göttingen: Vandenhoeck & Ruprecht, 1994); for Britain, see R. Pearson, 'Who Pays for Pensions? Das Problem der Alterssicherung in Grossbritannien im zwanzigsten Jahrhundert', *Zeitschrift für Unternehmensgeschichte*, 48 (2003), pp. 48–57; for Switzerland, see M. Leimgruber, '*Achieving Social Progress without Etatization'? A Political Economy of the Swiss Three-Pillar System of Old Age Insurance (1890–1972)* (Cambridge: Cambridge University Press, 2008); see also Lengwiler, 'Competing Appeals'.

50. *Transactions* (1937), vol. 2, pp. 161–2, 171–87; vol. 5, pp. 245ff., 249ff., 261ff., 268–9, 295ff.

51. C. Guinand, 'Zur Entstehung von IVSS und IAO', *Internationale Revue für Soziale Sicherheit*, 61 (2008), pp. 93–111; Internationale Vereinigung für Soziale Sicherheit [hereafter IVSS], *Historische Dokumente, 1927–1947* (Geneva: IVSS, 1977).

52. G. A. Johnston, *The International Labour Organisation: Its Work for Social and Economic Progress* (London: Europa Publications, 1970), pp. 199–200.

53. ILOLEX, www.ilo.org/ilolex/; Johnston, *The International Labour Organisation*, pp. 308–11.

54. Johnston, *The International Labour Organisation*, pp. 198–9.

55. Most of the conventions in labour legislation of the European Council were based upon expert opinions of the ILO; ibid., pp. 204–5.

56. Ibid., pp. 199–202.

57. IVSS, *Im Dienste der Sozialen Sicherheit, Die Geschichte der IVSS, 1927–1987* (Geneva: IVSS, 1986), p. 44.

58. Johnston, *The International Labour Organisation*, pp. 204–5; see also tables in M. Stack, *Vierzig Jahre im Dienste der Sozialen Sicherheit (1927–1967)* (Geneva: IVSS, 1967), p. 22; see also: IVSS, *Im Dienste der Sozialen Sicherheit*, p. 27.

59. Stack, *Vierzig Jahre*, pp. 17–18, 22.

60. Ibid., p. 22; IVSS, *Im Dienste der Sozialen Sicherheit*, pp. 25ff., 39–40.

61. Maul, 'Der Transnationale Blick'.

62. IVSS, *Im Dienste der Sozialen Sicherheit*, pp. 39–42, 51–3.

63. M. Ferrara, 'The "Southern Model" of Welfare in Social Europe', *Journal of European Social Policy*, 6 (1996), pp. 17–37; IVSS, *Im Dienste der Sozialen Sicherheit*, pp. 39–42.

64. Stack, *Vierzig Jahre*, p. 22.

65. Ibid., pp. 9–10.

66. IVSS, *Im Dienste der Sozialen Sicherheit*, pp. 42–3.

67. Source: *Transactions* (1895–1952).

WORKS CITED

Manuscripts

Banco de la Provincia de Buenos Aires, Argentina, Hugh Dallas Papers.

Brotherton Library, University of Leeds, William Lupton & Co. Papers.

Chilean National Archives, Valparaiso Judicial Papers.

Guildhall Library, Antony Gibbs & Sons Papers.

Guildhall Library, Huth Papers.

John Rylands Library, University of Manchester, Green, Hodgson and Robinson Papers.

Mutua General de Seguros Archive.

National Archives, Kew, Surrey.

Standard Bank Archives, Simmonds Street, Johannesburg.

SwissRe Archive, Zurich.

University College London, Special Collections, Huth & Co. Papers, English Letters.

University of Glasgow Archives, Wylie & Co. Papers.

Unternehmensarchiv Winterthur-AXA, Winterthur.

Zurich Financial Services, Zurich, Corporate Archives.

Printed Sources

Agarwala, A. N., *Insurance in India: A Study of Insurance Aspect of Social Security in India* (Allahabad: Allahabad Law Journal Press, 1960).

Alborn, T., *Regulated Lives: Life Insurance and British Society, 1800–1914* (Toronto: University of Toronto Press, 2009).

Ammeter, H., 'Grundlagen und Hauptprobleme der Sachversicherungsmathematik', *Mitteilungen der Vereinigung schweizerischer Versicherungsmathematiker*, 65 (1965), pp. 147–61.

—, 'Die Entwicklung der Versicherungsmathematik im 20. Jahrhundert', *Mitteilungen der Vereinigung schweizerischer Versicherungsmathematiker*, 70 (1970), pp. 317–32.

Armstrong, D., 'A History of the Property Insurance Business in the United States prior to 1890' (DPhil. dissertation, New York University, 1971).

Arndt, E. H. D., *Banking and Currency Development in South Africa* (Cape Town: Juta, 1928).

—, 'Safety for Savings', *South African Journal of Economics*, 2:3 (1934), pp. 273–87.

—, *An Analysis of the Investment Policies of Life Insurance Companies in the Union of South Africa: The Need for More Constructive Legislation*, 4th edn, Publications of the University of Pretoria series 3: Arts and Social Sciences 1 (Pretoria: University of Pretoria, 1938).

—, *Insuring our Insurance: A Survey of Insurance Legislation with Recommendations for the Union* (Pretoria: Union Booksellers, 1941).

Arps, L., *Auf Sicheren Pfeilern: Deutsche Versicherungswirtschaft vor 1914* (Göttingen: Vandenhoeck & Ruprecht, 1965).

Asahi Life Insurance Company, *The 80 Year History of Asahi Life Insurance Company* (Tokyo: Asahi Life Insurance Company, 1968).

—, *The Centenary History of Yasuda Life* (Tokyo: Asahi Life Insurance Company, 1975).

—, *The 123 Year History of Yasuda Life* (Tokyo: Asahi Life Insurance Company, 2003).

Ascoli, U., and C. Ranci (eds), *Dilemmas of the Welfare Mix: The New Structure of Welfare in an Era of Privatization* (Berlin: Kluwer Academic, 2002).

Aubrun, R.-G., *Mutual Aid Societies in France* (San Francisco, CA: Exposition Universielle De San Francisco, 1915).

Bajpai, O. P., *Life Insurance Finance in India* (Varanasi: Vishwavidyalaya Prakashan, 1975).

Baldwin, P., *The Politics of Social Solidarity: Class Bases of the European Welfare States 1875–1975* (Berkeley, CA: University of California Press, 1991).

Bankoff, G., 'Dangers to Going it Alone: Social Capital and the Origins of Community Resilience in the Philippines', *Continuity and Change*, 22 (2007), pp. 327–55.

Baranoff, D., 'Principals, Agents and Control in the American Fire Insurance Industry, 1799–1872', *Business and Economic History*, 27 (1998), pp. 91–101.

—, 'A Policy of Cooperation: The Cartelisation of American Fire Insurance, 1873–1906', *Financial History Review*, 10 (2003), pp. 119–36.

Barciela, C., 'Autarquía e Intervencionismo, 1939–1950', in C. Barciela, M. I. López, J. Melgarejo and J. M. Miranda (eds), *La España de Franco (1939–1975): Economía* (Madrid, 2001), pp. 23–154.

—, 'Guerra Civil y Primer Franquismo (1936–1959)', in F. Comín, M. Hernández and E. Llopis (eds), *Historia Económica de España, Siglos X–XX* (Barcelona: Crítica, 2002), pp. 331–68.

— (ed.), *Autarquía y Mercado Negro: El Fracaso del Primer Franquismo, 1939–1959* (Barcelona: Crítica, 2003).

Barnard, R. W., *A Century of Service, the Story of the Prudential 1848–1948* (London: Times Publishing, 1948).

Beak, G. H., 'South African Insurance Legislation and the Security of Policyholders', *Transactions of the Actuarial Society of South Africa*, 11 (1973), pp. 60–72.

Beck, U., *Risikogesellschaft: Auf dem Weg in eine andere Moderne* (Frankfurt am Main: Suhrkamp, 1986).

Beckmann, R., C. Eppendorfer and M. Neimke, *Financial Integration within the European Union: Towards a Single Market for Insurance*, Institut für Europäische Wirtschaft, Diskussionsbeiträge 40 (Bochum: Ruhr University, 2002).

—, 'Financial Integration within the European Union: Towards a Single Market for Insurance', in P. Cecchini, F. Heinemann and M. Jopp (eds), *The Incomplete European Market for Financial Services*, ZEW Economic Studies 19 (Heidelberg: Physica-Verlag, 2003), pp. 1–29.

Benfield, B. C., 'South African Life Assurance: Circumstance, Significance and Technique' (PhD dissertation, University of the Witwatersrand, 1987).

—, 'South African Life Assurance Legislation; A Survey', *South African Journal of Economics*, 65 (1997), pp. 568–94.

Benfield, B. C., and R. W. Vivian, 'Insurance in the 1990s', *South African Journal of Economic History*, 18 (2003), pp. 275–88.

Berghoff, H., and J. Sydow (eds), *Unternehmerische Netzwerke: Eine Historische Organisationsform mit Zukunft?* (Stuttgart: Kohlhammer, 2007).

Bernstein, M., 'The South African Insurance Market', paper presented to South African Actuarial Society, 13 December 1977.

Bernstein, P., *Against the Gods: The Remarkable Story of Risk* (New York: Wiley, 1996).

Bhave, S. R. (ed.), *Saga of Security: Story of Indian Life Insurance, 1870–1970* (Bombay: Life Insurance Corporation of India, 1970).

Bickelhaupt, D. L., and R. Bar-Niv, *International Insurance: Managing Risk in the World* (New York: Insurance Information Institute, 1983).

Booth, C., *The Aged Poor in England and Wales* (London: Macmillan, 1894).

Borscheid, P., *275 Jahre Feuersozietäten in Westfalen: Vorprung durch Erfahrung* (Münster: Westfälische Provinzial-Versicherungen, 1997).

—, 'Vertrauensgewinn und Vertrauensverlust: Das Auslandsgeschäft der Deutschen Versicherungswirtschaft 1870–1945', *Vierteljahrschrift für Sozial- und Wirtschaftsgeschichte*, 88 (2001), pp. 311–45.

—, 'Systemwettbewerb, Institionenexport und Homogenisierung: Der Internationalisierungsprozess der Versicherungswirtschaft im 19. Jahrhundert', *Zeitschrift für Unternehmensgeschichte*, 51 (2006), pp. 26–53.

—, 'A Globalisation Backlash in the Inter-War Period?', in Borscheid and Pearson (eds), *Internationalisation and Globalisation of the Insurance Industry*, pp. 129–41.

Borscheid, P., and R. Pearson (eds), *Internationalisation and Globalisation of the Insurance Industry in the Nineteenth and Twentieth Centuries* (Marburg: Philipps-University, 2007).

Braun, H., *Geschichte der Lebensversicherung und der Lebensversicherungstechnik*, Veröffentlichungen des Deutschen Vereins für Versicherungswissenschaft 70, 2nd edn (Berlin: Duncker & Humblot, 1963).

Bremborg Davidsson, A., *Yrke: Begravningsentreprenör* (Lund: Lund University, 2002).

Büchner, F., 'Die Entstehung der Hamburger Feuerkasse und ihre Entwicklung bis zur Mitte des 19. Jahrhunderts', in Hamburger Feuerkasse, *300 Jahre Hamburger Feuerkasse* (Karlsruhe: Verlag Versicherungswirtschaft, 1976), pp. 1–50.

Buck, N., *The Development of the Organisation of Anglo-American Trade, 1800–1850* (New Haven, CT: Yale University Press, 1925).

Bühlmann, H., 'The Actuary', *Insurance: Mathematics and Economics* (1992), pp. 223–8.

—, 'The Actuary, the Role and Limitations of the Profession since the mid-Nineteenth Century', *Astin Bulletin*, 27 (1997), pp. 165–71, also at http://www1.fee.uva.nl/ke/act/articles/Buhlmann.PDF.

Bulpin, T. V., *Die Southern 75 Jaar van Diens* (Cape Town: Southern Life Association, 1966).

Campbell-Kelly, M., 'Large-Scale Data Processing in the Prudential, 1850–1930', *Accounting Business and Financial History*, 2 (1992), pp. 117–39.

Cantwell, J., 'A Survey of Theories in International Production', in C. N. Pitelis and R. Sugden (eds), *The Nature of Transnational Firms* (London: Routledge, 1991), pp. 16–63.

Carreras, A., and J. Tafunell, *Historia Económica de la España Contemporánea* (Madrid: Crítica, 2003).

Carter, R. L., and G. M. Dickinson, *Obstacles to the Liberalization of Trade in Insurance*, Thames Essay 58 (London: Trade Policy Research Centre, 1992).

Chandler, A. D., *Scale and Scope: The Dynamics of Industrial Capitalism* (Cambridge, MA: Harvard University Press, 1990).

Claessens, S., and T. Glaessner, *Internationalization of Financial Services in Asia*, Policy Research Paper 1911 (Washington, DC: World Bank, 1997).

Clark, G., *Betting on Lives: The Culture of Life Insurance in England, 1695–1775* (Manchester: Manchester University Press, 1999).

Clavin, P., 'Defining Transnationalism', *Contemporary European History*, 14 (2005), pp. 421–40.

Cockerell, H. A. L., and E. Green, *The British Insurance Business, 1547–1970* (London: Heinemann Educational, 1976).

Cohen, P., *The British System of Social Insurance* (London: P. Allen, 1932).

Commission of the European Communities, *Insurance*, The Single Market Review, Subseries II (Impact on Services), 1 (Luxembourg: OOPEC, 1998).

Conrad, C., *Vom Greis zum Rentner, Strukturwandel des Alters in Deutschland, 1830–1930* (Göttingen: Vandenhoeck & Ruprecht, 1994).

—, 'Vorbemerkung zum Themenheft "Sozialpolitik Transnational"', *Geschichte und Gesellschaft*, 32 (2006), pp. 437–44.

Dake, K., 'Myths of Nature: Culture and the Social Construction of Risk', *Journal of Social Issues*, 48 (1992), pp. 21–37.

Danson, J. T., *Our Next War in its Commercial Aspect, with some Account of the Premiums Paid at 'Lloyd's' from 1805 to 1816* (London: Blades, East & Blades, 1894).

Davenport, H. J., 'Can Industrial Insurance Be Cheapened?', *Journal of Political Economy*, 15 (1907), pp. 542–5.

Davis, D. M., *The South African Law of Insurance* (Cape Town: Juta, 1993).

Davis, M. E., *Industrial Life Insurance in the United States* (New York and London: McGraw-Hill Book Co., 1944).

De Diego, E., *Historia de la Industria en España: La Electrónica y la Informática* (Madrid: Editorial Actas, 1995).

De Förenade, *Lifförsäkrings-Aktiebolaget De Förenade* (Stockholm: De Förenade, 1934).

De Kiewiet, C. W., *A History of South Africa: Social and Economic* (London: Oxford University Press, 1941).

De Rosa, L. (ed.), *International Banking and Financial Systems: Evolution and Stability* (Aldershot: Ashgate, 2003).

Defert, D., '"Popular Life" and Insurance Technology', in G. Burchell, C. Gordon and P. Miller (eds), *The Foucault Effect: Studies in Governmentality* (Chicago, IL: University of Chicago Press, 1991), pp. 211–34.

Dennett, L. *A Sense of Security: 150 Years of Prudential* (Cambridge: Granta Editions, 1998).

Desai, G. R., *Life Insurance in India: Its History and Dimensions of Growth* (Madras: Macmillan India, 1973).

Dickson, P. G. M., *The Sun Insurance Office, 1760–1960* (Oxford: Oxford University Press, 1960).

Dinsdale, W. A, *History of Accident Insurance in Great Britain* (London: Stone & Cox, 1954).

Douglas, M., and A. Wildavsky, *Risk and Culture: An Essay on the Selection of Technological and Environmental Dangers* (Berkeley, CA: University of California Press, 1982).

Drew, B., *The London Assurance: A Second Chronicle* (London: London Assurance, 1949).

Dublin, L. I., *A Family of Thirty Million: The Story of Metropolitan Life Insurance Company* (New York: Metropolitan Life Insurance Co., 1943).

Dürr, E., *Die Liberalisierung des Internationalen Versicherungsverkehrs* (Berlin: Duncker & Humblot, 1956).

Ehler, H. J., *Die Verbandszusammenschlüsse in der Privaten Lebensversicherung* (Karlsruhe: Verlag Versicherungswirtschaft, 2003).

Embrechts, P., *Revisiting the Edge, Ten Years On*, Research Paper (Zurich: ETH Zurich, 2008).

Engel, E., 'Die Unfallversicherung', in *Zeitschrift des Königlich Preussischen Statistischen Buraus*, 6 (1866), pp. 294–7.

—, 'Materialien zur Unfallversicherung', *Zeitschrift des Königlich Preussischen Statistischen Bureaus*, 7 (1867), pp. 171–85.

Epstein, A., *Insecurity: A Challenge to America* (New York: H. Smith & R. Haas, 1933).

Eriksson, K., J. Johanson, A. Majkgard and D. D. Sharma, 'Experiential Knowledge and Cost in the Internationalisation Process', *Journal of International Business Studies*, 28 (1997), pp. 337–60.

Erramilli, M. K., 'The Experience Factor in Foreign Market Entry Behaviour of Service Firms', *Journal of International Business Studies*, 4 (1991), pp. 479–501.

Fazio, A., 'Financial Stability and Growth', in De Rosa (ed.), *International Banking and Financial Systems*, pp. 225–32.

Fehlmann, H., 'Die Entwicklung der Unfallversicherung', in *Das Versicherungswesen in der Schweiz*, Sonderabdruck aus dem 'Bund' (Bern: Pochon-Jent, 1927), pp. 34–40.

Feinstein, C. H., *An Economic History of South Africa: Conquest, Discrimination and Development* (Cambridge: Cambridge University Press, 2005).

Ferguson, R. W., 'Consolidation in the Financial Sector', in De Rosa (ed.), *International Banking and Financial Systems*, pp. 233–8.

Ferrara, M., 'The "Southern Model" of Welfare in Social Europe', *Journal of European Social Policy*, 6 (1996), pp. 17–37.

Frankel, S. H., 'Review of E. H. D. Arndt', *South African Journal of Economics*, 9:4 (1941), pp. 313–14.

Frax, E., and M. J. Matilla, 'Los Seguros Negocios del Franquismo: El Proceso de Bloqueo, Expropiación y Liquidación de las Compañías de Seguros con Capital Alemán', ponencia de la sesión B17 ('El mercado de seguros en la España contemporánea', organized by M.A. Pons Brías and J. Pons Pons), VIII Congreso de la Asociación Española de Historia Económica, Santiago de Compostela, 13–16 September 2005.

French, S., 'The Cemetery as Cultural Institution: The Establishment of Mount Auburn and the "Rural Cemetery Movement"', in D. E. Stannard (ed.), *Death in America* (Philadelphia, PA: University of Pennsylvania Press, 1975) pp. 70–92.

Gales, B., 'Odds and Ends: The Problematic First Wave of Internationalisation in Dutch Insurance during the late Nineteenth and early Twentieth Centuries', in Borscheid and Pearson (eds), *Internationalisation and Globalisation of the Insurance Industry*, pp. 84–111.

Gales, B. P. A., 'A Fonds Perdu? The Business of Funeral Assurance in the Netherlands', in Núñez (ed.), *Insurance in Industrial Societies*, pp. 127–42.

García-Ruiz, J. L., and L. Caruana, 'The Internationalisation of the Business of Insurance in Spain, 1939–2005', in Borscheid and Pearson (eds), *Internationalisation and Globalisation of the Insurance Industry*, pp. 66–83.

Garrido Comas, J. J., *Notas de Andar y Ver: Memorias de J. J. Garrido y Comas* (Madrid: Fundación MAPFRE estudios, 1997).

Garriguez, J., and E. Maynes, *Dos Dictámenes sobre Liquidación de Pérdidas Sufridas por las Inversiones Afectas a las Reservas Matemáticas de los Seguros de Vida a Consecuencia de la Revolución Comunista Española* (Barcelona, 1940).

Gebhart, J. C., *The Reasons for Present-Day Funeral Costs: A Summary of Facts Developed by the Advisory Committee on Burial Survey in the Course of an Impartial Study of the Burial Industry* (New York: Metropolitan Life Insurance Co., 1927).

Gesellschaft fuer Feuerversicherungsgeschichtliche Forschung e.v., *Das Deutsche Feuerversicherungswesen*, 2 vols (Hanover: Staats- und Sozialwiss. Verlag, 1913).

Goedhuys, D. W., 'South African Monetary Policy in the 1980s: Years of Reform and Foreign Financial Aggression', *South African Journal of Economic History*, 9 (1994), pp. 144–63.

Goodall, B., 'Short and Long Term Insurers and Private Pension and Provident Funds', in A. Hamersma and N. H. H. Czypionka (eds), *Essays on the South African Financial Structure* (Johannesburg: SBSA, 1975), pp. 125–34.

Government of India, Controller of Insurance, *Indian Insurance Year Book*, 1933–56 (New Delhi, 1934–57).

—, Planning Commission, *Third Five-Year Plan* (New Delhi, 1960).

Grossmann, M., 'Rückversicherungszahlungen in Drittlandwährungen', *Schweizerische Versicherungs-Zeitschrift*, 17 (1949/50), pp. 331–7.

Guillem Mesado, J.-M., and J. Pons Pons, 'La Legislación en el Sector Asegurador (1935–1955): La Prolongación y Crecimiento de los Problemas Históricos del Sector', *Revista Española de Seguros*, 135 (2008), pp. 263–91.

Guillen, A. *ITT e IBM en España: El 'Holding' de la ITT y el Monopolio de IBM en España* (Bilbao: Zero, 1977).

Guinand, C., *ILO und die Soziale Sicherheit in Europa, 1942–1967* (Bern: Peter Lang, 2002).

—, 'Zur Entstehung von IVSS und IAO', *Internationale Revue für Soziale Sicherheit*, 61 (2008), pp. 93–111.

Guinnane, T. W., and J. Streb, 'Moral Hazard in a Mutual-Health Insurance System: The German *Knappschaften*, 1867–1914', Economics Working Paper 70 (Yale University, 2009).

Gulbin, A. M., 'From the Graveyard to the Cemetery: Evolving Attitudes that have affected American Funeral Rites and Customs from the Seventeenth through the Nineteenth Century' (MA dissertation, Keene State College, NH, 1986).

Gupta, L. C., *Corporate Management and Accountability: Towards a Joint Sector* (Madras: Macmillan India, 1974).

Gürtler, M., *Die Kalkulation der Versicherungsbetriebe* (Berlin: Mittler, 1936).

Habenstein, R. W., and M. Lamers, *The History of American Funeral Directing* (Milwaukee, WI: National Funeral Directors Association, 1981).

Haberman, S., *Landmarks in the History of Actuarial Science (up to 1919)*, Actuarial Research Paper 84 (London: Department of Actuarial Science and Statistics, City University London, 1996).

Hägg, P. G. T., 'The Institutional Analysis of Insurance Regulation: The Case of Sweden' (PhD dissertation, University of Lund, 1998)

Hamann, K., *Hundert Jahre Victoria Versicherung* (Berlin: Victoria Versicherung, 1953).

Henderson, C. R., *Industrial Insurance in the United States* (Chicago, IL: University of Chicago Press, 1909).

Hernando de Larramendi, I., *Así se hizo Mapfre: Mi Tiempo* (Madrid: Actas Editorial, 2000).

Herren, M., 'Sozialpolitik und die Historisierung des Transnationalen', *Geschichte und Gesellschaft*, 32 (2006), pp. 542–59.

Hoffman, B., 'Scientific Racism, Insurance, and Opposition to the Welfare State: Frederick L. Hoffman's Transatlantic Journey', *Journal of the Gilded Age and Progressive Era*, 2 (2003), pp. 150–90.

Hoffman, F. L., *History of the Prudential Insurance Company of America (Industrial Insurance) 1875–1900* (Newark, NJ: Prudential Press, 1900).

—, 'Industrial Insurance', *Annals of the American Academy of Political and Social Science*, 26 (1905), pp. 103–19.

—, *Pauper Burials and the Interment of Dead in Large Cities* (Newark, NJ: Prudential Press, 1919).

Hoken Ginko Jiho, *Honpo Seimei Hoken Gyoshi* [*History of Life Insurance Business*] (Tokyo: Hoken Ginko Jiho / Insurance and Banking News Report, 1933).

Hopkins, M., *A Manual of Marine Insurance* (London: Murray, 1867).

Horstman, K., *Public Bodies, Private Lives: The Historical Construction of Life Insurance, Health Risks and Citizenship in the Netherlands, 1880–1920* (Rotterdam: Erasmus, 2001).

Houghton, D. H., 'Economic Development, 1865–1965', in M. Wilson and L. M. Thompson (eds), *Oxford History of South Africa*, 2 vols (London: Oxford University Press, 1969–71), vol. 2, pp. 1–48.

—, *The South African Economy* (London: Oxford University Press, 1976).

Huerta Huerta, R., *Inversiones Extranjeras en España: Estudio Multidisciplinar* (Madrid: for the author, 1992).

ICEA, 'El Empleo de Máquinas de Fichas Perforadas en una Entidad de Seguros: La Utilización de Fichas Perforadas para las Operaciones de Emisión de recibos', report 3 (Madrid: ICEA, 1963).

—, 'Survey on Mechanisation in Insurance Institutions', report 94 (Madrid: ICEA, June 1971).

Inami, T., *Hoken ha dokohe* [*Where is the Insurance Company Going?*] (Bunga-Do, 1926).

International Congress of Actuaries, *Transactions of the International Congress of Actuaries* (London: IVSS, 1895–1952).

Internationale Vereinigung fuer Soziale Sicherheit, *Historische Dokumente, 1927–1947* (Geneva: IVSS, 1977).

—, *Im Dienste der Sozialen Sicherheit, Die Geschichte der IVSS, 1927–1987* (Geneva: IVSS, 1986).

Iserson, K. V., *Death to Dust: What Happens to Dead Bodies?* (Tucson, AZ: Galen Press, 1994).

James, M., *The Metropolitan Life: A Study in Business Growth* (New York: Viking, 1947).

Johanson J., and J.-E. Vahlne, 'The Internationalization Process of the Firm: A Model of Knowledge Development and Increasing Foreign Market Commitments', *Journal of International Business Studies*, 8 (1977), pp. 23–32.

John, A. H., 'The London Assurance Company and the Marine Insurance Market of the Eighteenth Century', *Economica*, n.s. 25 (1958), pp. 126–41.

Johnson, P., *Saving and Spending: The Working-Class Economy in Britain, 1870–1939* (Oxford: Clarendon Press, 1985).

Johnston, G. A., *The International Labour Organisation: Its Work for Social and Economic Progress* (London: Europa Publications, 1970).

Jones, G., 'British Multinationals and British Business since 1850', in M. W. Kirby and M. B. Rose (eds), *Business Enterprise in Modern Britain: From the Eighteenth to the Twentieth Century* (London and New York: Routledge, 1994), pp. 172–206.

Jones, S., *The Great Imperial Banks in South Africa: A Study of the Business of Standard Bank and Barclays Bank, 1861–1961* (Pretoria: Unisa Press, 1996).

Jones, S., and A. Müller, *The South African Economy 1910–1990* (London: Macmillan, 1992).

Jung, J., *Die Winterthur: Eine Versicherungsgeschichte* (Zurich: NNZ-Verlag, 2000).

Jungenfelt, K. G., *Löneandelen och den ekonomiska utvecklingen: en empirisk-teoretisk studie* (Stockholm: Almqvist & Wiksell, 1966).

Kaelble, H., 'Das Europäische Sozialmodell – eine Historische Perspektive', in Kaelble and Schmid (eds), *Das Europäische Sozialmodell*, pp. 31–50.

Kaelble, H., and G. Schmid (eds), *Das europäische Sozialmodell: Auf dem Weg zum transnationalen Sozialstaat* (Berlin: Edition Sigma, 2004).

Kang, Z., 'Assurances moderne en Chine: Une continuité interrompue (1801–1949)', *Risques*, 31 (1997), pp. 103–20.

Karup, W., *Handbuch der Lebensversicherung* (Leipzig: A. Fritsch, 1885).

Keller, M., *The Life Insurance Enterprise, 1880–1910: A Study in the Limits of Corporate Power* (Cambridge, MA: Harvard University Press, 1963).

Keneley, M. J., 'The Evolution of the Australian Life Insurance Industry', *Accounting, Business and Financial History*, 11 (2002), pp. 145–70.

—, 'In the Service of the Society: The Labour Management Practices of an Australian Life Insurer to 1940', *Business History*, 48 (2006), pp. 529–50.

—, 'Monitoring and Motivating Outworkers: The Case of the AMP and the Sale of Industrial Life Insurance 1905–1940', *Labor History*, 49 (2008), pp. 319–40.

Khan, M. Y., and P. Singh, 'Life Insurance Corporation and Corporate Control in India', *Indian Economic Journal*, 29 (1981), pp. 51–64.

Kingston, C., 'Marine Insurance in Britain and America, 1720–1844: A Comparative Institutional Analysis', *Journal of Economic History*, 67 (2007), pp. 379–409.

Knaggs, O., *Norwich Life 1706–1990* (Cape Town: Oliver Knaggs and Associates, 1990).

Kono, M., et al., *Opening Markets in Financial Services and the Role of the GATS* (Geneva: World Trade Organization, 1997).

Krüger, L., L. Daston and M. Heidelberger (eds), *The Probabilistic Revolution*, 2 vols (Cambridge, MA: MIT Press, 1987).

Kumar, D. (ed.), *Tryst with Trust* (New Delhi: Life Insurance Corporation of India, 1991).

La Estrella, *Medio Siglo del Seguro Privado Español* (Madrid, 1959).

Laing, A., 'Change and Development in Short Term Insurance in South Africa, 1950–1985', *South African Journal of Economic History*, 3 (1988), pp. 33–44.

Landis, A., *Friendly Societies and Fraternal Orders* (Winchester, TN: for the author, 1900).

Leimgruber, M., *'Achieving Social Progress without Etatization'? A Political Economy of the Swiss Three-Pillar System of Old Age Insurance (1890–1972)* (Cambridge: Cambridge University Press, 2008).

Lengwiler, M., *Risikopolitik im Sozialstaat: Die schweizerische Unfallversicherung 1870–1970* (Köln: Böhlau, 2006).

—, 'Competing Appeals: The Rise of Mixed Welfare Economies in Europe, 1850–1945', in G. Clark (ed.), *The Appeal of Insurance* (Toronto: University of Toronto Press, forthcoming).

Llorca-Jaña, M., 'British Textile Exports to the Southern Cone during the first half of the Nineteenth Century: Growth, Structure and the Marketing Chain' (PhD dissertation, University of Leicester, 2008).

Løkke, A., 'Tryghed og Risiko – Forsikring i Danmark 1850–1950', in O. Feldbæk, A. Løkke and S. J. Jeppesen (eds), *Drømmen om Tryghed: Tusind års Dansk Forsikring* (Gylling: Gad, 2007), pp. 262–78.

Lönnborg, M., *Internationalisering av svenska försäkringsbolag* (Uppsala: Uppsala University, 1999).

López, S., 'Los Precedentes de la Informática y la Automática en España (1925–1971)', in R. Enrich, G. Lusa, M. Mañosa, X Moreno and A. Roca (curators), *Tècnica i societat en el món contemporani: I Jornades, Maig 1992* (Sabadell: Museu d'Historia de Sabadell, 1994), pp. 211–28.

Lorenz-Liburnau, H., 'Integration der Europäischen Versicherungswirtschaft in Vergangenheit, Gegenwart und Zukunft', *Die Versicherungsrundschau*, 17 (1962), pp. 70–85.

Lubove, R., 'Economic Security and Social Conflict in America: The Early Twentieth Century', *Journal of Social History*, 1 (1967), pp. 61–87.

Maasdorp, G., 'Economic Survey, 1970–2000', in S. Jones (ed.), *The Decline of the South African Economy* (Cheltenham: Edward Elgar, 2002), pp. 7–30.

McCulloch, J. R., *A Dictionary, Practical, Theoretical, and Historical of Commerce and Commercial Navigation* (London: Longman, Brown & Green, 1852).

McLauchlan Slater, D., *Rise and Progress of Native Life Assurance in India* (Bombay, 1897).

Maclean, M., C. Harvey and J. Press, *Business Elites and Corporate Governance in France and the UK* (Basingstoke: Palgrave Macmillan, 2006).

MacPherson, I., 'The Origins of Cooperative Insurance on the Prairies', *Business and Economic History*, 26 (1977), pp. 76–87.

Maestro, M., *Formación del Mercado Español de Seguros* (Madrid: INESE, 1993).

Malaviya, H. D., *Insurance Business in India* (New Delhi: All India Congress Committee, 1956).

Martin, F. M., *The History of Lloyd's and of Marine Insurance in Great Britain* (London: Macmillan, 1876).

Martínez Ruiz, E., *El Sector Exterior durante la Autarquía: Una Reconstrucción de las Balanzas de Pagos de España (1940–1958)*, Estudios de Historia Económica 43 (Madrid: Banco de España, Servicio de Estudios, 2003).

Mathematical Investigations Regarding the Creation and Derivation of the Formulas to Calculate Net Premiums and Reserves for all Insurances Branches of the Swiss Rentenanstalt (Zurich, 1861).

Mathematical Investigations Regarding the Creation and Derivation of the Formulas to Calculate the Profit Reserves and Profit Commissions for the Respective Insurance Branches of the Swiss Rentenanstalt (Zurich, 1864).

Maul, D., *Menschenrechte, Sozialpolitik und Dekolonisation, die IAO 1940–1970* (Essen: Klartext, 2007)

—, 'Der Transnationale Blick: Die Internationale Arbeitsorganisation und die Sozialpolitischen Krisen Europas im 20. Jahrhundert', *Archiv für Sozial-versicherungen*, 47 (2007), pp. 349–70.

Meiji Life, *Meiji Seimei 50nenshi, 50 years History of Meiji Life* (Tokyo: Meiji Seimei Hoken, 1933).

Meller, H., 'Philanthropy and Public Enterprise: International Exhibitions and the Modern Town Planning Movement, 1889–1913', *Planning Perspectives*, 3 (1995), pp. 295–310.

Meyer, J. W., *World Society: The Writings of John W. Meyer* (Oxford: Oxford University Press, 2009).

Miranda, J. A., 'El Fracaso de la Industrialización Autárquica', in Barciela (ed.), *Autarquía y Mercado Negro*, pp. 95–122.

—, 'La Comisión Nacional de Productividad Industrial y la "Americanización" de la Industria del Calzado en España', *Revista de Historia Económica*, 22 (2004), pp. 637–68.

Mitchell, A., *The Divided Path: The German Influence on Social Reform in France after 1870* (Chapel Hill, NC: University of North Carolina Press, 1991).

Mitchell, B. R., *Abstract of British Historical Statistics* (Cambridge: Cambridge University Press, 1962).

—, *International Historical Statistics – Africa, Asia and Oceania 1750–1993*, 3rd edn (London: Macmillan, 1998)

—, *International Historical Statistics: Europe 1750–1993* (London: Macmillan, 1998).

—, *International Historical Statistics: The Americas, 1750–2000* (London: Macmillan, 2003).

Mitford, J., *The American Way of Death Revisited* (New York: Alfred A. Knopf, 1998).

Mohr, P., 'An Overview of the South African Economy in the 1990s', *South African Journal of Economic History*, 18 (2003), pp. 16–30.

Mohsin, M., *Investment of Life Insurance Corporation's Fund* (Aligarh: Aligarh Muslim University, 1966).

Morgan, J. M., *The Development of the Insurance Institute Movement in South Africa: A History* (Johannesburg: Cuppleditch Communication, 1992).

Morrah, D., *A History of Industrial Life Assurance* (London: Allen & Unwin, 1955).

Müller, A., *Ekonomiese Geskiedenis van Suid-Afrika* (Pretoria: Academica, 1982).

Muñoz Guarasa, M., *La Inversión Directa Extranjera en España: Factores Determinantes* (Madrid: Civitas, 1999).

Munro, A. R., and A. M. Snyman, 'The Life Insurance Industry in South Africa', *Geneva Papers on Risk and Insurance*, 20 (1995), pp. 127–40.

Murphy, S., 'Security in an Uncertain World: Life Insurance and the Emergence of Modern America' (PhD dissertation, University of Virginia, 2005).

Nichols, W. S., 'Fraternal Insurance in the United States: Its Origin, Development, Character and Existing Status', *Annals of the American Academy of Political and Social Science*, 70 (1917), 'Modern Insurance Problems', pp. 109–22.

Nicholson, D. T., 'Look at the Recent Changes in Banking Legislation in South Africa', *South African Banker*, 73 (1976), pp. 149–53.

Nicol, R., *At the End of the Road* (Sydney: Allen & Unwin, 1994).

—, *Final Pageant: The Past, Present and Future of Death* (Sydney: Uniting Church Historical Society, 1998).

Nippon Life Company, *The 100 Year History of Nippon Life: Its Growth and Socio-Economic Setting 1889–1989* (Osaka: Nippon Life Company, 1989).

Nissel, H., *Bombay: Untersuchungen zur Struktur und Dynamik einer indischen Metropole* (Berlin: Institut für Geographie der Technischen Universität Berlin, 1977).

Núñez, C. E. (ed.), *Insurance in Industrial Societies: Economic Role, Agents and Markets from the Eighteenth Century to Today* (Seville: University of Seville, 1998).

OECD, *Supervision of Private Insurance in Europe* (Paris: OECD, 1963).

Ogborn, M. E., *Equitable Assurances: The Story of Life Assurance in the Experience of the Equitable Life Assurance Society 1762–1962* (London: George Allen & Unwin, 1962).

Oriental Governmental Security Life Assurance Company Limited (ed.), *A Short History of the Oriental Governmental Security Life Assurance Company Ltd*, Silver Jubilee Souvenir (Bombay, 1924).

Panagariya, A., *India: The Emerging Giant* (New York: Oxford University Press, 2008).

Pearson, R., 'The Development of Reinsurance Markets in Europe during the Nineteenth Century', *Journal of European Economic History*, 24 (1995), pp. 557–71.

—, 'Towards an Historical Model of Financial Services Innovation: The Case of the Insurance Industry 1700–1914', *Economic History Review*, 50 (1997), pp. 235–56.

—, 'Growth, Crisis and Change in the Insurance Industry: A Retrospect', *Accounting, Business and Financial History*, 12 (2002), pp. 1–18.

—, 'Insurance: An Historical Overview', in J. Mokyr (ed.), *The Oxford Encyclopedia of Economic History*, 5 vols (New York: Oxford University Press, 2003), vol. 3, pp. 83–7.

—, 'Who Pays for Pensions? Das Problem der Alterssicherung in Grossbritannien im zwanzigsten Jahrhundert', *Zeitschrift für Unternehmensgeschichte*, 48 (2003), pp. 48–57.

—, *Insuring the Industrial Revolution: Fire Insurance in Great Britain, 1700–1850* (Aldershot: Ashgate, 2004).

Pearson, R., and M. Lönnborg, 'Regulatory Regimes and Multinational Insurers before 1914', *Business History Review*, 82 (2008), pp. 59–86.

Plaisted, H., *Prudential Past and Present* (Cardiff: Rees' Electric Press, 1916).

Planes, F. V., 'Panorámica Actual del Seguro Español', *Riesgo y Seguro* (1963), pp. 324–8.

Platt, D. C. M., *Latin America and British Trade* (London: A. & C. Black, 1972).

Pons Pons, J., *El sector seguros en Baleares: Empresas y empresarios en los siglo XIX y XX* (Palma de Mallorca: El Tall, 1998).

—, 'Jesús Serra Santamans', in E. Torres Villanueva (ed.), *Los 100 Empresarios Españoles del Siglo XX* (Madrid: Editorial Lid Empresarial, 2000), pp. 451–5.

—, 'Diversificación y Cartelización en el Seguro Español (1914–1935)', *Revista de Historia Económica*, 3 (2003), pp. 567–92.

—, 'Las Entidades Aseguradoras y la Canalización del Ahorro en España', *Revista Española de Seguros*, 115 (2003), pp. 337–58.

—, 'El Seguro de Accidentes de Trabajo en España: De la Obligación al Negocio (1900–1940)', *Investigaciones de Historia Económicas*, 4 (2006), pp. 77–100.

—, 'Mutua General de Seguros (1907–2007): Cien Años de Historia del Seguro Español' (unpublished manuscript, 2007).

—, 'Multinational Enterprises and Institutional Regulation in the Life Insurance Market in Spain, 1880–1935', *Business History Review*, 82 (2008), pp. 87–114.

—, 'Las Empresas Extranjeras en el Seguro Español ante el Aumento del Nacionalismo Económico (1912–1940)', in J. Pons Pons and M. A. Pons Brías (eds), *Investigaciones Históricas sobre el Seguro Español* (Madrid: Fundación Mapfre, 2010), pp. 191–226.

Rao, V. K. R. V., *India's National Income, 1950–1980: An Analysis of Economic Growth and Change* (New Delhi and Beverly Hills, CA: Sage Publications, 1983).

Raphael, L., 'Europäische Sozialstaaten in der Boomphase (1948–1973): Versuch einer Historischen Distanzierung einer "Klassischen Phase" des Europäischen Sozialmodells', in Kaelble and Schmid (eds), *Das Europäische Sozialmodell*, pp. 51–74.

Rau, M. C., *Jawaharlal Nehru* (New Delhi: Ministry of Information and Broadcasting, 1973).

Ray, R. M., *Life Insurance in India. Its History, Law, Practice, and Problems* (Bombay: Allied Publishers, 1941).

Raynes, H. E., *A History of British Insurance*, 2nd edn (London: Pitman, 1964).

Reber, V. B. 'Speculation and Commerce in Buenos Aires: The Hugh Dallas House, 1816–1820', *Business History*, 20 (1978), pp. 18–37.

Reinecke, M. F., S. van der Merwe, J. P. van Niekerk and P. Havenga, *General Principles of Insurance Law* (Durban: Lexis Nexis Butterworths, 2002).

Reserve Bank of India, *Handbook of Statistics on the Indian Economy 2002–03* (New Delhi: Reserve Bank, 2003).

Rohrbach, W., 'Von den Anfängen bis zum Börsenkrach des Jahres 1873', in W. Rohrbach (ed.), *Versicherungsgeschichte Österreichs*, 3 vols (Vienna: Holzhausen, 1988), vol. 1, pp. 46–432.

Roover, F. Edler de, 'Early Examples of Marine Insurance', *Journal of Economic History*, 5 (1945), pp. 172–200.

Rosa, M. L., *Central Banking and Banking Regulation* (London: LSE Financial Markets Group, 1996).

Rothermund, D., *An Economic History of India: From Pre-Colonial Times to 1991* (London: Routledge, 1993).

Rubinow, I. M., *The Quest for Security* (New York: Henry Holt & Co., 1934).

Ruffat, M., 'French Insurance from the *Ancien Régime* to 1946: Shifting Frontiers between State and Market', *Financial History Review*, 10 (2003), pp. 185–200.

Saito, O., *Hikaku Keizai Hattenron* [*Comparative Study of Economic Development: A Historical Approach*] (Tokyo: Iwanami, 2008).

Salmon, F., 'Recipe for Disaster: The Formula that Killed Wall Street', *Wired Magazine* (2 February 2009).

Sanchís Llopis, M. T., 'Relaciones de Intercambio Sectoriales y Desarrollo Industrial. España, 1954–1972', *Revista de Historia Industrial*, 11 (1997), pp. 149–74.

Sanlam, *Die weerste Vyftig Jaar* (Belvieel: Sanlam, 1968).

Schöller, P., 'L'évolution séculaire des taux de fret et d'assurance maritimes 1819–1940', *Bulletin de l'Institute de recherches économiques et sociales*, 17 (1951), pp. 519–57.

Schott, J. J., *The Uruguay Round: An Assessment* (Washington, DC: Institute for International Economics, 1994).

Schumann, C. G. W., *Structural Changes and Business Cycles in South Africa, 1800–1936* (London: Staples Press, 1938).

Schweizerische Lebensversicherungs- und Rentenanstalt Zürich, *Fünfundsiebzig Jahre Schweizerische Lebensversicherungs- und Rentenanstalt Zürich 1857–1932* (Zurich, 1932).

Scott, P., 'Towards the "Cult of the Equity"? Insurance Companies and the Interwar Capital Market', *Economic History Review*, 55 (2002), pp. 78–104.

Select Committee on Marine Insurance, 'Report from the Select Committee on Marine Insurance, 1810', *British Parliamentary Papers*, VII:298 (1824), pp. 1–11.

Shelp, R. K., *Beyond Industrialization* (New York: Praeger, 1981).

Sivasubramonian, S., *The National Income of India in the Twentieth Century* (Oxford: Oxford University Press, 2000).

Skipper, H. D., 'Protectionism in the Provision of International Insurance Services', *Journal of Risk and Insurance*, 54 (1987), pp. 55–85.

—, 'International Trade in Insurance', in C. E. Barfield (ed.), *International Financial Markets: Harmonization versus Competition* (Washington, DC: AEI Press, 1996), pp. 151–224.

Sloane, D. C., *The Last Great Necessity: Cemeteries in American History* (Baltimore, MD, and London: Johns Hopkins University Press, 1991).

Slovic P., and E. Peters, 'The Importance of Worldviews in Risk Perception', *Risk, Decision and Policy*, 3 (1998), pp. 165–70.

Söhner, P. A., *Die Private Volksversicherung, ihr Wesen und ihr Wert und die Wichtigeren Reformbestrebungen* (Tübingen: J.C.B. Mohr, 1911).

Soto Carmona, Á., 'Rupturas y Continuidades en las Relaciones Laborales del Primer Franquismo, 1938–1958', in Barciela (ed.), *Autarquía y Mercado Negro*, pp. 217–45.

South African Government, *Summaries of Returns Deposited with the Treasury by Insurance Companies* (Pretoria: Government Printer, 1925–44).

—, *Annual Report of the Registrar of Insurance Companies* (Pretoria: Government Printer, 1944–2001).

—, Bureau for Census and Statistics, *Union Statistics for Fifty Years, Jubilee Edition, 1910–1960* (Pretoria: Government Printer, 1960).

—, *Third Report of the Commission of Enquiry into Fiscal and Monetary Policy in South Africa (Franszen Commission)*, RP87/1970 (Pretoria: Government Printer, 1970).

—, Department of Finance, *Report of the Commission of Inquiry into the Long Term Insurance Industry* (Pretoria: Government Printer, 1976).

—, *Final Report of the Commission of Inquiry into the Monetary System and Monetary Policy in South Africa (De Kock Commission)*, RP70/1984 (Pretoria: Government Printer, 1984).

South African Reserve Bank, *Quarterly Statistical Bulletin* (1950–2002).

—, *A Statistical Presentation of South Africa's National Accounts for the Period 1946 to 1970* (Pretoria: Government Printer, 1975).

Sprecher, A. von, *75 Jahre 'Zürich'. Band II – Aus der Werkstatt der 'Zürich', 1872–1947* (Zurich, 1948).

Sprecher, H. von, *'Zürich': Die Gesellschaft in den Ersten Fünfzig Jahren ihres Bestehens 1872–1922* (Zurich: Buchdr. Berichthaus, 1923).

Spyrou, H., 'The Development of Insurance Business in the Union of South Africa', *South African Journal of Economics*, 23 (1955), pp. 325–40.

Stack, M., *Vierzig Jahre im Dienste der Sozialen Sicherheit (1927–1967)* (Geneva: IVSS, 1967).

Stalson, J. O., *Marketing Life Insurance: Its History in America* (Cambridge, MA: Harvard University Press, 1942).

Supple, B., *The Royal Exchange Assurance: A History of British Insurance 1720–1970* (Cambridge: Cambridge University Press, 1970).

—, 'Insurance in British History', in O. M. Westall (ed.), *The Historian and the Business of Insurance* (Manchester: Manchester University Press, 1984), pp. 1–8.

Surminski, A., *Im Zug der Zeiten: 150 Jahre Victoria* (Düsseldorf: Victoria Versicherungs-Gesellschaften, 2003).

Taylor, M., *The Social Cost of Industrial Insurance* (New York: A. A. Knopf, 1933).

Thakore, D., 'The Case for Deregulating the Insurance Sector', at http://www.rediff.com/business/1998/aug/08dilip. htm [accessed 8 January 2010].

Thomasson, M. A., 'From Sickness to Health: The Twentieth-Century Development of U.S. Health Insurance', *Explorations in Economic History*, 39 (2002), pp. 233–53.

Torres Villanueva, E., 'La Empresa en la Autarquía, 1939–1959. Iniciativa Pública versus Iniciativa Privada', in Barciela (ed.), *Autarquía y Mercado Negro*, pp. 169–216.

Trebilcock, C., *Phoenix Assurance and the Development of British Insurance*, 2 vols (Cambridge: Cambridge University Press, 1985–98).

UNCTAD, *Insurance in the Context of Services and the Development Process*, TD/B/1014 (Geneva: UNCTAD, 1984).

—, *Services and the Development Process*, TD/B/1008 (New York: UNCTAD, 1985).

—, *The Outcome of the Uruguay Round: An Initial Assessment. Supporting Papers to the Trade and Development Report 1994*, TDR/14 (New York: UNCTAD, 1994).

United States Congress, Bureau of the Census, *Insurance Report* (Washington, DC, 1890).

—, Bureau of Manufactures, *Insurance in Foreign Countries*, Special Consular Reports 38 (House of Representatives Document 165 (Washington, DC: Government Printing Office, 1905).

Usera, G. de, 'El Seguro Privado y el Desarrollo Económico', *Anales del Instituto de Actuarios Españoles*, 4 (1964), pp. 1–15.

Vakil, C. N., *Economic Consequences of Divided India: A Study of the Economy of India and Pakistan* (Bombay: Vora, 1950).

Valenzuela de Quinta, E., *Protagonistas del Mutualismo de Accidentes de Trabajo: 100 Años de Historia (1900–2000)* (Madrid: Asociación de Mutuas de Accidentes de Trabajo y Enfermedades Profesionales de la Seguridad Social, 2000).

Van Selm, R., *History of the South African Mutual Life Assurance Society, 1845–1945* (Cape Town: Mutual Life Assurance Society, 1945).

Verhoef, G., 'The Dynamics of Banking in South Africa, 1980–1993', *South African Journal of Economic History*, special issue (1994), pp. 84–109.

Vilar Rodríguez, M., 'Mercado de Trabajo y Crecimiento Económico en España (1908–1963): Una Nueva Interpretación del Primer Franquismo' (PhD dissertation, University of Barcelona, 2004).

—, 'El Sistema de Cobertura Social en la Inmediata Posguerra Civil (1939–1958): Una Pieza más de la Estrategia Represiva Franquista', in *VI Encuentro de Investigadores sobre el Franquismo* (Zaragoza: Fundación Sindicalismo y Cultura. CCOO, 2006), pp. 619–36.

—, 'El Mercado de Trabajo como Estrategia Política del Régimen Franquista (1936–1975)', in J. De la Torre Campo and G. Sanz Lafuente (eds), *Migraciones y Coyuntura Económica del Franquismo a la Democracia* (Zaragoza: Prensas Universitarias de Zaragoza, 2008), pp. 153–77.

Vivian, R. W., *The Story of Mutual and Federal 1831–1995* (Johannesburg: Mutual and Federal Insurance Company, 1995).

—, 'A History of the South African Fire and Life Assurance Company', *South African Journal of Economic History*, 11 (1996), pp. 145–57.

—, *Morgan's History of the Insurance Institute Movement of South Africa, 1898–1999* (Cape Town: IISA, 2001).

—, 'A History of the London and Lancashire Fire Insurance Company in South Africa', *South African Journal of Economic History*, 17 (2002), pp. 138–61.

—, 'A Royal Farewell', *FA News* (April 2004), pp. 12–13.

—, 'Anniversaries', *Cover*, 19 (2006), p. 44.

—, 'South African Insurance Markets', in J. D. Cummins and B. Venard (eds), *Handbook of International Insurance* (New York: Springer, 2007), pp. 677–738.

Vogel, J., 'Von der Wissenschafts- zur Wissensgeschichte: Für eine Historisierung der "Wissensgesellschaft"', *Geschichte und Gesellschaft*, 30 (2004), pp. 639–60.

Walford, C., *Insurance Cyclopaedia*, 5 vols (London: Layton, 1871–8).

Walker, F. A., 'Compulsory Health Insurance: "The Next Great Step in Social Legislation"', *Journal of American History*, 56 (1969), pp. 290–304.

Werner, W., *Das WTO-Finanzdienstleistungsabkommen* (Munich: Oldenbourg, 1999).

—, *Handelspolitik für Finanzdienste*, Schriften zur Monetären Ökonomie (Baden-Baden: Nomos, 2004).

—, 'Öffnung der Versicherungsmärkte bei OECD, EU und WTO: Mühsamer Abschied vom Finanzmarktprotektionismus der Bretton Woods Periode', *Zeitschrift für die gesamte Versicherungswissenschaft*, 94 (2005), pp. 841–64.

Westall, O. M., *The Provincial Insurance Company, 1903–1938* (Manchester: Manchester University Press, 1992).

Whaples, R., and D. Buffum, 'Fraternalism, Paternalism, the Family, and the Market: Insurance a Century Ago', *Social Science History*, 15 (1991), pp. 97–122.

Wilkins, M., *The Emergence of Multinational Enterprise: American Business Abroad from the Colonial Era to 1914* (Cambridge, MA: Harvard University Press, 1970).

Wilson, A., and H. Levy, *Burial Reform and Funeral Costs* (London and New York: Oxford University Press, 1938).

Witherell, W., 'The Liberalization of International Service Transactions: The Experience of Developed Countries', in United Nations Centre on Transnational Corporations, *Services and Development: The Role of Foreign Direct Investment in Trade*, ST/CTC/95 (New York: United Nations, 1989), pp. 143–50.

Wright, C., *A History of Lloyd's* (London: Lloyd's, 1928).

Wright, R. E., and G. D. Smith, *Mutually Beneficial: The Guardian and Life Insurance in America* (New York: New York University Press, 2004).

Yates, J., 'The Structuring of Early Computer Use in Life Insurance', *Journal of Design History*, 12 (1999), pp. 5–24.

—, *Structuring the Information Age: Life Insurance and Technology in the Twentieth Century* (Baltimore, MD: Johns Hopkins University Press, 2005).

Yui, T., and M. Tatsuki (eds), *Historical Documents of Japanese Life Assurance in the Early Period* (Tokyo: Meiji Life, 1981).

—, *Meiji Seimei 100-nenshi* [*Documents of Meiji 100 Year History*] (Tokyo: Meiji Seimei Hoken Sogogaisha, 1982).

Yunus, M., *Grameen Bank, as I See It* (Dhaka: Grameen Bank, 1994).

Zappino, J. S., *El Instituto Mixto Argentino de Reaseguros: La Formación de un Mercado Nacional de Seguro, 1946–1952* (Buenos Aires: Ediciones Cooperativas, 2007).

Zelizer, V. A., *Morals and Markets: The Development of Life Insurance in the United State* (New York: Columbia University Press, 1979).

Zeuner, G., *Abhandlungen aus der Mathematischen Statistik* (Leipzig: A. Felix, 1869).

INDEX

Foundation dates are given for companies and other organizations, life dates for people, where known.

For Product Safety Concerns and Information please contact our EU
representative GPSR@taylorandfrancis.com
Taylor & Francis Verlag GmbH, Kaufingerstraße 24, 80331 München, Germany